WITHDRAWN

BETWEEN
ADOLESCENTS
AND
PARENTS

Between Adolescents & Parents

Moshe Smilansky

Psychosocial & Educational Publications
Gaithersburg, Maryland

Printed in the United States of America

Published by:

Psychosocial & Educational Publications
P.O. Box 2146
Gaithersburg, Maryland 20886
(301) 869-4454

ISBN 0-9625963-4-5
Library of Congress Catalog Card Number: 90-72146

*To Sara, my wife, for her love,
sharing and motherhood.*

Contents

Preface

THE PURPOSE OF THIS BOOK, *BETWEEN ADOLESCENTS AND PARENTS*, IS TO help the reader to understand, both in terms of theory and practical experience, the development of interaction between children and parents from the period of early adolescence to the stage of transition to adulthood.

This work focuses on themes occurring during this developmental process: the needs of both children and parents; mutual expectations of one another and of oneself; feelings of satisfaction and/or frustration, love and/or anger, both separately and inextricably mixed; expressions of both negative and positive behavior; occurrence of problems and crises; signs of growth and progress in shaping personal identity and attaining coping capability as opposed to the negative phenomena of regression and deviance. Personal interviews, case studies and theoretical explanations from various sources provide material presented in the text. The approach is to offer practical coping methods useful in both individual counselling frameworks and in group work and which can be applied in a class in school or in a positive peer support group in a social setting outside the school structure.

The book is divided into two major sections: the first section is aimed at the general public which is interested in learning about and understanding the complexity of the development of the child-parent relationship. Its provision of comprehensive theoretical, practical and diverse information should provide help to aid all those involved in this process. The second section is aimed more at teachers, guidance counselors, psychologists and youth group counselors who are interested in material which could enrich, deepen and enliven their work; it will provide them a detailed, systematic guide for conducting groups on the various subjects-themes such as listed above; the overall purpose of such groups is to develop social perspective and social skills.

The material on which both sections of this work are based comes from a series of cross-cultural studies and records of activities in practical group facilitation carried on in the United States and Israel. Systematic field work in facilitation and supervision was carried out throughout the 1970's and 1980's, initially at schools in Ohio, later across the United States in US Department of Labor education and training centers, and finally at schools and secondary level educational institutions under the auspices of Israel's Ministry of Education.

Not only did the results of the various studies demonstrate the significance and positive influence of our approach and facilitation methods but they clearly indicated the unique quality of group learning experiences. The positive appraisal of principals, educators, guidance counselors and psychologists in the US and Israel earned by the earlier, experimental edition which appeared in mimeographed form encouraged us in bringing out this more complete version.

Contributions by educators, counselors and therapists, adolescent boys and girls, parents, researchers and others in both countries by consenting to be interviewed, by participating in active groups, by completing questionnaires and assessment forms, etc. have immeasurably aided in the unraveling of this complex and intricate subject. We must content ourselves with extending our most heartfelt thanks to them as a group, anonymously.

We would like to express our appreciation for the help and contribution of our colleagues in the US and in Israel who were active partners in fashioning the approach, the curricula, workshops, supervision of facilitators, research, assessment and preparation of the report for publication. The project for encouraging adolescents at schools in socially disadvantaged areas of Ohio was begun with the assistance of the late Prof. Ross Mooney, Prof. Dan Sanders and Dr. Deborah Coleman. Upon the invitation of Dr. Richard Jaffe, Director of the National Education System of the US Department of Labor's Job Corps I set out to assess the educational programs included in this rubric, to develop the course of study, *Self-Development and Coping Competence*, and to supervise group leaders in 24 education centers in across the North American continent.

In Israel I direct my greatest debt of gratitude to the former Directors-General of the Ministry of Education and Culture: Eliezer Shmueli and Dr. Shimshon Shoshani, to the Directors of the Department of Curriculum: Dr. Shevach Eden and Navah Segen, and to the heads of the Psychological Counseling Service: Dr. Kolodner and Dr. Norman. Thanks are also due to the Mayor of Tel Aviv, Mr. Shlomo Lahat; to the director of the Association for Advancement of Education, Dr. Palti Stavi; to the directors of the Tel Aviv University School of Education, the late Prof. Shimon Reshef, Professors Rina Shapira and Michael

Chen; and to the directors of the Curriculum Development Unit, Prof. David Chen and Prof. Mordechai Miron. Each of them has contributed greatly, from the context of his or her position, to the establishment of the Project for Advancement of Youth from Deprived Areas, in which we tested the significance of our educational approach and the effectiveness of the curricula we developed over five consecutive years.

All the staff members of Project NETA deserve special thanks for development of curricula and carrying out the day-to-day application of the Project for Advancement of Youth from Deprived Areas within the Israeli educational system, and especially for their support on which I came to depend during the years I directed the project.

This book, one of six volumes of the overall course, *The Challenge of Adolescence*, is intended to promote cognitive, emotional and social development of students in grades 7-12; it attempts to deal with all the issues significant during adolescence and the period leading towards the transition to adulthood. In particular the contributions of Dr. Moshe Yisraelashvili, Shoshana Feldman, Rachel Weiser-Gernak, Michal Rozenman, Alina Brookman-Shelkes and Prof. Sara Smilansky should be mentioned in this regard.

Furthermore, I would like to thank psychoanalyst Dr. Yolanda Gimpel, clinical psychologist Prof. Yona Teichman, and the head of the educational counseling department, Dr. Zippora Magen for their reading the manuscript of this book in its entirety, assessment of its contribution and significance for facilitators in adolescent groups, and suggestions of various alterations which improved its focus and validity.

Karen and Roy Abramovitz prepared and edited the translation into English, and Jeremy Kay of Bartleby Press has prepared the printed edition. Although many people have contributed to our ideas, plans, activities and preparation of the book, responsibility for any shortcomings is wholly the author's.

MOSHE SMILANSKY

Introduction

Topic under Discussion

THE TOPIC OF THIS VOLUME IS THE DEVELOPMENT OF THE NETWORK OF relationships between adolescents and their parents. Although the centrality and crucial quality of this primary subject is generally agreed, it has not been discussed on a theoretical level appropriate for classroom teachers and counsellors within the educational system, and a practical curricular program remains to be developed.

We have based this work on field studies carried out among various target groups. We hope to demonstrate how purposeful development of psychological differentiation from parents is a basic psycho-social task of adolescents in modern society. Once we have dealt with the theoretical and empirical definitions of the topic, we will make recommendations which we hope will facilitate the promotion of such a process.

About 20-25%, a significant number, of adolescents undergo a period of differentiation which can be characterized as one of "storm and stress" and which is extremely difficult for adolescent and parent alike. Those adolescents who do not make an active and/or effective attempt to deal with this task may encounter emotional and social difficulties at a later stage of their development. For some who seem not to "need" to differentiate and seem to be free of the usual parent-adolescent problems, growing up appears to be simple and easy. However, when they reach the stage of having to assume responsibility, to make decisions regarding their personal identity and to choose a career or a life-partner and establish a family, the consequences of having skipped over this life-task become evident. They have not attained the prerequisite autonomy and psychological differentiation from their parents. Clinical studies and research show that such decisions are often influenced by an over-identification or a negative perception of a particular parent. Thus, the decision may actually be inappropriate to one's individual needs, to one's basic personality characteristics or to the sociocultural milieu in which one must find a place. Our assumption is that every adolescent is entitled to support during the process of identity formation, which reinforces the sense of being able to handle such a decisive developmental stage. Our assumptions include the consideration that basic components of sound adolescent development include a broad social perspective and a readiness for significant, reciprocal communication within the sphere of adolescent-parent relationships.

Our approach considers the secondary school system as responsible for ensuring that each adolescent receive the support required for such development. Classroom teachers and counsellors must, therefore, understand the meaning of the term "individuation," including all its implications, and should learn how they can become effective facilitators of the process by means of working with groups and individuals.

Programs confronting adolescent-parent relationships have not been established anywhere else, as far as we are aware. We had no parallel, normative models with which to compare our premises and suggestions for intervention. Therefore, in order to check our starting points, we distributed duplicated copies of the previous version of this book to counsellors, psychologists and classroom teachers, who had already participated in training courses preparing them as facilitators for adolescent groups in Israel and in the United States, and asked for their reactions. We received some very positive responses along with some questions on basic content. This edition takes into account various suggestions for additions and changes. The theoretical introduction— Part One of the book—has been designed for classroom teachers, counsellors and psychologists as well as others with a basic knowledge of the behavioral sciences.

Part One of this book consists of five chapters. Chapter One discusses psychological differentiation occurring between parents and children, in general terms. It represents an integrative view of various theoretical assumptions, according to which differentiation between parents and children is a multifaceted, complex and protracted process, mainly unconscious, which begins at birth and continues throughout one's life. The process originates with the family-of-origin and occurs throughout the period when the individual becomes integrated into various social systems, builds a family and fulfills the tasks of parenthood. In psychological literature this process is called "separation-individuation." We have included both terms in the more general term, "differentiation" trying to include the significance of the term "individuation," referring to the process whereby the child/person deals with becoming "somebody," an individual, an entity possessing a personal identity, an ability to cope and a readiness to assume social responsibility as well as the significance of "separation," whereby the child defines the boundaries between himself and his parents.

Chapter Two shows how adolescents perceive their parents, what their general expectations are, how they define the differences between the mother and the father, and how they see the constellation of interpersonal relationships within the family at any particular stage in their lives. Data cited in this chapter come from research carried out for the purpose of designing this study-program and from other researchers and therapists.

Chapter Three describes conflict patterns occurring in the adolescent-parent relationship. Some are applicable universally: they are the norm for all societies at a certain stage of development. Others are unique to particular social and/or family patterns occurring in Israel or in the United States.

Chapter Four focuses on parent-adolescent communication patterns. It is recognized that both adolescents and parents are deeply involved in each others' lives; both parties are interested in and demand mutual recognition, understanding and support. Therefore, there must be mutual, significant communication between adolescents and parents if the differentiation process is to continue and the quality of family life remain at a high level. Communication will enable the adolescent to negotiate conditions of autonomy and the parent will know how much responsibility to transfer to the adolescent at the appropriate time.

Chapter Five concludes Part One, including a summary of previous material, further generalizations, and the formulation of assumptions concomitant with our approach. It is hoped that the principles outlined in this chapter will foster the development and use of our approach in an appropriate context in order to support and promote continuing adolescent individuation.

There are four factors which must be considered whenever dealing with the topic of adolescent-parent relationships.

a. Culture patterns of a particular society
b. Unique history of the family
c. Basic personality traits and the unique network of relationships between the adolescent and his/her parents
d. Influence of the theoretical point of view.

The Effect of Culture Patterns on the Development of Interpersonal-Relationship Networks

Differences in family culture patterns show up in almost every anthropological or sociological study. The origin of these differences can be historical-ecological, religious, racial, ethnic or class-based;

they influence family composition, role definition and role distribution within the family, the network of relationships among family members, expectations regarding reciprocal expression of emotions, etc. A more wide-ranging discussion of the subject can be found in *Three Generations of Israeli Families* (M. Smilansky, in process).

The Unique History of the Family

When we work with adolescents, we face needs, emotions, expectations and responses of specific young people who have each grown up in a unique environment. We must be conscious of the fact that although each individual family history has developed according to macro-factor influences, it is still a unique system which must be understood and supported for what it is. In Positive Peer Support group work, the purpose of which is to promote adolescent development, the implications go far beyond the limits of anthropological, psychological or sociological research. We are dealing with experiential learning of individuals who need understanding, someone who will listen to them and make responses which are significant for each one as an individual. Our experiential exercises are based on material learned from personal interviews carried out among members of the families: the mother, the father, the adolescent. We interviewed approximately 450 members of 150 families, and, using a psycho-historical reconstruction process, we formed a picture of how members of various families perceived their own development as well as that of other significant family members. At that point we completed our picture with information garnered through additional interviews and discussions in peer groups. This material was the basis for the theoretical data found in the first part of this work and helped us formulate some of the experiential suggestions embodied in the second part of this work.

Basic personality traits and the unique network of relationships between the adolescent, his/her parents and siblings

The facilitator focuses on the development of a particular youngster and how he/she deals with difficulties, while at the same time becoming acquainted with the youngster's behavior at school and within his various peer groups. However, one cannot lose sight of the fact that the young person also exists within the context of a unique family system which is a complex and partially closed entity. What goes on in the family system will directly and/or indirectly, consciously and/or unconsciously, affect adolescent behavior both in school and among peers, and affect interpersonal interaction with peers, friends, teachers and counsellors. Similarly, experiences in school, in the neighborhood and in wider society are reflected within interpersonal relationships in the family.

Theoretical stand necessary for our understanding of the situation, for formulating our assumptions, and for developing sensitivity and concomitant activities

There are many theoretical propositions regarding human development and relationship formation within the family. One's commitment to the principles of a specific proposition will influence one's particular view of a situation, interpretation of developmental tendencies and expectations of change, and selection of alternative interventions and support structures. We do not intend to present an overall, systematic picture of all possible alternatives according to all possible theories, but, rather, where appropriate for our discussion we will cite particular assumptions. We will often refer back to classical psychoanalytic as well as revised psychodynamic theories, since they represent some of the most searching and provocative ideas in the field. Of course, we will also state our own assumptions and propositions. Although it is impossible to generalize when dealing with adolescent-parent relationships, we can employ particular theoretical assumptions in order to reach a general understanding of the phenomena.

The Importance of the Topic

Adolescent-parent relations actually deal with an essential and possibly critical developmental stage of a more comprehensive relational network—that of parent-child relations. Parents are disturbed by various aspects of the problem long before they begin to fulfill their parental role. During the course of their development and the shaping of their patterns of living, from childhood to adulthood, they repeatedly ask themselves or are asked by others: What type of father or mother will I be for my children? When this question is raised, the discussion of which is part of the individuation process and the shaping of each one's identity, expectations develop regarding the manner in which the universal role of parenting will be fulfilled. These expectations may be conscious or remain unconscious. Throughout one's life, from birth on, the parent has struggled with the issue of motherhood or fatherhood—an issue which is the basic component in the process of forming a sexual identity and in one's socialization toward fulfilling a sexual role. Children play "house" and "family" constantly, and through such makebelieve play they cope with the roles of father and/ or mother. From early adolescence until entering the parental role, they asked themselves, by chance or intentionally: Do I want children? How many children? Boys or girls? What will I give them that will be like or unlike what my parents gave me? What will I *not* do with them that my parents did with me? What do I expect to get from fulfilling the social role of parent?

There is no more universal, central or problematic issue in each person's life than that of parenthood. In modern societies 80-90% of the population fulfill the parental role. Indeed, most of those who do not eventually fulfill this role have struggled with the issue, either deciding that they do not want parenthood or having had to reconcile themselves to a biological or social situation which prevented them from fulfilling this role. Thus we can see that understanding the subject is essential for facilitators, parents and adolescents.

There are, in our view, three reasons why it is vital for adolescent development that there be a conscious effort to come to terms with adolescent-parent relationships.

- Purposeful, significant progress through the differentiation process is necessary for adolescent identity formation and consequent development of mature adolescent-parent relationships.
- The quality of present-day life for the adolescent, the parents and the entire family depends on the ability to deal with various aspects of the role issue and thus negotiate desired norms of each role. At that point a situation in which there is mutual understanding of needs, recognition of each one's formulations of his needs and acceptance of responsibility to fulfill mutual expectations can be encouraged.
- Mature choosing of a life-partner and building a future family depends on working through adolescent relationships with one's mother and father and developing both cognitive and emotional faculties.

The developmental sequences described above constitute the process of separation-individuation by which we refer to the differentiation from parents. See Chapter One, "Stages and Patterns in the Lifelong Differentiation Process," for a further description of the process.

In a social context the parental role is complex, multifaceted and laden with expectations. In view of the multiplicity of parental expectations of themselves and the expectations of the children of their parents, we designed an empirical research project with 150 families, noted above, to clarify the cross-generational connection between vertical influences—what is transmitted from one generation to the next—and horizontal influences—intra-familial transactions. We administered additional questionnaires dealing with the adolescent's view of his parents in order to round out the scope of our data. We will use examples from this research to illustrate how the adolescent's perception of his/her parents and the network of relations between them affect the adolescent's life theme, identity formation and its behavioral expression, dreams for the future and expectations of his "niche" in life.

Another important issue is the balance within the family vis a vis the father's role vs. the mother's, which includes the adolescent's perception of his parents as a unit. At this stage the adolescent is in an anomalous position, expecting greater parental support while at the same time expecting the granting of autonomy with its concomitant responsibility, power and authority. We will also discuss the influence of adolescent-parent transactions on the child's vision of the future, methods of choosing a partner and patterns of parenthood.

Chapter One

Stages and Patterns in the Lifelong Individuation Process

THE PROCESS OF PSYCHOLOGICAL DIFFERENTIATION BETWEEN CHILDREN and their parents begins with conception and birth and continues throughout the life span of each family member. Although largely unconscious, it is central to the development of the child's ego and superego, the crystallization of a unique self identity, and the gaining of cognitive, emotional and social difference and distance from each of the parents. It is also the foundation for the development of appropriate, mutually satisfying relationships for the child—a maturing and coping person—and each of his parents, siblings, relatives and life associates.

Although the focus of this book is on adolescent-parent relationships, it is necessary to discuss those early stages which serve as a foundation and address, in short, the transition to adult maturity-the gradual integration of identity and the capacity for autonomy in decision-making and coping.

Six Theoretical Resources for Understanding the Individuation Process

Various theories have contributed to the overall understanding of the differentiation process as it occurs between parents and children. The process in question is multifaceted, complex, protracted and, generally, unconscious.

Each of the psychological and sociological theories described below provides a partial explanation of the essence of the process. These theories are mostly significant for their clarification of the developmental patterns of particular ages, for their in-depth description of certain developmental levels, or for their specific approaches to certain populations. Any contradictions appearing in the generalizations presented below are due, to a certain degree, to the variable reliability of different measurement tools and to perceptual differences between clinical practitioners, who are working with adolescent patients at a crisis point in their lives, using an approach which involves in-depth digging into the secret places of the patient's psyche, and researchers, who are conducting a more objective investigation, using certain types of questionnaires, scales or tests and/or interviews.

First Theoretical Resource: Classical and Modern Psychodynamic Approach

We have drawn the terminology and concepts used in our discussion from classical and modern psychoanalytic theory as our first theoretical resource (cf. Freud, 1905; Erikson, 1950; Freud, 1958; Blos, 1962; Erikson, 1968; Mahler, 1977; Blos, 1979; Josselson, 1980). Psychoanalysis points up the many difficulties attending the multifaceted, complex process of separation-individuation, which tends to cause normative crises and even regression in the developing individual. This process influences children's psychological distancing from their parents as well as the formation of character traits and individual behavior patterns. Beginning with birth it continues throughout life and does not cease even with the death of the parents.

Although research of the past twenty years has called into question the degree of universality psychoanalysts ascribe to a number of the concepts applied to certain developmental phenomena, there has been nothing of comparable depth to replace these concepts.

Second Theoretical Resource: Psycho-social Developmental Approach

Psycho-social developmental theory covers the entire life-span (cf. Erikson, 1950; Gould, 1978; Levinson et al., 1978). This approach extends the concept of development beyond early childhood and adolescence. It describes maturation tasks and coping with normative crises in terms of discrete stages of development, ranging from the period of late adolescence to old age. Note that Erikson appears in both the first and second level of resources.

Third Theoretical Resource:
the Family as a Developing Social System

This approach (cf. Boszarmanyi-Nagi, 1965; Satir, 1967; Minuchin, 1974; Kantor & Lehr, 1975) not only deals with an expanded age range, from that of early childhood to that of adolescence, but also broadens the concept of human development to include both the sociocultural and the dynamic interpersonal context. Thus the adolescent must cope with separation-individuation tasks not only in terms of his personal, inmost needs, but also in terms of his membership within an integrated and dynamic interpersonal entity where everyone is involved in the process—mother, father, sisters, brothers; these others not only actively influence, but are also recipients of influence and they themselves go through stages of development by fulfilling their own roles, sexually determined and otherwise, within the family and society-at-large.

Fourth Theoretical Resource: the Development of Social Cognition

This approach (cf. particularly the works of Selman (1980) and Youniss & Smaller, 1985) enables us to perceive the development of a social perspective throughout the life-cycle and to appreciate the unique role the period of adolescence can play in developing an even higher level of social perspective. Through this approach an adolescent can begin to perceive his parents as human beings, composite personalities with their own needs, existing within a context of a past, present and expectations for the future. Developing social cognition enables an adolescent to learn systematically how to develop a new, more mature network of relationships with his parents, based on his achievements within a social perspective.

Fifth Theoretical Resource:
Theories of Role Fulfillment and Communication

The significance of these theories lies in their recognition that individual development is not simply a personal, inner process, taking place, as it were, in a vacuum. It is also the experience of fulfilling social roles, communication and transactions with others, which is crucial. The child first experiences mutual transactions with his parents and afterwards with others. Progress in adolescence is marked by differentiation from parents, attaining psychological autonomy and forming a personal identity. These goals are achieved through coping with friendship tasks, social relationships, and social activities outside the family while, at the same time, dealing with confrontations over roles, i.e., positions of power and responsibility, within the family. Therefore, within the framework of the Supportive Peer Group, which we have developed, the approach and the activities focus on communication and learning how to perceive roles. In the experiential segment of this unit we work towards developing the adolescent's ability to understand his/her parents as human beings who fill social-sexual roles in the family and in society-at-large and who have needs, problems, frustrations, successes and failures arising out of the fulfillment of their roles. According to our approach, the adolescent at this stage of social-sexual role-fulfillment must understand other members of his family and perform his roles in family interpersonal transactions, in the youth society and in society-at-large. He must negotiate for power and authority within the family system just as within other systems and form new and more desirable sets of relationships.

Sixth Theoretical Resource: Theories of Group Dynamics

According to this approach, the rules of the development of group dynamics or group process applies to the family as well. The adolescent develops his personal identity and individuates while coping with several temporary groups or subgroups: his original family group, his class at school, his youth group, his sports team, his neighborhood group, his friends from the community, etc. Later he will have to cope with other, more or less stable groups: his roommates at university, his comrades in the army, his colleagues at work, his spouse and family, his community. Inasmuch as, while filling his own needs and expectations, he understands the needs and expectations of other participants in the groups of which he is a member, he will be able to proceed towards individuation and concomitant discovery of a life-theme or "niche." The fact that we give such a central position to supportive peer group experiences reflects how important we consider coping within a group framework.

In addition to the theoretical basis described above, our approach is also predicated on research which we have undertaken, some of which was intended specifically as preparation for this program and some of which was intended for more general purposes.

Stages in the Development of Separation-Individuation Throughout the Life-cycle

Two basic concepts in the psychological description of human development are *separation* and *individuation*. They refer to a generally unconscious, complex and multifaceted developmental process by which the infant separates from his/her mother and seeks the rudiments of autonomy from both mother and father. Later, during adolescence, this process involves a conscious freeing of oneself from the image of the omnipotent, larger-than-life mother and father, internalized as a child, which consequently frees oneself from psychological dependence on real-life parents and encourages the formulation of a personal identity and the development of the ability to cope as an autonomous entity.

The term "individuation" was coined by Mahler (1977) in order to describe a stage in the development of a child from birth to the end of his third year. Blos (1962, 1979) describes the psychodynamic process at the beginning of adolescence, defining this period as "a second individuation stage." We will use the term "individuation" as a general heading which describes man's lifelong task of achieving psychological differentiation and autonomy—the way man is active in formulating his identity, determining his life-style and taking responsibility for his own decisions. In general it is possible to describe 11 stages of individuation, each of which represents a turning point in the process of psycho-social child-parent differentiation. Of course, the age at which a particular event occurs, the form each stage takes in terms of its concrete expression and the significance of such expressions are different for each individual within each family—they are unique to a particular child, his mother and father, his siblings and even those members of the extended family who have a significant role in the family. These patterns are also different, to a certain degree, in different cultures.

Stage One of Individuation—from birth through the age of three.

Stage Two of Individuation—from 3-4 to 10-11 years of age, the beginning of adolescence.

Stage Three of Individuation—from the beginning of adolescence to age 14-15, completion of eight-year elementary school or junior high school.

Stage Four of Individuation—Adolescence, 15-18 years of age. Adolescence includes the development of social skills and a more complex social perspective, involvement in peer groups and initial development of intimate ties with members of the opposite sex, and beginning to establish a personal identity (such as, choosing a major or type of secondary school) which may affect one's future career choice. This stage marks the beginning of political involvement and confrontations with parents about equality as a human value. At this stage some youth begin to work full time, having reached the legal age at which one is allowed to work, and others may move from the house into a dormitory setting. For Europeans, Israelis and some Americans this stage ends with preparations to enter the army and making decisions concerning one's national service.

Stage Five of Individuation—Advanced Adolescence, from the age of 17-18 to 20-21 years: acceptance of the right and obligations of citizenship by fulfilling obligatory army or national service, exercising full political rights and obligations of a citizen through voting in both national and local elections. At this point the individual attains certain legal rights: to marry without parental consent, to change one's religious values without parental intervention, and to leave the country without parental consent.

Stage Six of Individuation—Transition to Early Adulthood, from 20-21 to 23-24 years of age, which is characterized by renewed conflict arising from adjustments in the relationships between the younger and older generations. Development in this stage focuses on leaving the parents' home and conditions therein, the decision whether to continue in higher education of some sort or to go out to work, the continuation of one's personal-sexual, professional, political, economic identity formulation and a crystallization of one's mature worldview in all dimensions and within all one's activities.

Stage Seven of Individuation—Early Adulthood, the second half of the 20's through the 30's, choosing a mate and establishing a family. At this stage the focus on mutual responsibility of parents and children changes into the measure of involvement of the parents in their children's decisions, the ties that the young person establishes with his spouse and his/her parents, how the young couple copes with the difficulties of establishing a new network of relationships with their parents and relatives.

Stage Eight of Individuation—Pregnancy and Becoming Parents. This stage is sometimes simultaneous with the previous stage, depending on the individual situation. It includes the new mother's establishing relations with her parents (and those of her husband) in their new roles as grandparents.

Stage Nine of Individuation—The 40's—Middle Age. Theoreticians and therapists have called this stage the "Mid-Life Crisis." A central characteristic of this turning point in the developmental road is critical reevaluation of early decisions which were taken for the most part before the young person had progressed very far on the differentiation road and during a period when his life-focus or youthful dreams were forcing him into intensive coping with psycho-social maturation tasks.

Stage Ten of Individuation—Later Adulthood, Aging and Death of Parents.

Stage Eleven of Individuation—The Period Between One's Parents' Death and One's Own Death.

After enumerating a possible definition of developmental stages through the life-span, we shall describe the main features of childhood and adolescence.

Stage 1: Primary Individuation

The first stage begins at birth. The beginning of the process is marked with the severing of the biological connection of the infant from its mother with the cutting of the umbilical cord and the creation of a psychological symbiosis with the mother during the first month of life as a substitute. Subsequently, a psycho-social tie develops, first with the mother and then with the father. These ties are responsible for the formation of a primary sense of "self," of an actively coping "I."

What we have here is an example of the basic human, mutual development of deeply significant social-emotional ties the effects of which are felt throughout the lifetime of both parties to the relationship. The wife-mother and, sometimes, the husband-father, develop a bond with the infant. Psychological literature employs two terms to express this connection (Bowlby, 1969).

The first psychological term is the "natural maternal bond" and describes the bio-psychological sensation which appears in women at childbirth. It is the result of an immediate psycho-biological sensitivity to the significance of confronting the fruit of her own body. The second term refers to the tie which develops gradually during the first year of life between the mother and the father (or another, regular primary care-giver) and the child. This tie is physical and psychological. Bowlby (1951) termed this "attachment" and considered this tie crucial for the normal development of the child. If the physical aspect of the tie is not accomplished, the phenomenon which Freud called "separation anxiety" is liable to appear. Failure to develop such a physical tie between parents and the child in the first year of life results in other negative behavior patterns such as fear and anxiety in the presence of strangers, a phenomenon which is called "xenophobia."

A report presented by Bowlby to the World Health Organization (1951) describes the problems of children deprived of this basic tie with their mothers. Severe effects associated with such deprivation include retarded emotional, intellectual and social development of the child. Since this report was published, additional evidence has been collected. Following are three general comments:

- empirical research in recent decades has aided our understanding that a child is an active, social agent from birth—he establishes social ties with those around him and uses his behavior to influence his relationship with his mother, father, and other caregivers.

- mothers treat male babies differently than female (Goldberg & Lewis, 1969; Lewis, 1972); they treat babies of different temperament in different ways and the care, e.g., the social tie with the infant, is different in situations where the mother is alone with the baby and when the father is present. In other words, from the very beginning of life we are speaking about interpersonal transactions within an active social system and not about a unidirectional model in which the child's development can be ascribed only to the way the mother raised him.

- every parent who has raised more than one child knows that individual differences exist between infants from the very beginning; research has indicated that different infants establish different modes of interaction with their parents. For example, Schaefer & Emerson (1964 B) reported how it is possible to define certain infants as "loving to be hugged." Rutter (1947) described how differential qualities of infants influenced how the relationship with the mother proceeded. Thomas, Chess & Birch (1968, 1977) followed the development of children from birth until elementary school age and concluded that temperament was a basic part of the personality, remaining constant for most of the subjects (138 infants) over the years.

Mahler's (1977) description of the relationship between a child and his mother expresses the modern psychoanalytic approach. She claimed that by the second month of life the infant already recognizes the mother as the one who provides for his needs. The origin of the lengthy process of defining boundaries and borders between himself and others begins when he realizes that his mother exists as a separate being. Mahler called this process "separation-individuation." According to her view the infant's perception is fuzzy for several long months and the lack of differentiation between the "I" and the "not-I" is characteristic of this initial period of individuation.

Mahler held that separation and individuation are two complementary processes: the separation process characterizes development of the child as he frees himself of the diffuse symbiosis with the mother, and individuation is the process in which the child develops an awareness of his own individual characteristics. This integrated development is what brings about the feeling of differentiation for the child, the feeling of being a separate individual.

According to Mahler, it is possible to divide the infant and toddler's process of the development of psychological individuation into three central stages: *the autistic stage, the symbiotic stage* and *the separation-individuation stage*.

The autistic stage defines the situation of the infant at the age of one month. During this stage the infant sleeps most of the time and, even when awake, does not seem to be aware of the mother. The infant perceives himself as an autarchy, as supplying himself with everything necessary. The mother, however, by caring for him, provides him satisfying experiences and enables him to become aware of the significance of a tie with her and with that which surrounds him.

The symbiotic stage develops from the second month and lasts until the fifth month. It begins with the infant employing his various senses to explore the significance of the mother and ends with sensory awareness extending to contacts beyond the mother. The term symbiosis describes the dependency relationship between the mother's energy and the child's energy. Such a relationship expressing the integration of the mother with the child becomes a vital all-purpose system—a bi-polar unity within shared borders, which contributes initially to removal of the autistic shell. Mahler claims that in this period the baby is completely dependent on the mother, who is his partner in the symbiotic system, since he still lacks a perceptible "self." In different terms, the mother acts as an auxiliary ego at this stage, filling developmental roles for the child of which he is not yet capable. She is sensitive to feelings of frustration and aggression, establishes boundaries and helps govern impulses. Winnicot (1971) completes the picture and claims that the symbiosis, which from a psychological point of view is the lack of a feeling of boundaries, is felt mutually by the child and the mother. The loss of boundaries brings about a temporary psychological regression in the mother, expressing itself in recollections of her earlier childhood experiences, a phenomenon which contributes to the child's development by enabling the mother to give the child supportive empathy. This is a preparatory situation, of consolidation leading to formation of the nuclear self vis-a-vis the parental object.

The climax of the childhood development process, is that of separation-individuation. This period, which begins around the age of six months and lasts until the child is about three years old, is decisive with regard to normal ego development. Physical, cognitive, emotional and social development during this period contribute to the psychological readiness of the child to be separated gradually from his mother and father and to act as required in the school's social system.

Mahler notes that during this period the child enjoys his discoveries, systematically practicing the new skills he has acquired, but constantly tests whether his libidinal needs are continuing to be met by the mother. The child tries to distance himself from his mother and at the same time watches to make sure she doesn't get too far away from him. His goal at this point is to feel in control over the ambivalence involved in his need to distance himself and maintain closeness, which is a pleasurable feeling. Also in this period the child gradually gains control over most of the tasks that the mother had fulfilled for him in the past, internalizing her image along with those functions.

This process strengthens the "I" as his ability develops to withstand internal and external stimuli. Now the "I" also has the ability of access to sublimation, a more accurate, objective perception of reality, a greater control over feelings, a much greater ability to withstand frustration. At the end of the period he should have achieved development of a stable emotional relationship with the mother and father, despite fluctuations, anxiety and frustration in the realization of needs. Mahler, like other psychoanalysts before her, speaks about the relationship of the infant and toddler with the mother while ignoring the father. But, according to her view, the father also fulfills roles in the process.

The father is the one who can and needs to bring the child out of the symbiotic relationship with the mother, and supports the child in his absorption into the real world of things and people. The father is the "not mother." When he is active, loving and persistent, he has the ability to create the necessary balance to the regressive attraction of the mother, who does not adequately support progress in separation-individuation. The father also creates a balance of alternative, loving image which may be internalized in the process of securing confidence in man and developing an autonomous "I" during the second year of life. Erikson (1950) emphasizes the blending of relationships between the mother and the baby and defines the maturation task of the first year of life as the initial fundamental attempt to formulate an identity separate from the mother. The central problem of the child at this stage is acquiring a basic trust that his needs will be met. From this, in his words, springs the psychological basis for trust in the future, in man and in society.

The basic period of the individuation process reaches its peak in the second year of life, when with the acquisition of language and loco-motion, the child is ready to differentiate between himself, his parents and significant others. He can express his perceptions, his desires and his decisions in his own words. In a practical sense, he can attempt to establish personal autonomy in his clothing, in food, in forming rela-tionships and in preferring relationships (such as showing a preference for father over mother). Mahler describes this period in the develop-ment of individuation in detail and indicates that it generally concludes toward the end of the third year of life. This process is characterized by the acquisition of "object permanency" and the ability to distin-guish between inner and external reality, between "I" and "not I." A result of the initial individuation process is an independence from the mother's concrete, physical presence, whom psychoanalysts define as an "object." The physical separation from the mother is facilitated by the perception of the permanence of the object, that is to say, the mother exists even when she isn't there, because the child has inter-nalized her image.

According to Erikson's view (1950), this is the second of eight devel-opment stages of "ego identity." Its focus or maturation task is the attainment of psychological autonomy from the mother. According to Erikson those who have not coped successfully with this task remain prey to a sense of embarrassment and self-doubt.

Stage Two of Individuation: From the Age of 4 until 10 or 11

Development from the first stage of individuation to the beginnings of maturation is characterized by four major dimensions:

Physical, biological development—which gives the child a growing ability of personal activity, gradually becoming free of the need to depend on a parent or other adult. He is then able to distance himself from the parent and home and to experience the significance of what he sees, of people and of activities which are different from those he has encountered or seen at home or in his own surroundings.

Cognitive development—which enables the development of self per-ception as well as perception of others and the learning of language and other necessary skills. This includes the gradual acquisition of the basics of one's heritage and the culture in which one is raised and the development of mutual communication with one's parents and other adults as well as with one's peers and others. The latter items will be brought up in Part II of this book and will be further explained and illustrated by writings from various schools of thought.

Emotional development—which enables the child to separate from his mother and from other members of his family and to fashion emotional ties with children he meets on the street, in the neighborhood, in kindergarten and in school.

Social development—which could be called learning the "rules of the game" with reference to learning how to participate in the various socio-dramatic games, to the development of friendship and group ties and to integration into the life in kindergarten and in school, etc.

It is understood that these dimensions are integrated and expressed within each child in a different pattern and at a different rate. We will present only the general outlines of the things by means of an essential description as supported by various theoretical thinkers before continuing on with the main focus of our discussion: stages in the period of adolescence.

Freudian Theory and Later Psychodynamic Propositions

Freud saw sexual power as a central force in human behavior. Growth takes place according to stages of psychosexual development which are identified by the erogenous zone dominant in each stage. Thus the child will pass from the oral stage (during which gratification comes from the mouth) to the anal stage (during which gratification comes from the process of producing bodily excretions) to the "phallic" stage (during which the focus of gratification is on the male sexual organ).

During the oral and anal stages the mother is the main "love object" and the primary relationship formed with her is the basis and the model for all the later interpersonal relationships.

The phallic stage, generally characterizing the period between the ages of three and six, the period following the primary individuation stage, involves the parent of the opposite sex as the child's major "love object." Thus, the "Oedipal situation" occurs when a son finds himself in conflict: on the one hand, the boy identifies with his father and loves him; on the other hand, the father is the boy's major competitor for the mother's love as well as the major obstacle preventing him from attaining his desire with regard to the mother. At this stage the child fears that his father, who is stronger than he is, will take revenge and punish him for forbidden sexual desires. Freud argues, that castration fears, characterizing this stage of development arise from this situation.

Girls, according to Freud, show a different dynamic during this stage of development. Girls discover that they are missing the male sexual organ. They blame their mother and turn for compensation from their father. This is called the "Electra Complex" in psychoanalytical literature, parallel to the "Oedipus Complex" for boys, and is characterized by penis envy.

The normal resolution of the oedipal conflict is found in the child's identification with the parent of the same sex. This identification involves internalizing parental values and the development of a superego. With such a solution the child is able to enter the relatively tranquil latency stage.

Latency (ages 6-10 or 11) encompasses a lessening in the pressure of sexual urges. Identification with parents is strong; the child's energy is channeled into the areas of learning and developing social skills and becoming an integrated member of elementary school.

Such integration is significant in terms of the child's ability to identify with learning and performance tasks required by that societal institution. The developmental focus is the ability to carry out requisite tasks without developing an inferiority complex.

Damon (1983) notes the importance of social development—the relationships with friends—at the transition point from home to nursery or kindergarten and defines three prominent psychological changes which characterize the quality of the interaction with friends. His definition of the development of individuation is based on these changes:

- daily events have greater and greater symbolic significance as social cognition develops. Such symbolic significance changes the meaning of life events of the child, opens him up to new possibilities of interpersonal interaction with others and weakens his psychological dependence on his parents.
- a sense of moral obligation develops at this stage, which enables the child to understand the deeper significance of such activities as role-playing, sharing (toys, food, clothing), etc.
- the capacity of a nursery or kindergarten-aged child to perceive interpersonal interaction as part of a stable system of social relations, which lays foundations for the development of friendship.

In addition to the ability to perceive roles, a significant stage in the child's social-cognitive development occurs now which enables the child to enter another's shoes, to feel the other's relationships and emotions. This is the beginning of the development of social perspective. This stage also marks the beginning of a change in self perception and perception of the parent—a process of individuation through which the child moves in three sub-stages:

From age 3-6 he still has an egotistical view of the world. However, the child discriminates between himself and others although he cannot yet distinguish between his own social perspective (in terms of thoughts and feelings) and that of another. He can label the external expression of different types of behavior (like anger, sadness, joy), but he has no perception of the cause-effect relationship existing between the cause of feelings and the reactions to the cause.

From age 6-8 the child develops perception of social-informative roles. He understands that it is possible that there could be a social perspective different from his, based on a different perception and interpretation of reality. But he still focuses on isolated perceptions and is unable to adapt to different perceptions.

At the age of 8-10 the child arrives at the "Reflective Stage," meaning that the child can now reflect on his role and that of others in a comparative way. The child is aware now that each person has a different social perspective and this influences both his perception of others and of himself in relation to others. He understands how putting himself in another's place is a way of judging aims, intentions and actions. He is able to create a chain of parallel perspectives but he is not yet able to abstract the process.

It is also necessary to consider the aspect of pro-social development which is based on the formation of an affective element called empathy: the readiness to identify with the needs of another person and to give him the support he needs.

As children grow in age and cognitive development, they become more capable of engaging in systematic cooperative activity with others. Pro-social behavior, a characteristic which develops gradually from age four until 12 and is expressed by showing empathy and mutual support, becomes the dominant trait of stable friendships and social relations. As we described earlier (Smilansky, 1988), any discussion of the development of friendship and social relations must include the implications social development has for the child's progress in psychological separation from his parents.

Stage Three of Individuation—Early Adolescence

The third stage of separation-individuation begins at the beginning of adolescence (age 11-12), parallel to biological development and the awakening of sexual urges, and it continues on the average to age 13-15.

In classical psychoanalytic terms this stage is a period in which there is a regression to the oedipal stage, a struggle with psychological separation and the formation of a new network of relationships with each of the parents. Freud claims that the adolescent period is characterized by maturing sexual drives. As in the phallic stage the child's sexuality continues to be expressed towards the parent of the opposite sex. Therefore, oedipal conflicts appear once again. However, unlike during the phallic stage, the superego, which came to the fore during the latency period, does not allow conscious expression of forbidden sexual desires; drawing on a defense mechanism called repression, early adolescent children project their desires onto other objects which serve as substitutes for the parent of the opposite sex. The degree of identification with one's parents drops at the beginning of the adolescent period, and the adolescent begins to identify with other models: a youth group counsellor, a teacher, a counsellor at camp or in the dormitory of a boarding school, sports stars, popular singers, movie stars, etc. Sometimes the adolescent may fall in love with an adult man or woman who is unaware of becoming the object of such feelings. The task of the adolescent is to break free of his emotional dependency on his parents and attain mature sexual relationships with members of the opposite sex. It is up to him to break off the love tie with his mother and to free himself from the father's dominance. This process of emotional breaking away can show up as alienation, rebellion, hostility toward the parent or toward any other social authority.

Classical analysis emphasizes the "generation gap" during adolescence and especially the conflict between children and their parents. It characterizes adolescence as a stage of "storm and stress" across all cultures and historical periods. Freud perceived the individuation process occurring at the beginning of adolescence as accompanied universally by a profound crisis. He considered it as one of the most painful psychological attainments which concluded the period of distancing oneself from parental authority, a process which alone ensured that the new generation would oppose the old and which was of utmost importance for the progress of civilization (Freud, Z., 1905).

Anna Freud (1958), who was a psychotherapist who treated adolescents, thoroughly investigated their problems and described the difficult nature of the maturation process. The following excerpt presents her point of view that the adolescent period is a universally troublesome stage, a generalization which undoubtedly reflects her treatment of troubled adolescents who served as examples from which she generalized about the rest of their peers.

She notes that the adolescent period constitutes, by definition, the cutting off point of a tranquil growth process and its external indicators resemble various manifestations of emotional and structural disturbance. The behavioral expressions of adolescents are similar to that of neurotic, psychotic and sociopathic personalities, and are combined in a nearly incomprehensible way with primary borderline states, frustration or full blown expressions of nearly all mental illnesses. As a result, differential diagnosis between a disturbed adolescent and actual pathology is an extremely difficult task.

The clearest and most detailed articulation of the psychoanalytic concept of individuation during adolescence is presented by Peter Blos (1963, 1979) in various articles and his most recent book, in which he integrates concepts from modern theories of ego psychology. Unlike Freud, who claimed that the personality is essentially formed in the initial years of childhood, Blos attaches great importance to the influence of the processes taking place during adolescence and considers this period as a critical stage in personality formation.

Blos describes the central task of adolescence as breaking away from an emotional dependency on parents and finding a love object outside the family. Picking up on Mahler's definition of the early development period as "Primary Individuation," Blos defines the beginning of adolescence as "Secondary Individuation." He further describes the process of secondary individuation as involving a partial regression to earlier developmental stages, a regression which brings with it reawakened, unresolved conflicts. This regression is not pathological, but rather it serves a positive function in ego development during adolescence. Such a regression allows a reorganization of the personality, facilitating the finding of solutions to previously unresolved conflicts. As do other modern psychoanalysts, he claims that during adolescence the person attains psychological independence from internal infantile objects, i.e., from a childish perception of mother and father stemming from the first stages of childhood ego development. This process ends when the adolescent finds a love object outside the family. He claims that psychological release from dependency on parents, the foundation of which is in immature relationships with "internalized familial objects," enables the adolescent to perceive his parents and himself anew, to appreciate them differently and conceptualize his place in the adult world. Thus, psychological individuation occurring during the adolescent maturation process supports and furthers the crystallization of a personal, sexual-social identity. Differentiation from parents compels the young person to distance himself from them, even if he fails to attain sufficient internal autonomy. The adolescent turns for the most part to his peer groups and these fulfill important functions in furthering his development. Thus, for example, a social group (or friends from within it) can help the adolescent to break away, to a great extent, from emotional dependence on his parents and can supply him with the support and feeling of confidence that his parents had previously provided within the framework of the family.

Blos describes several stages within the ongoing adolescent period. He begins with a description of the characteristics of the preadolescent period and concludes with a definition of the transition to maturity. This division also provides us with a bridge between the description of childhood development and that of adolescence.

Blos delineates six developmental stages, at the center of which is the adolescent process:

Latency—During this period the libidinal drive is not intense and may be directed towards constructive educational goals. The child identifies greatly with his parents and internal conflicts are nearly undetectable. This period is one in which the ego develops greatly and increases its autonomy. At the same time there are significant developments in cognitive areas: memory, judgment, empathy, planning, self-awareness, the ability to distinguish between reality and imagination and between thoughts and actions. These developments prepare a positive basis for normal development during adolescence and prepare the way toward resolution of conflicts.

Preadolescence—A significant change takes place, as a result of physical maturation and an increase in the intensity of sexual urges and feelings of aggression. These urges are still not consolidated and are not focused on any specific object. At the same time there are strong regressive tendencies which are sometimes expressed in external forms, such as overeating, neglecting one's body and personal hygiene, etc. The child begins to distance himself from the family and ignores his parent's attempts to control him. The parents respond for the most part with ambivalent feelings. Parental inconsistency, arising from this ambivalence, may contribute to exacerbating the rift between them and their adolescent children.

During this period a son directs his aggression toward his mother and women in general. There are fewer conflicts with his father. According to Blos, the adolescent boy, fearing his father's jealous reaction, tries to defend himself from the father. He is often unaware of this background to his friendly relations with his father. At this stage some young boys exhibit idealizations of their fathers.

The crisis in daughter-parent relationships begins during this period as well, especially between daughters and mothers. The daughter, who has been encouraged to remain passive and dependent since childhood, attempts to free herself, and she begins to identify with her father or with someone of the opposite sex. Thus, we find the daughter who tries to act as though she were a son and, the opposite, the daughter who acts as though she were a "little wife."

Early Adolescence—In contrast to the previous stage, maturation of aggressive drives, especially the libidinal drive, become more focused. The awakening sexual drive is directed to finding love objects outside of the family. There is a sharp drop in the degree of identification with parents, and the search for others with whom to identify through friendships, idealizations and hero-worship becomes even more intense. This period is characterized by a proliferation of incidents of a bisexual nature, reflecting the fact that these identifications are not necessarily heterosexual. Such occurrences arouse frequent conflicts at this stage. In order for the adolescent to be able to form a heterosexual relationship, he must overcome his homosexual or bisexual tendencies and give up his preoedipal and oedipal love objects for a love object from outside the family. In order to do this he must break his psychological dependency on his parents. In early adolescence conflict with parents is primarily in terms of the relationship with the mother.

Adolescence—At this stage heterosexual tendencies become stronger than bisexual ones. The sexual drives mature further and are directed at finding a heterosexual object. Acknowledgment of heterosexual tendencies requires differentiation from the family of origin and the finding of a final resolution for oedipal conflicts. A reorganization of personality begins at this stage. The reorganization process is characterized by confused identification and extreme swings in opinions and moods—a situation which is broadly referred to as development of feelings of "storm and stress." Typical of this period is unpredictable and rebellious behavior of the adolescent.

Although the adolescent is searching for an alternative heterosexual object to love outside the family, at this stage he is still afraid of deep involvement with and dependence on the new object. The conflict-laden struggle to free himself from dependence on his parents, which has reached its peak at this point, gives rise to such fears. The adolescent's view of achieving independence is intertwined with his separation from his childhood parental image, previously the source of guidance, understanding and feelings of confidence.

Advanced Adolescence—It is now possible to discern a drop in the degree of intensity of the "storm," the confusion and the reorganization which characterized the previous stage. The adolescent's sexual identity is beginning to coalesce, opposing tendencies of the id are being integrated to a greater degree, the existence of an ego and superego is evident, and a harmonious personality structure is forming in which the id and the superego serve the ego.

The sexual drive and the ego have united for the purpose of seeking a heterosexual love object; thus, ambivalence in the relationship with parents and the intensity of conflicts related to the search for ties and identities outside the family both drop distinctly.

Transition to Pre-Adulthood—This stage marks the transition from adolescence to adulthood. This stage sees the achievement of the final goals of adolescence: a stable organization of sexual drives in harmony with ego organization. During this period self assessment becomes more stable and consistent, and less influenced by outside sources.

The developmental task of this period is the establishment of identities, loyalties and intimate relationships outside of the family. At the same time, the level of conflict and rebelliousness toward the parents decreases, and the perception of the parents is more realistic and is characterized by greater readiness to recognize the parents' positive qualities and not just their negative qualities.

Criticism of the Classical Proposition that Adolescence is Universally a Period of "Storm and Stress"

Cumulative evidence from studies carried out since the 1960's (Douvan & Adelson, 1966; Masterson, 1967; Offer, 1969; Offer & Offer, 1975; Josselson, 1977; Vaillant, 1977; Flaherty & Dusek, 1980; Smilansky, 1984; Youniss & Smaller, 1985) has contradicted the hypothesis regarding the universality of the identity crisis and of "storm and stress" syndrome. It seems that such a phenomenon is characteristic of only a small portion of the research subjects (approximately 25% of all adolescents). This population, it would seem, is well known to psychoanalysts and it was on the basis of their therapeutic experience with these adolescents that the problem was generalized. Most adolescents don't hate their parents, don't reveal instability or maladjustment, and go gradually through each developmental stage. During the process they settle into peer groups, differentiate without a rift from their parents, form relationships with the opposite sex, choose a vocation (those who opt early for work and vocational schools) or begin the process of forming their professional identity and enjoying their leisure time (sports, cars, entertainment, movies, etc.).

Josselson (1980)'s summary of this criticism is harsh, but nevertheless correct in our view:

> [The psychoanalytic] literature, although added enormously to our understanding of defenses, drew an extremely skewed picture of adolescents. The adolescent was seen to be desperately warding off a revival of the Oedipus

complex by choosing a "non-incestuous sexual partner." All other aspects of adolescence, such as interests, friendships, or identity, were either overlooked or treated as sublimations designed to contain Oedipal dangers. The adolescent was seen to become autonomous from his parents because repudiating the incestuous (Oedipal) tie also involved relinquishing all ego ties to the parents (Josselyn, 1952; Balser, 1966). This repudiation of the parents was viewed as a necessary means to avoid regression to Oedipal fixations" (Josselson, 1980, p. 188).

Josselson also argues that these descriptions of the "weak ego of the adolescent" are based on clinical evidence and mentions empirical studies which contradict this assumption. She claims that the theory of "storm and stress" has misled an entire generation of researchers in adolescent development.

Douvan and Adelson (1966) studied a sample of approximately 3500 "normal" young adolescents and did not find any evidence of their being occupied with problems of inhibiting their drives vis a vis the parent of the opposite sex. Offer (1969, 1975), a psychiatrist, designed a long-term, intensive study, using various types of research tools, with a regular population of adolescents studying in a high school in the United States. He did not find a universal phenomenon of the development of signs of "storm and stress" or of weak egos and rejection of parents. He and his colleagues concluded that this phenomenon characterizes, to one degree or another, about 22% of the study sample.

Adelson (1979) concludes, based on all of the above evidence, that the existence of "storm and stress" as a universal phenomenon of adolescence is a kind of psychoanalytic myth, and describes further limitations of the classic psychodynamic approach. In another article (1980) he notes that the use of clinical procedure, including lying on the couch and encouraging concentration fixed on the child's relationship with his parents and on conflicts during childhood, can in themselves contribute to the appearance of regression noted by the psychoanalysts as characterizing that very stage of development. He notes also that the same theoreticians ignore the revolutionary development which occurs in the level of social thinking and cognition, a claim which is also made by Selman (1980) in his work on the development of social perspective during adolescence, as we shall describe below.

Social-Psychological Theories: Focus on Late Adolescence and Transition to Adulthood

Despite different theoretical formulations, there is considerable agreement about defining psycho-social maturation tasks and about the primary role of the differentiation process from parents as a basis for individuation, formation of personal identity and building an adult life-style. The later theories also agree in their stress on the fifth and sixth stages of individuation, or according to our classification, the period of Late Adolescence and Transition to Early Adulthood.

Erikson (1950, 1968) notes that from ages 19-22 young people cease using their parents as models and begin to build their personal identity. Havighurst (1953), representing an anthropological and sociological approach, speaks about developmental tasks of adolescence and defines the age range of 16-22 as a period during which the adolescent must attain emotional independence from his parents and acquire an independent system of values. Levinson (1978), a social psychologist, defines the period between 17-22 as a "transition period" between adolescence and adulthood, focused on psychological differentiation from parents and formulation of an independent "dream." Gould (1978), a psychiatrist with an analytic background, defines the years 16-18 as a period of striving for autonomy from parents, during the course of which bridges are built with members of the peer group.

Erikson states that the concept of ego identity formation is part of an emotional process of self development from age 16-22. At a time when one is dealing with preparing for a career, one is coping with a complete and more independent development of mature awareness. In this process one copes with the challenge of the assumptions and world-view of parents while developing one's own beliefs and values. The individual acquires his independence and afterwards shares it with his social groups or voluntarily limits it within an intimate relationship. The adult consciousness is formulated gradually over the years as, step by step, parents are abandoned as models and a personal identity begins to be built. By about the age of 22 the individual must abandon the world as half child-half adult, in which form he had lived in until now and he must decide to be someone (1968).

We would add that Erikson considers differentiation from parents as a secondary component of personal identity formation, which he sees as the central task of late adolescence.

Cognitive Theory: the Development of Social Perspective in Parent-Child Relations

Cognitive theory assumes that development of the child's ability to perceive himself and others on a higher level enables him to understand who his mother and father are, as well as to become aware of his own self. Having attained this insight, he can then proceed in a more conscious way in his differentiation from each of his parents.

Selman (1980) developed a scale of development of social perspective, based on the theories and research approaches of Piaget and Inhelder (1969) and Kohlberg (1969). We presented his hierarchical and structured scale of perception of friendship elsewhere (Smilansky, 1988); here we shall present his scale of the perception of parent-child relations. We will focus on the issue of punishment to illustrate this approach, and show the development of the child's perception of the meaning of punishment as his parents apply it to his behavior. The overlap of ages within the different stages illustrates the existence of individual differences in developmental rate and patterns.

The Egocentric, Non-Differentiating Stage (ages 3-6)

The child cannot distinguish clearly between the object and the subject or between his perception of social situations and those of others. He cannot understand why his perception may not necessarily be the correct one.

The child is aware of the connection between punishment and forbidden behavior; however, he is not aware of the meaning of the motives which led his parents to punish him.

The Stage of Subjective, Discriminating Ability to Observe from Someone Else's Point of View (age 5-9)

Children of this age know that another person has his own personal point of view which is different from his. He is still unable to determine exactly what the other person's method of adapting is, and he likewise assumes that only one point of view can be correct—his, or that of some authority.

At this stage the child recognizes the motivation behind his parents' punishments. He perceives punishment as serving three ends: to learn a lesson, to protect him from danger, to redress the balance—a sort of settling of accounts.

The Stage of Dual Perspective and of Introspection (age 7-12)

The child perceives that the other person is capable of thinking about *his* way of thinking and understanding his perspective in different social situations, but this ability is still limited to a relationship between two people. At this stage he still cannot grasp more than one point of view which differs from his own.

Parental punishment is perceived as an expression of worry on the part of the parent for his child. The child understands punishment as a type of communication the purpose of which is to make him think about a certain aspect of his behavior. Punishment is perceived as a deterrent which will later become an internal agent of control in similar situations.

The Stage of Mutual Perspective Including a Third Person (typical of the adolescent period)

During the adolescent period the adolescent develops a higher, more abstract level of perceiving interpersonal perspective. Thus, when conflicts arise, composed of moral, social or legal perspectives common to everyone, he is able to grasp the different points of view in the abstract, including the varying degrees of depth within the different opinions. At this stage the adolescent may be aware of the psychological forces, at least a portion of which are unconscious, underlying the activities, motivations, thoughts and feelings of others. One who achieves this stage of social cognition is able to grasp that personality is a complex network of qualities, beliefs, values and approaches which are themselves the result of a unique developmental history.

At this stage the realization of punishment as an unconscious attempt to maintain psychological control over another person develops. Not every adolescent is able to arrive at this conceptual level, which corresponds to a great extent to Piaget's Stage of Formal Operations and to Kohlberg's Level of Post-Conventional Moral Judgment.

An Approach Viewing the Family as a Developing, Dynamic System in the Process of Individuation

As with psychodynamic and cognitive theories, the variations of the approach of viewing the family as a network share an attempt to understand human development within man's basic ecological context—the family. This is seen initially as the family of origin and subsequently as the family which is built by the new adult.

We are presenting this approach last because its theory and application developed mainly in the 1970's and because it has unique significance for our topic of parent-child relations.

Our study of adolescent-parent relations was based on viewing the family as a dynamic, developing system. In order to test our basic assumptions we interviewed an adolescent and each of his parents, concomitantly but separately. We requested that each adolescent relate to his own adolescence and his relationships with his parents. We asked the parents to describe their relationships with their own parents during their adolescence and with their own adolescent children. Because of the significance we attach to this approach in our series, we will discuss it in considerable detail.

We conceive of the family as a partially closed social system of people who themselves change and develop while engaging in ongoing transactions among themselves. These transactions are based on the following factors: the capacity for social perception, sensitivity and empathy; a sense of autonomy, self confidence and mutual recognition; the struggle for increasing autonomy in order to advance individuation; power and authority in fulfilling sexual roles; mutual support or establishment of limits for inner struggles or coping with external parties.

Perceiving the family as a system has led to several assumptions on the subject of individuation.

The first assumption is that the absence of significant progress in the individuation process during adolescence is liable to have negative consequences for selecting a mate and building a family (Bowen, 1976; Stierlin, 1981; Maier, 1982). Therefore, we feel that the lack of positive family or school support during adolescence is not only potentially harmful to the adolescent, but an expression of lack of social responsibility for the character of the family's second generation. In addition to Erikson's assumptions regarding the link between ego identity formation in adolescence and the development of intimacy, Maier (1982) and Teyber (1983) argue that significant progress in individuation is a precondition for development of the capacity for intimacy, building a family and parenthood.

The second assumption asserts that inadequate individuation during adolescence has implications for the "dream" of the future and formation of professional identity and career development. As a result, it is liable to have a negative effect on shaping the family's life style.

The third assumption: scholars claim that from the very first year of life separation from the symbiotic state of mother-infant relations is a function of the mother's and infant's basic needs, but differentiation also depends on the father's view of his role and his activity. Thus, the gestalt of husband-wife relations is integrated into the mother-infant relations system. Thus combined, they influence the individuation process of the children.

The fourth assumption takes in consideration the siblings in most families. Their birth order, the constellation of relations of each one with the mother and father, and the relationships of one or more of them with the child whom we are discussing, may have implications for the individuation process.

The fifth assumption is that every family has unique patterns of differentiation and integration. Kantor & Lehr (1975) and others have demonstrated that different families maintain fixed patterns, not only for role definition but also for delimiting the boundaries of involvement in the inner system of relations. The expectation of autonomy and psychological or behavioral differentiation can be perceived as a threat to the existing balance of role distribution, power and authority, sometimes even to the family's stability in families which demand total involvement in each member's life and where there is no place for autonomy of thought or behavior.

An adolescent in such a family must attain individuation without capitulating to the constant threat that the family is disintegrating because of him; at the same time the family makes every effort to withhold the autonomy required for developing his identity and his coping ability. By contrast, there is an assumption that flexible families adapt better to the changes occurring in its members' needs, enabling a more dynamic and appropriate balance for their joint and differentiated needs (Teyber, 1983; Sabatelli & Mazor, 1985). During the adolescent period, more flexible and adaptive families learn to create a balance of expectations and reactions which is appropriate to the adolescent's developing needs for individuation, without reducing the extent of their responsibility for the socialization process.

The sixth assumption considers the capacity for physical separation from the home (separate living quarters, school dormitories or military service) as not proof of progress in the individuation process. Even an individual who has left home may continue to be quite dependent emotionally on a parent. Such feelings are likely to be expressed in some cases by anxiety and internal stress, or in other cases by a reaction which is manifested as expressions of anger (Boszormanyi-Nagi & Spark, 1973).

The seventh assumption: Special patterns of individuation develop in single parent families. With the increase of divorce in recent years and the increasingly common phenomenon of single parent families, research has spotlighted the effects on the individuation process of being in a single parent family (Hetherington, 1971, 1972; Wallerstein & Kelly, 1980; Smilansky, 1990).

A difference has been found in individuation patterns according to sex in single parent families. For example, boys find it harder to leave home at the end of adolescence (ages 18-21), whereas girls show no such influence. Ckzenmihalyi & Larson (1984) found evidence that children in single parent families mature more quickly in terms of willingness to take on tasks in the family, and sometimes even to meet the mother's needs as a person who will support her psychologically in her isolation. Coles & Stokes (1984) found that adolescents from divorced families are involved in twice as many sexual experiences (ages 14-17 in a national American sample). This finding has been interpreted in several ways: the adolescent emulates the parental model, who has such relations out of wedlock; the adolescent is punishing the parent, consciously or unconsciously; the adolescent feels that he/she has permission for early individuation in the framework of a disturbed balance of family relations.

The eighth assumption: In many families the extended family has significant influence on the transactional process. This is prominent in cases where a parent of one member of the couple lives with the family. This intervention has both direct and indirect influence on individuation processes.

Among the interviews we conducted, there are various cases of a parent, generally the mother, who continues to interfere with the life of a son or daughter, especially on the threshold of a significant decision. Or the grandparents may provide shelter for a grandson or granddaughter, offering an array of supportive guidance for coping with one of their parents. Grandparents may fill an essential and positive role for their grandchildren, but that is not our concern here. We just mention the possibility that they might interfere with the individuation process of their children, who are the parents of their grandchildren.

The ninth assumption: A known phenomenon in many problem families is that one of the children becomes the family's "scapegoat" (Vogel & Bell, 1967; Ackerman, 1967). This demonstrates how the need for maintaining a family balance in problematic relations between the couple places the focus on an unwanted child or on one who has become unwanted in consequence of his developmental process. According to the clinicians, in such cases this phenomenon commonly replicates a situation which was typical of one of the parents' status in his family of origin. It tends to consist of an attempt to make the child realize he is problematic and is harmful to the family's life style. It sometimes happens that the child or young person accepts the role and proves by his behavior that he is indeed as they declared. In other cases the family treats him very strictly and follows him around; he is filled with anxiety about his behavior and adjusts until a blockage occurs in meeting his basic needs in the course of individuation.

The tenth assumption: Lidz (1968) coined the term "distorted" families. This refers to a situation in which one of the parents has a strong personality and is dominant, while the other one is weak, defeated and appears powerless. This imbalance in distribution of power and authority in the family system has many implications for the sexual role of the adolescents and for relations between the sexes. It clearly has a direct implication for development and identity formation during adolescence and on continuation of the individuation process. In our interviews we encountered clear instances of its influence on adolescents' decisions to leave home during this period and on the nature of mate selection. Some women told of their adolescence thus: "I couldn't stand seeing my mother as a doormat, I tried to push her to be something, to oppose him," adding that they left home at the earliest possible opportunity. Others related that they tried to take over the mother's place and cope with the father in her stead, while still others were heard to say: "I looked for a friend-husband different from my father, who would be a decent person and respect my needs . . ."

In the random sample with which we conducted approximately 450 interviews with about 150 families, it appears that the number of adolescent girls who suffer from a domineering mother and weak father is greater than those who complain of a domineering father. The developmental scenario for the individuation process in their families is similar to that reported in the previous scenario.

The eleventh assumption: In many families the family balance develops and is maintained by means of coalitions. We learned from our discussions with adolescents that their composition can be different and even strange: a mother and child versus the father; parents versus a daughter or son, usually the oldest son or the "problem" son; a father and daughter versus the mother, or a mother with two sons, etc.

Temporary coalitions are sometimes formed due to a crisis caused by the behavior of one parent, or the children, which aroused objections and brought about this sort of organizing. But in other cases this is a regular phenomenon of the family's differentiation pattern. One of the women interviewed put it this way: "For as long as I remember, Father was on my side and Mother was against me. It was as if she didn't want me to develop, and she tried to prove to me that I was not worthy. If Father hadn't stood by me I would certainly have fallen apart . . ."

The twelfth assumption: Closed families. A family is in a favorable situation when both parents maintain mutual understanding and willingness for mutual responsibility, when they learn to enjoy the contribution of the outside world, which is open and changing; when they go out to have a good time, invite guests, allow their children to maintain open ties with others, and when necessary regulate the flow in order to ensure there will be a desirable balance between involvement and autonomy. Attempts to isolate are common in problem families. Instead of an appropriate balance between togetherness and the differentiation of outside contact, a common phenomenon in the latter families is creation of a closed social climate, worrying about the adolescent's going out, fear of harm to the family's image, so that there is a need for a wedge between it and the outside world. Adolescents attest that they felt "choked in the family, a need to get out, to breath different air." In some instances the girls' reaction was sexual permissiveness.

The thirteenth assumption: A narcissistic parent, around whom the family's problematic developmental formation takes shape. In such cases there are many possible transactions. Among the interviews conducted, we encountered the case of a father who maintained a nearly symbiotic relationship with his divorced and loving mother until adolescence. He was separated from her only by a decision to send him to a boarding school. The price for his suffering was paid by his wife and each of his children in turn, while the focus was always on him and his problems. Family life revolved around the questions: How does he feel, what does he eat, how are they disturbing him, how others in the outside world don't understand him, etc.

The fourteenth assumption: A family with rigid role division. Clearly defining roles has advantages and disadvantages, but rigid definitions are liable to have a deleterious effect on development of individuation at the stage of a son's or daughter's marriage. It frequently happens that the patterns of the family of origin are transferred to the new family, and the husband expects that his wife will continue to act with him as his mother did. Rubin (1976) describes this phenomenon extensively, as it appears among the blue collar worker class.

Similar phenomena were found in our interviews, generally among blue-collar workers or those with little education. There was a recurrent complaint in those interviews, voiced primarily by young women: "He thought I was his mother . . . that I would prepare his clothes, or foods or bath, like she did."

There were frequent cases of young men or young women who were not prepared by their families, or by anyone else, for the necessity of individuation after marriage. The most prominent examples are those of women whose ties with their mothers had implications for the couple's relations. Thus, for example, we heard a young husband state in an interview: "Every other sentence from my wife is, 'Things aren't done that way in our family . . .' or 'We only do it this way,' as if God himself had come down and revealed it to her mother." Another husband related that when he and his wife quarrel, it seems to him that "he is sitting and listening to her mother rather than her." A third husband complained that "my wife talks for hours with her mother every day, like my 14-year old sister used to talk with her girlfriend." He then continues to complain that "it's as if her mother were living in our apartment—she brought food, interfered with arranging objects, and sent her cleaning woman to clean, because according to her, she, the mother, can't stand such lack of cleanliness." On the other hand, women complained: "It's as if my husband hadn't married—he brings his friends home, just like they used to come to his parents' house; he continues to play basketball as though he were still in his youth group; he goes to eat at his mother's as if I didn't exist; he throws things around as if I were his mother, who would go pick them up, even though he knows that I work just as hard outside the house as he does; and he expects me to take care of his younger brother."

Proposal for an Integrated Model

We have based our conception of the stages of individuation through the extended adolescent period on various factors:

according to what has been stated above,

according to information we have gathered concerning adolescents' perceptions of their parents as they relate with them and concerning development of conflicts between adolescents and parents at different stages and around different focal points, and

on reports and interpretations which we have distilled from a prolonged process of educational and therapeutic work with adolescents in the Israeli and American educational systems.

In our opinion adolescence is characterized by a similarity and variety of patterns among age cohorts, who are members of the same generation or *horizontal age stratum*. Development occurs at different rates for different traits of psycho-social maturation throughout the process of adolescence. This may be considered a *vertical maturation* pattern. We discuss the connection and mutual influence of these developmental factors in the chapter on the Process of Adolescence. At this time, keeping in mind the principle that the interaction of parents, adolescents (and the facilitators supporting them) is the way to ensure a unique differentiation process for the family, we will simply present a general survey of the six developmental stages of the process;

we will note prominent phenomena and summarize important principal trends. We wish to point out that this process does not move along rapidly and is not basically destructive in nature, but, at the same time, it must not impede growth and avoid creating any developmental delay which might plant the seeds of a pathological crisis during adolescence.

The third stage of individuation, which is the first of the adolescent period, is characterized by the adolescent and his parents experiencing a new reality, different from that which characterized their relationship during childhood. New needs and pressures, both internal and external, are awakened by the beginning and development of adolescence. "Significant others," now external to the family—peers, friends, teachers, counsellors and advisors—intervene and introduce new expectations into the child's life. Suddenly, parents are faced with a "new" child, whom they hardly know, with new needs and a different relationship with his friends. Feelings of anxiety and/or resistance to these new phenomena arise in the parents. At this stage the parent-child relationship sometimes takes on a spiral form of development, accompanied by separations, outbursts and regressions of all concerned. In general all those with a developmental approach to adolescence would agree that there are four stages in adolescence: an initial stage corresponding to early adolescence, an intermediate stage corresponding to middle adolescence, a late stage corresponding to late adolescence, and a fourth stage corresponding to a transition to adulthood.

The Initial Stage (the third life stage)—Early Adolescence

The adolescent feels a need for autonomy in his attempts to adopt new behaviors and to develop new relations as he copes with new internal and external developments in his and his parents' world. He tests the limits of his abilities: what he does, what he can do and what he should do. A considerable part of this development is unconscious and his attitude toward the environment is ambivalent.

The adolescent experiments with different sorts of peer relations and friendships and is influenced by both the rewards and the difficulties which arise in his new social experiences. Doubts about his self-image and the way he is perceived by others come to the fore. Although biological, cognitive and social development leads to new possibilities, approaches and behavior, it also arouses anxieties and questions about his attitude toward the new opportunities he faces and about his readiness to respond to them.

The adolescent's parents are also undergoing new experiences; ambivalence characterizes their attitude toward what is happening as well. They don't know how to respond, are anxious about this or that development and are unsure if their reactions are appropriate. Adolescents act as if they are capable of being independent, as though they don't need their parents, and are offended by parental interference. Yet, at the same time, they also need their parents' support and expect recognition of their right to autonomy along with any help necessary. A process of mutual attraction and rejection develops, with adolescents moving towards autonomy and pushing the parents away, while, unwilling to let go entirely, pulling them along after them. Parents pull the adolescents toward them, in order to protect them or to fill their own needs of having a child with them, but, at the same time, they push them away recognizing their need to develop themselves, acquire friends, gain social experience and share experiences and impressions.

In the great majority of cases both sides adjust to the new reality. Thus, despite adolescent regression, when the child tries to break out and win greater autonomy, authority and responsibility, and/or parental reactions trying either to stop him or to guide him according to their own views, development does take place.

The Second Stage (the fourth stage of individuation)—the Period of Middle Adolescence

Social perspective and social skills develop from age 14-16 to a point at which the adolescent is capable of understanding the complexity and intricacy of interpersonal relationships on a higher plain. Such understanding is gained through his experiences with peers, friends and parents and devolves from his trying to act according to expected norms in various areas. Adolescents understand their parents better than before, and make use of communication to convince them to fulfill their needs and to note their progress toward differentiation and individuation. Parents understand that their children have reached a new stage in life, that their capability is developing and their life-situation is changing. Parents become cognizant of their own need to learn how to cope with this new reality.

Whereas parent-child relations in the first stage focused on rights of autonomy and individuation, the focus in the second stage is on different subject-areas through which personal identity is developed. In the first stage mothers and daughters clashed over the right to their own territory, dress-style, etc. But, in the second stage, clashes concern essential matters: mothers and daughters express different ideas in terms of their taste in clothing and cosmetics, the nature of girl-boy relationships, the nature of the mother's involvement in her daughter's life and with her daughter's friends, etc. Fathers debate with their sons and daughters about politics, idealism versus realism, study goals, study and professions appropriate for career development, life styles, etc. As conflicts become more severe, many adolescents break with behavioral norms, trying to prove their separateness and their power, and are prepared to pay any price to win these conflicts. Some complain about their parents' lack of candor and credibility claiming that there is a gap between their ideology and their behavior, others employ actual or psychological denial, and still others are anxious to make decisions and to fight for their beliefs or rights.

Development continues in the same direction from ages 16 to 18. However, the adolescent's readiness to choose between alternatives makes this period unique. Such readiness develops out of his cognitive and social development as well as from significant experience in various areas of activity. At this stage adolescents begin to enter into temporary, even experimental, life-style patterns as a means of fashioning a preferred way of life. Some adolescents try out new directions in their style of dress, hair and cosmetics within the bounds of their cognitive and social development. Others try out new ideologies, which are sometimes extreme and on the edges of what is socially acceptable. Some join together in anti-establishment peer groups, and others are active as youth movement counsellors or in community social service groups. Some experiment with sexual activity or even drugs and alcohol, and others isolate or seclude themselves with a boy/girl friend, with books, a computer, music or some other activity in which they excel. Some succeed in formulating their ultimate goals in life and also possibly selecting an intermediate vocation and a major study area, while others put off all decisions, choosing to enjoy a social moratorium until the conclusion of their high school studies and military service.

As in the earlier stages, a wide variety of adolescent-parent relations is also apparent in this stage, ranging from outspoken, bitter rebellion to quiet, apparently problem-free adjustment. It is important to recall that just as rebellion is not necessarily a negative phenomenon, adjustment does not have to attest to a positive individuation process. The existence of a "generation gap" or an apparently abysmal lack of understanding, described by the adolescent as a chasm between himself and his parents, is not necessarily the result of the phenomenon of conflict accompanied by upheaval in relations with the mother or father. It may often happen that the same adolescent, when at school, at a friends' home or in a youth group, will present a position not essentially different than that of his parents. In many cases the need to go to extremes, to escalate and to discriminate is an external indication of differentiation, and the process expresses itself in attempts at conflict and validation in order to mark the limits of autonomy and to consolidate an independent personal identity.

Whereas the adolescent needs to prove his uniqueness and distinctness in a parent's presence or in various situations in the parents' home, most adolescents need to prove the opposite in their peer groups—their belonging, adaptation and compatability—in order to be accepted and worthy of support. This support is necessary in their struggle in two areas of the establishment: the parents' home and the school; it is particularly important in terms counteracting the anxieties, doubts and ambivalent feelings characterizing their inner emotions.

However, as adolescents develop further, they face a new task: establishing intimate friendships. Moving towards that task, the adolescent reveals himself ready to free himself, at least in part, from peer group pressures. Similarly, conflict and validation patterns develop vis-a-vis dominant friends in the class, age cohort, the youth group or peer groups dominant in the neighborhood or community. The school-based division into major areas of study or into subject areas which may become significant in terms of future life choices, advances social individuation and focuses attention on the adult world. In those countries where there is compulsory national military service, reporting to the draft office plus the emotional and/or practical preparation for military service encourage individuation from the adolescent world by focusing anxieties, planning and behavior toward expectations in an adult context. Upon seeing their son or daughter with an intimate partner and/or witnessing their children's preparations for matriculation examinations or military service, parents are forced to come to terms with and develop considerable readiness to support this significant stage.

In the case of working youth, leaving school and the transition to working life usually create a transformation or at least a change in expectations and behavior.

The Third Stage (the fifth stage of individuation)—the Period of Late Adolescence

The age 17-18 to 20-21 is characterized by a change in social and civil status and in the consolidation of cognitive, emotional and social differentiation and individuation. This stage is the outcome of the combined influences of external factors along with intrafamilial status changes. In Israel and most European countries the dominant factor is military service. The army demands physical, emotional and social separation, and integration into the world of basic trainees and soldiers. The situation of young Israelis at this stage differs from that of young Americans or Englishmen, who continue to study or go off to private civilian employment. Those conscripted into the army move into a radically new and different social system, in terms of authority, power, array of tasks and human challenge. Many receive adult responsibility in the army which may even be greater than that of their parents. They feel differently than in the past, understand more in many areas of interpersonal and intergroup relations, and experience the meaning of conflict and validation of individuation. Military service also separates most of them from their previous peer group which had influenced their values and behavior. For most it opens up new opportunities and confronts them with a new test of companionship and friendship. They develop contacts with adults whose background, jobs, values and behavior is different from their own. The latter may be different in many ways from their parents, neighbors and teachers. The unique significance of this stage will be discussed at length in a special monograph on preparation toward adulthood (Volume 6 in the series, *The Challenge of Adolescence*, 1991).

At this point, we can recount several assumptions briefly which illustrate the special nature of the experience (Lieblich, 1987):

1. Basic training is a difficult physical and emotional test for most of the young men, particularly in combat units, both regular and special (voluntary).

2. The army draws most soldiers into direct conflict with human, social problems involving a personal challenge: commanding or being commanded, putting one's ethical values to the test. Most of the young men pass these tests of male adulthood, but a minority fail and in some cases there are implications beyond the maturation period.

3. A new type of comradeship and friendship develops in the army, especially in field and special units, which is often very deep, lasting into later life stages.

4. Many women soldiers face the test of living in a male-oriented society, sometimes being faced with sexual harassment. Many are troubled when confronted with the limited jobs available to women. Others tell about their speedy maturation upon leaving the protection of the parental home and about their involvement in relationships different from those to which they had been accustomed.

5. Finally, these three to four years of intensive social service constitute a focus for consolidation of personal identity for many individuals, but for others it serves as a moratorium for decision-making.

Military service also has implications for the adolescent's feelings toward his family and his status within it. At the same time that the young person leaves home and wins independence, a new bond is created with the parents. At first, when confronting the difficulties of basic training and later, when struggling with the problems we have noted, the soldier finds cognitive and emotional support in his parents: they worry about him, identify with him, try to understand him, advise him, accept his weaknesses and experience his anxieties as best they can.

The Fourth Stage of Adolescence (the sixth stage of individuation)— the Transition Period to Early Adulthood

Between the ages of 20-21 to 23-24 another period characterized by conflict over formation of new relationships between young people and their parents occurs.

In the Israeli social system this is marked upon completion of military service. Some young people, primarily young women, continue to live at home during their national service, and, in a few cases, continue to do so even during university studies. These young people have not experienced a separation crisis, and the conclusion of their military service, which did not involve returning home, did not constitute a milestone. But among those who served away from home, some come back to live at home and to study at post-secondary schools and universities. Others live at home and go out to work, while still others do not return to the parental home. In some cases they even free themselves from economic dependency, while others continue receiving their parents' full or partial economic support. For the purpose of our discussion, what is important is the degree of consolidation of the individuation process in the young adolescent's understanding, feelings and behavior, and of the parallel counterdevelopment of the mother and father.

The developmental focus in this stage is further cognitive development of social perspective, and the affective reaction to the individuation process. Acknowledgment of the young person as an adult rather than a child is prevalent for most families in this stage. Therefore, the issue becomes the degree of mutual acknowledgment which depends on the young person's readiness to act like an adult, i.e., to perform the tasks which require psycho-social maturity, and on the extent of the parent's readiness to believe in his child's ability and to support his advancement and the realization of his individuation.

Various affective reactions are familiar to us at this stage. Young people and parents reflect back, angrily in some cases, on attitudes and behavior in the past, while others do so nostalgically. Some young people understand the ambivalence of their parent's reactions, even trying to understand them and their current needs. There are others at this stage, distracted by problems of relations with the other sex, selecting a mate, fashioning a career and other tasks, who continue to harp on issues which were not resolved in an earlier stage. Actually, they are now struggling with shaping their identity as a result of the social moratorium previously made possible. Most adolescents and parents do in fact return to nostalgia, in both positive and negative senses, but they live in the present and act for the future. The evidence we have attests to a positive development in most adolescents' view of their parents, and to most parents' willingness to recognize their sons or daughters as young people who need to bear the responsibility for consolidation of their identity and their struggles.

Problems in differentiation and fashioning a new relationship, appear, manifesting itself in depression, isolation, the severing of relations or making mutual accusations and continuing to struggle over power and authority appear in a minority of cases. The latter struggles carry with them a range of guilty feelings, anger, denial or of blame and punishment. In such situations young people and parents need support and professional guidance in order to prevent mutual blame and to be enabled to cope with maturational tasks and with the normal commitments of this stage. Otherwise, there is a question of the ability to progress to the next stage.

Stages in Adult Development

The Seventh Stage of Individuation—Early Adulthood occurs between the ages 24 or 25 and extends into the thirties. In most cases this is a stage of mutual acquaintance, mutual acceptance and the initial formation of a new set of relationships.

Once decisions have been made in the areas of choosing a field of study or work, selecting a mate, setting up living quarters separate from one's parents and completing tasks successfully, a willingness to free the self from the inhibitions and limitations of the past ought to develop. We see the formation of a new, more adult system of ties and relationships with parents. Young people tell of their capacity for differential identification with their parents: they recognize the parent's strengths and discern his limitations, and they reach a new understanding of the parent as a person. Young people, who have married, perceive the parent's influence on their selecting a mate and shaping the pattern of their new home; those, who have themselves become parents, sometimes discern how they have integrated the values and behavioral patterns of their parental home into their new function. Since these processes develop at least in part unconsciously, these young people are sometimes surprised when an outsider, such as a relative, friend or therapist, draws their attention to the continuity, or differential reorientation, in their behavior. It would seem that those who had raged and rebelled against certain manifestations of parental behavior are now acting in the very same way.

Concomitantly, parents often try in different ways to come to terms with the facts of psychological and physical differentiation, striving towards creating a new system of relations. We refer here to very different processes, which are also in part unconscious. Parents who attempt to adjust by trying to act like young people frequently fail, since role play of that kind has a poor chance of success. Others use financial means to try to ensure continued contact; they usually fail as well, because it is basically an attempt to reestablish a dependency relationship with their daughter or son. Generally, parents who build a new life style, gradually developing ties of equality and mutual commitment with their son or daughter and with their child's spouse are the most successful.

Thus, we can see how most young adults in their twenties and thirties are struggling to form an independent life style. The tasks of this stage: shaping a professional identity and developing a career, establishing a home separate from that in which they grew up, experiencing an intimate commitment and becoming involved in community or political life all contribute to further development of the separation-individuation process and to greater readiness of both young adults and parents to form a new, more mature system of relations. According to various evidence, existence of an intimate commitment and a spouse's support in coping with individuation are strong factors in promoting the process.

Selecting a mate and building a family has special significance for the process of differentiation from parents. People bring the past from their family of origin along to their marriage in order to recreate it. Hence, the task, function and destiny of the newlyweds is to try to control that influence.

Marriage constitutes a parting of the ways which demands a further degree of psychological separation from the family of origin. Unconscious conflicts from earlier stages of psychosexual maturation are reawakened during this stage. The roots of the capacity to establish mutual, enduring love relations with a spouse are connected with progress in the separation-individuation process, which includes renewed coping with the oedipal conflict. That very coping with differentiation, which is involved with defining the boundaries of personal identity vis-a-vis the parents' identity, is what enables emotional intimacy and sexual ties without fear of loss of self. It also enables the partners to suspend their own needs, as contrasted with the other's needs, for a certain period of time.

Our interviews help to demonstrate the effect of relations with either or both parents on the process of mate selection. Some respondents declared explicitly, in retrospect, that they were looking for an instant substitute as an escape from conflicts with parents. Others sought the family warmth which they sensed in the cultural climate of their partner's family and which was absent in their own family. Still others told how they had sought a particular image of a spouse which, according to their perception at the time, would be similar to or contrast with the image of their own mother or father. Thus, we find evidence for the transfer of emotions from the mother to the wife, the development of a differential perception of commitment toward the mother as opposed to commitment to the wife, and the establishment of a new balance between the limits of mutual commitment within the family of origin and the demands of building a new family.

Our interviews revealed variations in terms of the timing of the development of this differentiation stage. For one individual the decision to marry may appear to cause a positive crisis in promoting differentiation, whereas for others long years of inner struggle or of direct strife with a spouse, accompanied by pressures or even threats of separation are required.

The eighth stage evolves with pregnancy and parenthood. At this point the young adults enter still another stage of psychological differentiation from their parents: they form a personal identity and progress in building a family, and they develop a new system of relations with their parents, who, in turn, begin to fill their new role as grandparents. Our discussion of this stage and those after it will be quite brief, but they are of great importance in the differentiation process. Psychological development in this stage is multi-dimensional, since, as the young couple enters into parenthood, they evolve a new identity for themselves and accept responsibility for forming the identity of their children. But beyond that, the young husband senses in his wife the development of a future mother, comparing her consciously or unconsciously to his mother. As they experience parenthood, the young adults begin to understand the feelings and behavior of their parents which in the past they had been unable to understand or accept. As their parents settle into their new roles and status as grandparents, a new balance of mutual dependence and authority develops. In other words, the kaleidoscope of the family system changes with regard to family composition, distribution of tasks, the position of brothers and sisters, the balance of power and authority, patterns of communication, etc.

The ninth stage, the transitional stage of middle age evolves within the framework of a process defined in the past decade, and which has been described extensively in the studies of Stewart (1977), Gould (1978), Levinson, *et al.* (1978), and others. There remain differences of opinion concerning the meaning of the term "middle age" and its connection with a chronological age. However, it is clear that a considerable portion of the population included in the research samples attested that, when faced with taking stock and when appraising the significance of past decisions and perceptions of the future, a person examines things both in comparison with his parents as well as in contradistinction with them.

It is possible to generalize and conclude that the first choice of profession and life style is influenced by parents' images or expectations. It seems that what is involved is a conscious imitation of the parent, a model unconsciously internalized during childhood, or a perception of parental behavior as transmitting a message of status and role expectations. Only after many years of living out that role did they examine the meaning of their choice in terms of their basic personality needs. They then were able to progress in differentiating from their parents, feeling they were prepared to shape an independent dream and to select anew the pattern of their lives.

The tenth stage continues through life until the parents' death. In Halpern's clinical work, *Cutting Loose*, (1977) the relationships of adults coming for therapy with their parents are described. There is a remarkable continuity in Halpern's description of what he terms "the dance" and "the music" accompanying the child-mother or child-father relationship, mutual expectations—either conscious or unconscious—for fulfilling the parent's expectations. Based on significant examples, he argues that parents continue to expect understanding and consideration from their children, even though the child is an adult and usually a parent in his own right. The adult/child feels as though the "dance" and the "music," with him since childhood continue on, and his personality lacks the strength to free itself psychologically, and thus is unable to change behavior patterns formed during childhood.

In our interviews we detected, among other things, the phenomenon of a chain of relationships including the connection between the system of relationships of the fathers' and mothers' generation together with their parents along with their system of relationships with their adolescent sons and daughters. We will discuss this phenomenon in the next chapter.

The eleventh stage evolves upon the parents' death. It is expressed, consciously or unconsciously, in continued cognitive and emotional stocktaking and even in attempts to translate the event of the death into inner decisions and messages to himself and his children. In continuing education seminars we have conducted, participants described the affects of a father's or mother's death close to the occurrence of the death or during a particular range of time or, sometimes, after several decades. One woman mentioned the Sabbath and Festival tradition her mother had cultivated at home, which she had given up when she married a non-religious man. Since her mother's death, she has blamed herself and her husband for deviating from tradition, which she felt had caused her children to lack a life-style in which the Sabbath and Festivals were significant. Another person told of his returning to traditional religion when his father died. He added that he had a profound sense of guilt toward his parents; they had cultivated a tradition thousands of years old in order to bequeath it to him, and he had abandoned this cultural richness, without transmitting anything meaningful to his children.

One woman claimed if her mother were still alive, her husband would not treat her as he does. Another woman blamed herself for not having understood her mother and not providing her what was needed. Another woman related how she had transferred the furniture from her parents' home to her own house, turning one section into a sort of continuation of the parental home. This was in contrast to the description in her interview of how she had rebelled against her parents and left them feeling that she wanted nothing to do with them. Yet another described how she continued to call her father to account for what he did or did not give her and her children during his lifetime, and what he bequeathed to her as compared to her brother. Thus it is possible to see how psychological differentiation from a parent does not conclude upon the parent's death and how each of us maintains a psychological link with his parents as long as he lives.

Concluding Remarks and Supplementary Notes

Having described the separation-individuation process, based on assumptions of our own and others' findings, we will attempt to summarize several issues and make some observations, not necessarily in order of importance.

- The concept of individuation has been defined and developed by psychoanalytic theoreticians. The basic assumption in this primarily unconscious process is that the child has internalized his parents' images and their expectations, has identified with their values system and with their behavior patterns. Influenced by the latter, he consolidates the basic components of his values, expectations and behavior. According to modern dynamic theories, the adolescent is faced with two tasks: to effect a conscious release from the image of the large, omnipotent mother and father, internalized during his early childhood years; and at the same time to unravel the psychological intertwining of his personality with that of his parents as they really are. In other words, he must create psychological distance between himself and his parents, analyzing the difference between himself and his mother or father in terms of basic personality traits, needs and difficulties. He must develop autonomy in order to create a bond of love with a member of the opposite sex and progress in the formation of a personal sexual identity and the shaping of a personal "dream" and an independent, unique life-style.

  We may add that the significance of acceding to the need for differentiation, autonomy and forming a personal identity does not mean that adolescents must differ from their parents in values, attitudes or behavior patterns. It certainly does not require that they hate their parents or distance themselves from them physically, as certain theoreticians have assumed.

- The process referred to is complex, intricate, prolonged, and emotionally difficult; this is because it is primarily unconscious and also because, in most cases, it involves a discontinuing of dependence on love objects, with whom the tie is perceived as essential or even obligatory.

- The assumption of a universal phenomenon of "storm and stress" and even hatred of parents is no longer acceptable. The current tendency is to view the latter as a stereotyped generalization and myth which was the outgrowth of clinical treatment of problematic adolescents. The clinical picture of "storm and stress" depicted by classic psychoanalysts fits only 20-25% of adolescents. All the others undergo the process with different patterns.

Our study of adolescents and their parents also shows that most adolescents maintain a positive feeling toward their parents, even after conflicts arise over authority and power in the family.

- Progress in the individuation process is essential, and in many cases even critical, to the adolescent's ability to feel sufficient autonomy in order to bear responsibility for shaping a personal identity, for creating a bond of intimate, mutual commitment and for building an independent life style.

- The psychoanalytic view has been formed based on clinical work with adolescents and adults, but in recent years several aspects of this view have also been examined in empirical research. Similarly, the assumption that various patterns of adolescence and individuation exist has been verified by research evidence. Therefore, recognition of the various patterns and understanding their significance is important for the educator and counselor, so they will not apply generalized labels to adolescents, will understand their needs better, and will adapt the possible methods of support accordingly. The contributions of investigators from other schools of thought broaden our view and further our understanding of the unique significance of adolescence as a meaningful period for shaping the adult as well.

- A general phenomenon during adolescence is ambivalence in the adolescent's behavior and appraisal of his parents, as well as in that of his parents with regard to him. Ambivalence is manifest in different areas; various theories explain it in different ways according to the basic concepts of each theory. For example, classic psychoanalysts describe ambivalence as a phenomenon originating from the sexual tie with the parent of the opposite sex. Social psychologists, such as Kurt Lewin, ascribe it to lack of confidence stemming from the new arrangement of the "social field" where the adolescent is in a marginal position. Cognitive psychologists demonstrate the gaps in perception of others' feelings, thoughts and behavior, and the discrepancy in expectations between those involved. What is common to all the theories is a description of the ambivalence regarding autonomy. On the one hand, the adolescent wants people to trust him, to recognize his responsibility to mature and to offer him freedom of action without interference. Concomitantly, the parent wants his child to grow up and bear responsibility for his behavior. However, at the same time, the parent does not yet believe enough in the adolescent's ability to accept responsibility. He fears peer influence on his child, is wary of the outcomes of certain experiences, and frequently does not know how to maintain meaningful contact in this variable, transitional situation.

- Physical separation (leaving home in its various forms) and emotional separation ("I've gotten over them and I don't want to know about them") does not necessarily indicate progress in the inner process of separation-individuation, which is essential for development of personal identity and the formation of relations of equal human value between adolescents or adults and their parents. We will limit ourselves here to presenting the modern psychoanalytic claim that the primary task is differentiation from the parent's image, as perceived by the adolescent. In other words, the process referred to is an internal, cognitive and emotional working through of perceptions and emotions, rather than escape by tearing off an old mask and choosing a new mask behind which past emotions remain. Our work with peer groups in boarding schools in Israel and the United States, showed in a very striking way how physical escape from home provides only a partial solution for territorial conflicts, and does not usually contribute to advancing the struggle for autonomy or solving the deeper conflicts.
- It is important to differentiate between the terms "generation gap" and "adolescent rebellion." In modern society in general and particularly in Israel, we see a remarkable variation in the possible alternatives for experience between the adolescent generation and that of their parents. Hence, we may refer to the possibility of an experiential generation gap.

Examples of this gap may be found in various areas of social life: the economy (poverty or a declining standard of living as opposed to affluence), transportation (private cars, trips abroad) and communications media (the advent of television, video, transistors, etc.).

In contrast, compared to the accepted norm in contemporary Israeli society, a higher proportion of youth rebelled against parental values and behavior patterns in turn-of-the-century Eastern Europe, influenced by the Enlightenment, Zionism, socialism and communism. Studies of the youth rebellion in Western Europe and the United States yield similar findings. The "youth rebellion" as it was termed in the sixties (Keniston, 1968, 1970) did not turn against the parents. It was, rather, a temporary phenomenon originating from the condition of the universities in France or Italy (crowding, an unwilling to cope with expectations of democratization, etc.) and economic expectations of the welfare state. In the United States it contained an expression of wide public opposition to the Vietnam War, students' and parents' fear of the draft, and lack of willingness of administration and faculty in high schools and universities to cope with the expectations aroused by democratizations of secondary and higher education. The fact is that this phenomenon disappeared shortly after confirmation of defeat in Vietnam and the end of the compulsory draft.

In addition, it appears from various evidence about the "rebellion" in Europe, that only about 10% of the age cohort was involved, and half of those were the children of liberal and leftist parents who had educated them to oppose the establishment. This same "rebellion" actually adds significant evidence that most adolescents do not rebel against their parents even during a period of social crisis.

- Responsibility for affirmative progress in the individuation process is the overall responsibility of the family. However, in our experience it is not always possible to ensure that parents will be capable and ready to participate in this learning process. Therefore, we suggest that the adolescent become an active and responsible agent in shaping his identity and his struggle through participating in a program entitled "The Challenge of Adolescence". While being trained to accept this responsibility, he will learn to develop communication with his parents, to conduct transactions with them in a manner appropriate to his needs, and to develop his social perspective and his social skills. Our task is to teach him to assume this responsibility, which we will describe further in Chapter 4 below.

Chapter Two

Adolescents' Expectations of Their Parents and Their Perception of Parents' Expectations of Them

Methods Used for Problem Identification

WE APPLIED FOUR PARALLEL APPROACHES IN ADDITION TO REVIEWING the existing literature in our probe of adolescent-parent relations.

- We assembled four concurrent groups of adolescents and parents from a district school with a heterogeneous population. During the course of the school year, we met with student peer groups one morning a week at the school and with parents' groups in the evening. We held open discussions with them based on the following question: What disturbs you about adolescent-parent relations?
- Questionnaires were prepared to examine adolescents' expectations of their parents and to understand their perception of parents' expectations. Using these questionnaires we sought to find out whether any differences existed based on variation in sex, age, ethnic background or as a result of the effects of leaving home to study in a boarding school. In our view the influence of leaving home for a boarding school would be particularly important, since adolescents in such an institution apparently did not require parental support in various areas. They were not dependent on parents on a day-to-day basis in many ways (provision of clothing, supplying nutrition, setting times for getting up and going to sleep, controlling the opportunities for meeting with members of the opposite sex, etc.), nor were they affected by conflicts over territorial struggles or by differences of values in various areas. Similarly, they were not immediately affected by a parent's deviant or problematic behavior, as would be the case for adolescents in a family setting.

  Respondents to the questionnaire consisted of 433 young men and women aged 15-16, from ten schools of two types: five were boarding schools and five were regular schools (Mazor, Geva &

Smilansky, 1981). Then at a later point, appropriate sections of the questionnaire together with additional questions were administered to 16-17 year old students from a regional school serving seven kibbutzim, and, at the same time, students of the same age at an urban high school were interviewed (Platek, 1984).

- Comprehensive interviews were conducted with approximately 150 adolescents; parallel interviews were held separately with each parent, using questions relating to the development of each of the three respondents, to his perception of the development of the other two family respondents and of adolescent-parent relations.

- The group exercises prepared by the staff were carried out in peer groups at different schools. Feedback received from the adolescents and counsellors helped the preparation of the exercises appearing in the second part of this volume and the clarification of issues.

Patterns of Adolescent Perceptions of Parents and Parental Expectations

Research findings in all population groups

Research findings show that adolescent expectations of parents are high in all population groups.

In a comparison made between 15-16 year old adolescents' expectations both in the urban environment and at boarding school (Mazor, Geva & Smilansky, 1981), the average expectation score (on a scale from 1-5) was 3.7. Although students from a boarding school setting come from different background and exhibit particular problems, no significant difference was found between the expectations of students living with their parents and those in a boarding school setting. Adolescents living at the regional educational institution of the National Kibbutz Movement had higher expectations of parents than those of members of the urban control group (Platek, 1984).

These findings are significant in that they show that adolescent boys and girls in urban areas, at boarding school and on the kibbutz expect a high level of parental involvement in various areas of life.

These expectations include:

- Providing a feeling of security in maintaining a positive balance in the family. Adolescents from both urban and kibbutz background expect *not* to discover that relations between their parents have been upset, that their parents will discuss with them problems associated with interpersonal relations between the couple, the family's financial situation (on the kibbutz, ways to spend the personal-family budget), etc. In other words, they see themselves as part of the family and expect to be recognized as an equal partner in coping within the family system.

- Providing help with school subjects—the expectations of urban and kibbutz youth are similar: parents will be interested in their child's studies and show involvement. Kibbutz youth tend to expect more support in the area of preparing homework than do urban youth, despite the fact that grades are not given in the kibbutz setting as they are in urban schools; moreover, competition like that related to the matriculation examinations does not predominate on the kibbutz.

In this sense, it is interesting to note that 16-17 year olds at the kibbutz regional educational institution seek maximal autonomy in matters connected with their private lives: their ties with friends, their appearance, and their leisure time activities. The average score in this area was 2.63 for kibbutz respondents as compared with 1.87 for urban students. However, at the same time, they expect to share in the family's troubles and problems; the average score of kibbutz youth on the 5 point index comprising this category was 2.51 as opposed to 2.04 for urban youth. It would seem that kibbutz youth seek to be involved as much as possible in family life and request openness from their parents in terms of hearing their criticism. They expect to be involved in deciding the allocation of the family monies and to be consulted by their parents about both interpersonal problems between the parents and work problems (average score of 3.38). Finally, both kibbutz and urban youth express the expectation that "parents will show their love for them, will see them as a source of pride, will be available to them and accept them as they are" (Platek, 1984).

The problem of individuation in the process of adolescence, as perceived by adolescents, would appear to be basically similar to that of the first years of life. It is typified by a desire for autonomy mixed with a need to feel secure; the adolescent does not wish to lose his parents' support by becoming more remote. The difference is that during adolescence social perspective develops which allows differential perception of the complexity of problems, awareness of the need for and problematic nature of forming a personal identity, and responsible struggling to shape a life-style.

Another difference arises from the complexity and intricacy of the social skills required to be a member of a youth society and to engage in relations with members of the opposite sex.

Comparison of Adolescents in Residential and non-Residential Schools

Research findings show that adolescents studying in residential schools have higher expectations of parental involvement than do adolescents in regular schools (s.d. = 0.40). Apparently, youth who study in a setting where interaction with parents is neither daily nor intensive express higher expectations of parental involvement in the areas of life presented in our questionnaire (average score was 3.7 on a scale of 5). In contrast, youth attending regular schools, who interact daily and even engage in conflicts with their parents, have somewhat lower expectations for parental involvement (average score: 3.5).

It is noteworthy that, when the first residential school was opened in the early sixties as part of an enrichment project for "gifted" children from culturally deprived backgrounds (Smilansky, 1961), there were some who argued that we would bring about "a separation of adolescents from their families." We, however, proposed a different and more complicated set of theoretical assumptions than did the critics. It became clear that adolescents who were away from home actually began to appreciate their parents more. Although they missed their parents' concern and support, especially that of their mothers, they clashed with counsellors, aides, teachers and friends daily over meeting their needs instead of with their mother or father. Frustration with their own limitations, adjustment difficulties and problems of identity formation were aimed at the Significant Others at hand. When they left for weekend vacations and holidays, an average of once in three weeks, they were met by a family which is anticipating their arrival, celebrating their visit home, identifying with their difficulties, and providing them with love. Family members relay messages about their own difficulties in facing the world outside: bureaucracy, bosses, limited budget, etc., and expect their understanding and help. Residential school students returned to their dormitories longing for the warmth of home.

We learned that students from families in which there was serious marital strife generally had difficulty in identity formation and functioning at the residential school. Interviews conducted after the first graduating class had completed four years in the residential school, indicated that more than half of the students noted an increase in ties with their families, approximately one quarter noted a decline, and the others reported no change.

Residential school populations differ from regular school populations in various ways. The great majority of the former come from a religiously traditional background, their parents' level of education is lower, and there are generally marked difficulties in family relations, which was one of the reasons for referring their children to residential education. All these factors, separately and combined, affect the possibility of finding different expectations in various directions. In this limited framework we can only note that, in theoretical terms, in-depth research is required regarding the problems emerging from this different reality of adolescent patterns. Since in Israel nearly every fifth adolescent experiences separation from his family during the adolescence process, these young people deserve more understanding and professional support better suited to their needs. In our opinion it would be worthwhile to investigate thoroughly the nature of adolescent-parent relations among residential school students as a basis for systematic educational activity.

It is clear from our findings that urban and residential school adolescents attribute a high level of expectations of themselves *from their parents*, with the mean score in different populations ranging from 3.75 to 4.05 on a scale of 1-5. It should be noted that many girls and boys answered without differentiating between the set of expectations and pressures of their fathers as compared with those of their mothers. This may be due to limitations in the questions we created or because the 15-16 year old's perception of expectations is still included within the concept of "adolescent-parent relations." By contrast, this distinction becomes gradually more prominent between the ages of 16-18. Residential school adolescents attribute a higher level of expectations to their parents than adolescents in regular schools. Expectations attributed to parents are in the areas of studies and of empathy and involvement within the family.

Three basic premises, used either singly or in combination, may explain this finding: first, going away from home to a residential school makes adolescents internalize a less realistic picture of the parent, to whom he then attributes less realistic expectations. Adolescents in residential schools are in a situation where parental expectations are not declared on a daily basis but are transmitted to them through meta-communication. In other words, this occurs during visits at home or in letters and phone calls in this sort of form: "I love you and miss you" and at the same time, "I'm sure you can succeed; you promised me to behave yourself, and you will carry through on that";

or, "Remember, this is your last chance! If they expel you, it will reflect on the whole family;" etc. Adolescents conclude from such meta-communications that "My dad expects higher grades from me than my brothers had"; "Father wants me to be the best, and he doesn't take reality into account"; "My mother could just 'die' because I'm in a residential school," etc.

The second premise is that most of the residential school population comes from families which are both traditional and from a culturally deprived background. In most cases the typical communication is conducted in extreme terms. Emotional messages are conveyed such as: "I am sacrificing my whole life for you," along with unequivocal threats: "If you don't succeed, or if you don't behave properly, your father will break your bones." There are fewer tender or equivocal formulations, in either a negative or positive sense, with more expressions of social and psychological dependence accompanied by clear reminders of use of force and authority by the educational institution and the parent.

Third, most students in residential schools are there because of family problems, learning difficulties, or behavior problems at school. In most cases the educational institution is perceived by the adolescent as a necessary refuge/solution, even if it is neither desired or ideal. Parents reinforce absorption into the particular institution and the child's stay within this setting in general as well on the basis of their expectations that he will fulfill his obligations, show responsibility and not bring about any crisis which might result in difficulties for the family and the adolescent.

This unique residential school reality deserves special research and subsequently a special support program. We will limit ourselves here to the generalization that in many instances the adolescent's perception of parental expectations generates positive motivation in their adjustment. It produces motivation for achievement, increases willingness to weather crises and encourages positive development; this stands in contrast to the negative feelings it sometimes arouses with regard to the various kinds of educators, advisors and counsellors. As in every case of counselling and treatment, the meaning of any particular perception must be viewed in terms of that particular adolescent.

Alienation from the Family

There are no indications of alienation from the family or of hatred of parents in the great majority of cases. Also, there is no alienation from the family in a considerable proportion of cases where the adolescent pattern of "storm and stress" is evident.

The foregoing generalization must be accompanied by two qualifications:

- No comparison may be drawn between the research methods and tools we have employed and the intensive, prolonged work of the psychoanalysts or other clinicians who have presented these phenomena as universal. However, every form of our test yielded a clear picture of this phenomenon, including more than 100 cases where the interviewers knew the family very well, either as relatives, as longtime close friends, or as advisors or psychologists who have maintained a long-term relationship with the adolescent. As previously noted, this finding has been reinforced by similar results obtained in parallel studies conducted in the United States.
- The various questions posed or statements presented in the questionnaires to which the respondents reacted, undoubtedly contained an expression of social volition and/or painted a more positive picture than the actual state of relations in those families. But while recognizing the existence of social volition, it is important to acknowledge that this in itself is a positive expression of the state of family relations. The significance of the fact that adolescents from urban areas, residential schools and from the kibbutz say they expect parental involvement, recognition and support is that the social climate in the age cohort, which influences social volition, supports the direction of our finding.

This is not to deny the existence of a minority of cases in which the picture is different, nor does it contradict the fact that many adolescents hate certain parental behavior and may rebel against it, isolate themselves from that parent or even complain to an outside interviewer once the latter has promised that their personal statements will not be made public. Furthermore, it is important to note that many different conflicts arise during adolescence, some as structural phenomena and others which are unique to adolescents in particular families. Most of these conflicts are structural, and some are desirable in terms of advancing individuation in the adolescent process. The typology and description of conflicts will be dealt with in the next chapter.

Parental Authority

Adolescents acknowledge parents' authority and their good intentions, even when appealing against their behavior in certain situations. Various theories of psychological development assume that when

the biological balance shifts during adolescence, expectations of autonomy develop and peer group pressures increase along with the influence of movies and television, all of which undermine parents'
hierarchical and unidirectional authority. More egalitarian communication might then be expected to develop in response to this situation.
All available evidence indicates that this is not the case during early
adolescence or mid-adolescence of Israeli high school students.

Similar findings have also been clearly obtained in the American
educational system, which is even likely to include exposure to influences liable to precipitate the undermining of the family and parental
authority. In order to support our generalization, we would like to cite
the statement of Youniss & Smaller (1985), summarizing research
based on population samples defined as "white" and "middle class"
in Washington and New York. They describe how when comparing
adolescents in the samples, parents maintain their authority status.
These adolescents perceive their parents as having the right to criticize,
direct and supervise behavior; to set rules and demand they be kept;
to present expectations and advise about things like preparing school
work or doing household chores. Moreover, adolescents say that they
seek advice from their parents, especially concerning everything connected with their plans to choose a profession or plans in other areas
of their future.

We may add three secondary conclusions to this, formulated in
accordance with our data and the findings of Youniss & Smaller:

- During adolescence differentiation develops in the perception of
  the extent of parental authority over various areas of behavior.
  While children accept the assumption of total parental authority,
  adolescents gradually develop criteria about where parents are
  allowed to intervene or give orders; about what parents are permitted to advise, but not to demand acceptance; and about what
  they may claim total autonomy. Basing their behavior on these
  assumptions, they engage in self exposure, expecting their parents to act accordingly. When they feel that the parent does not
  meet their expectations, they burst out with what seems to be a
  general challenge to the area of parental authority an outburst
  because of its emotional expression. The exclamation, "You can't
  tell me what to do!" is one such response, after which there
  emerges a willingness to negotiate the limits of authority in the
  area under discussion.
- There is a certain amount of variation in this process within
  subgroups and of course between individuals, but the general

democratization of interpersonal family relations in the present generation, as contrasted with relational patterns prevalent in the previous generation, reduces these differences.

In most of the evidence we have, both adolescents and parents depict communication patterns which attest to manifestations of parental willingness to listen to the adolescent, to discuss with him and reach some compromise. In contrast, parents do not cede their authority in the area of studies and are supported by the teachers' authority in demanding completion of assignments, being willing to compromise only with regard to due-dates and the amount of time allowed. In the area of opposite-sex relations, both sides are cautious about exposure and expectation of involvement. There is also a group of parents and adolescents conspicuous by their permissiveness rather than exercise of parental authority. Members of this group usually come from the higher educated social strata of European origin.

- There is a prominent difference in the degree and the patterns of authority according to the parent's sex. In a detailed discussion about differences found in Israel and the United States, two prominent patterns appear:

In nearly all instances the mother is the active agent in communication.

In educationally deprived strata, in middle class and in highly educated homes she exercises authority from the onset of adolescence in the areas of organization of space, cleaning, keeping the room neat, clothing, eating, relations with friends, preparing homework, ties with relatives, etc. She is sometimes aided by the father in maintaining her authority, generally so that he will support her demands, and in certain instances she requires him to act as a "beat cop" and representative of the "sheriff's department." From the adolescent's point of view, most fathers try to evade this responsibility, playing an active role only in special situations, primarily when they are concerned about the mother's vulnerability, that she might hurt the adolescent's feelings, or after the mother has complained to the father that he must fulfill his duty and make his presence felt.

The father usually limits his intervention to two areas.

Fathers will only intervene in school issues (homework preparation and behavior) and planning for the future (achievement motivation, choice of major area of study, selection of profession, beginning to work, etc.). In religiously traditional families fathers may intervene in the area of religious observance, and in many families, in matters of political ideology as well.

- As the process of adolescence progresses, many mothers reach a positive balance of equality and cooperation with the adolescent regarding realization of his authority, whereas most fathers are perceived as maintaining their authoritarian pattern or as being "distant."

There are some who explain this difference as resulting from the different socialization patterns men and women have experienced in forming their identity and perceiving their sexual role. However, Youniss & Smaller (1985) explain it also by the nature of role division in a modern family. They are referring to the same structural differentiation which, according to Parsons & Bales (1955) and the sociologists and social biologists who came after them, is perceived positively in terms of preserving the balance of power and authority in the family. The latter has consequences for the development of interpersonal conflicts and for the shaping of adolescent sexual identity in this generation.

In our opinion adolescents are influenced more by what happens in their family than by political demands for equality like those of the women's liberation movement. Adolescents claim in the interviews, and both parents bear this out, that a father/male who has not learned to reveal himself to his son and daughter and to enjoy deep, effective communication with his adolescent and adult children is handicapped.

- Concomitant with their acknowledgment of parental authority, adolescents expect their parents to recognize that they are no longer children, to honor their demand for autonomy, and not to interfere in certain areas associated with identity formation and developing their own coping patterns. We will cite three prominent areas of the expectation of autonomy:

Outward Appearance

Outward appearance includes dress and accompanying accessories (clothing, hair style, decoration, cosmetics, earrings, belt), body posture (how they stand, sit or walk) and verbal communication patterns (vocabulary and method of expression). One's outward appearance is an expression of one's personal identity. Adolescents are struggling with fashioning their identity, playing daily with various images including presenting an alternative visages to the world and developing expectations of being acknowledged.

Maintaining One's Own Territory

"In *my* room I want things arranged like *I* want"; "It's *my* room and not hers"; "The furniture, decoration and way things are arranged is *my* business, and I don't expect anyone to help me"; "What I do in my room is my business, just like what she does in her room is her business"; "I hang pictures of heroes in my room for myself, like Dad hung a picture of his hero in his office."

Desiring an autonomous territory (one's own "space") and protecting the right to shape it and make it unique, begins in early adolescence. During that stage it serves as a focus for a considerable proportion of the conflicts, primarily with the mother, as discussed in detail below.

In addition to the evidence obtained from questionnaires and interviews, role play revealed similar scripts for families in which the mother stays home and is a housewife, families in which the mother works outside the home, families with a developmental pattern of "storm and stress" and for families in which adolescence is undergone tranquilly and slowly. In families where the adolescent does not have his own room due to economic reasons, a desire appears for "at least my own corner—so others won't touch my table and shelf, and so they won't open my drawer." This need is conspicuous in residential schools where several adolescents live in one room. Some institutions have learned to build a bi- or tri-level room, or to divide the room using furniture or bookshelves, etc. in order to ensure each student's privacy. A follow-up study of adolescents who left residential schools revealed evidence that the lack of territorial privacy not only disturbed them, but was one of the causes of their leaving.

Relations with peers and friends

The choice of friends, receiving friends at home and particularly in their rooms, and what is done in the company of their peers and friends are all considered as their rights. They therefore serve as an index of the extent of parental recognition of their autonomy. There is a need for negotiation over recognition, equality of human worth and gradual transfer of authority and responsibility. In the vast majority of cases adolescents and their parents may be supported.

Each party involved in the process must clearly learn the fundamental principle of adolescent responsibility for forming his own identity and for his behavior. At the same time they can clarify the parental responsibility for socializing his children, taking into account anxieties about security, social standing and the future. These issues bear special impact regarding adolescent daughters.

Problems unique to adolescent girl-parent relations often pit girls against their mothers, and the girls cite three especially hurtful issues:

Mothers who do not recognize their daughter's private life— "My mother reads my diary," and "My mother cross-examines me after a date with a boy as though I were a criminal."

Mothers who do not recognize their daughter's private life— "My mother talks with my girlfriends or boyfriends using slang as though she were one of the crowd, as if she were twenty years old." The evidence in these cases clearly carries this message: "I want a mother, not a problematic adolescent," or "I don't need another friend; she should keep on being a mother," or "she embarrasses me in front of friends."

An analysis of the interviews indicates that this phenomenon is particularly frequent among mothers who are housewives, mothers who have gone through a divorce crisis and mothers of only daughters. They seem to need support in order to understand that they hurt themselves and their daughters and must learn other modes of behavior.

Mothers who manage things for their daughters, mothers who are domineering—"she tries to run the house and Dad and thus the children as well." Others feel that their mothers don't trust them and therefore try to ensure success: "She tries to mediate between me and my girlfriend or my boyfriend," or "She requests other girls to intervene for me." Others describe how their mothers try to get a detailed report of what happened on a date with their boyfriend, then expanding on what she ought to have done in the past and what she is destined to do in the future. It would appears that in many instances the daughter's complaint expresses her own lack of confidence, and the mother's behavior not only does not improve but contributes to a worsening of their relations. In many cases it even causes the creation of conflicts which exacerbate the condition of both mother and daughter.

The Individuation Process

The process of individuation is expressed by gradual differentiation from parents and between parents, paralleled by formation of mutual relations with peers and friends.

Adolescents are engaged in shaping their identity, for which they need the family as a basis for emotional confidence. The adolescent continues to internalize and be influenced by his parents' values. As his social perspective develops, he begins to differentiate between his mother and father as people and the patterns of transaction between them within the overall family system. Due to the adolescent's ego-centricity, his view is affected by his status, fulfillment of his needs, his modes of observation and the feedback he receives from outside the family. He expects his parents to acknowledge his autonomy and equal worth in the family. He cannot build his identity without gaining perspective on his parents, without the possibility of criticizing them, or without coping in conflicts with them. He needs their approval since even though he is different and goes into the outside world, they love him and support his independence. At the same time he is active in his peer group, establishing ties with peers and friends. He borrows from them, internalizing values and behavior patterns, copes with them in various experiences, and borrows appropriate ingredients for shaping his identity. As we have described in detail in a discussion of companionship and friendship and in a discussion about the formation of a sexual identity, differentiation within the family is a process of mutual struggle and mutual recognition of adolescents by parents and of parents by adolescents. The pattern of family relations is linked to the balance of mutuality in the adolescent's coping with peers and friends. This integrated, systemic viewpoint is what brought us to investigate the family and relations within the family as well as within peer and friendship systems.

An analysis of the interviews seems to indicate that it is possible to make a general statement that the individuation process proceeds in a positive direction when the adolescent develops according to the following seven criteria:

- Making a transition from perceiving a parent as functioning as a stereotyped parent to relating differentially and humanly to the parent as a person—"I understood that Dad has problems at work, and when Dad comes home tense from work, I ask him what happened before I raise my own needs"; "Now Mother and I talk about what happened with her at school and not only about what happened to me"; "It's funny to say this, but it's as if I found out in one day that my Dad is a human being. It happened when he told about something, and I interrupted and asked him why he believed this man, and he simply said that he had made an error in judgement."

- Continuing to expect recognition and support, but with a readiness to understand the parent's needs and his viewpoint— "Although I am still Daddy's girl, he talks to me like a person.

He explains, asks and discusses"; "I have achieved an ability with Mother to tell her what I feel and to listen to her without being hurt"; "I know that what I feel is also of concern to him, and not only what he thinks. He just doesn't know how to show feelings."

- Perceiving the parent's readiness to transfer responsibility and to give support—"Now Mother talks directly with me, and doesn't just preach"; "Now Dad also respects my judgement"; "Now Dad understands that I am already a young woman and not a little girl"; "Dad also asks me what I think and doesn't just preach to me"; "Dad believes me when I tell what happened at school, without immediately justifying the teacher and jumping on me"; "Mother demands more from me and trusts me more"; "When Dad asks me to do something for him, without explaining it to me like a child, I know that he trusts me."

- Disappearance of fear of the parent and continued expectation of his approval, primarily in the case of fathers—"My father never raised his hand to me, but I was afraid he would hit me if I wasn't good"; "I don't know why, but it's important to me that Dad tell me that the paper I wrote is good"; "I've somehow reached the point of doing things without being afraid of what Dad will think of me"; "Listen, it's not that I don't care what he thinks—I care very much, but I know he will understand even if I have made a mistake"; "I do care what Mother says, but I'm no longer afraid that she will let loose"; "Dad knows already that he can't talk all the time without listening to others; and I know that there are things about which I want to hear what he thinks"; "Just when I left Dad to go to the army, he said to me that he depends on me to know how to judge what is right and what's not"; "I'll tell you straight—I'm not afraid of him anymore, but I accept him as my father."

- Ability to discuss subjects and problems without defensiveness or outbursts—"Today Mom and I simply talk like two women. It's not that I agree with what she says, but I am prepared to listen. Previously I just didn't hear what she said, because I knew beforehand what I could expect"; "I know I can talk seriously with Dad, without immediately having to prove to him that I am right"; "Even now Dad and I don't talk much, but it's a conversation between people, not a conversation between a father and child"; "Dad understood that I am a person and not a little girl, now he speaks with me and doesn't lecture me like a history teacher"; "It's simple, Dad used to be like a sort of 'assistant God' to me, distant but admired. Later, I began to learn to understand him, and he became a regular person. I can listen to him without getting excited, accepting or compromising" or "We get along because she accepts that I am no longer a little girl, and I learned to accept that I will be dependent on her until I leave home and become independent."

- A viewpoint that on certain subjects there is agreement and accepting the lack of agreement about other areas—"I really have just about the same opinions as my Dad, about many things: sports, Arabs and religion. But I didn't used to see that because he always argued with me, and I argued with him"; "There are also things we don't agree about, like clothing and music. But I don't try to convince him, and he doesn't bring up the subject, but says rather that it doesn't have to happen in the living room with voices raised"; "There are some subjects that I don't tell mother about, like what happens between me and my boyfriend, and she accepts that. There are other things that I want to hear her opinion about, like buying dresses, and she agrees that I don't have to accept her opinion."

- A gap in trust, without problem-centered conflicts—This category is characteristic of only a tiny minority of the families we interviewed. These are the adolescents and young people who have lost trust in their parents, reaching a psycho-social severance of contact with them. "Mother and I used to quarrel about putting the room in order, about choosing a garment or some other behavior, either of hers or of mine. Now things are different—I simply don't trust her intentions, reject her interference and accept her authority only because I still have to stay in her house for two more years"; "Dad and I have reached a sort of truce after bitter quarrels. He knows that he can't hurt me, since I'm no longer a child. I accept that he is my provider and father, and this is certain to continue until I leave home. The reason is that I have simply understood that there is nothing behind his words, that he doesn't act or think like he talks. I have friends and counsellors I can rely on"; "She was everything for me—an example, an ideal, God—and that has broken down, since I gradually understood that she is domineering, manipulative and treats Dad like a dish rag. Since she's like that for me, I can only accept orders from her and compromise about arrangements, because I've lost her in the most important sense."

Sex Differences

We find differences between the sexes primarily in two areas: the level of expectations from parents and in communication patterns with the mother and father.

Expectations and communication patterns

According to the questionnaires we administered, girls' expectations were found to be higher than those of the boys. This finding applies to both girls in residential schools and to girls learning in regular schools (girls scored about 3.75 as compared with the boys' score of about 3.55). This finding is supported by those of Dreyfus (1976), which indicated that girls are more dependent on parents than boys, leading to the conclusion that they have higher expectations of parental involvement in their lives. However, based on the interviews we conducted, discussions held in peer groups and various studies touching on this subject, the actual situation was found to be more complex and far more positive.

1. Most girls are more involved in the family. They have a deeper individual connection, primarily with the mother.

2. The parents, both mother and father, are more concerned about the daughter's social development, primarily regarding relations with members of the opposite sex. Therefore, parents are more critical of a daughter and limit her actions more. But in order to do so, they also maintain more intensive relations with her through which they express their love, concern, dependence on and expectations of her. Thus, this contributes to their showing interest in her and to mutual involvement. Thus, for example, two girls interviewed in the family study explained the process in different but complementary ways. According to Rachel, "Every time I went out on a date with a boy, I saw my mother's agitation and heard her warnings to be careful. And when I returned she would be waiting for me, apologizing for her interference. Although I was terribly angry with her, I knew she cared, and that she was experiencing my life more than any other person. Now that I am more than ten years older, looking back during my conversation with you (the interviewer), I think that I had already begun to understand then that she is a person with fears and worries like myself" (interview 75). Drora stated, "I will tell you when I really began to grow up and become a woman. It began one night when I came back late; my father yelled and then went back to reading the newspaper and watching television. I fled upstairs to my room. Mother came and wanted to come in, but I wouldn't let her. She said she wouldn't budge from the door until I let her in, and then I opened the door. She began to tell me about herself and her adolescence, about how they didn't understand her and wouldn't let her go out; and also about how she met Dad on a trip and about the problems she had in connection with him until they married. We sat that way on the bed for a long time, hours, and talked woman to woman" (interview 18).

3. The rate of psycho-social development for girls is faster. This is expressed in various ways, among which is the fact that girls in the upper division of high school form friendships with older boys, through which they participate in general social and heterosexual interaction at a level different from that of most boys of their age. Rachel, for example, tells of her boyfriend: "He was a Haganah commander and I was a 16 year old girl. However, in the friendship between us he poured out his heart about problems in his family, about problems in the Command, and I shared his struggling. . . ."; or Dina: "He had already been a soldier for years in Egypt, Crete and Italy, had experienced life, and I was a 17 year old girl who had just joined the [political-nationalist] movement, but he would tell me about his life as a child in a broken family, about coming to Israel and his loneliness, about problems in the army, etc. I understood things that no school taught me. . . ."

The same variation is repeatedly expressed in the transition from adolescence to adulthood and in early adulthood during the twenties.

4. In most cases communication within the family develops between girls and their mothers. This phenomenon is typical of families from all social strata. Although there are conflicts in mother-daughter communication which sometimes leave the hard feelings characteristic of adolescence, it is a human, mutual transaction. It contributes to the girl's psycho-social development in three ways: development of social perspective, development of the social skill of face-to-face communication and increasing expectation of readiness for personal involvement. The beginning of this readiness is focused on the human needs of the mother and daughter, but during transition to the stage of early adulthood it is transferred to the process of developing intimate relationships with men generally, and in particular with the man whom the girl intends to marry.

It is important to add here that the social relations which girls develop in this developmental stage contain considerable mutual communication and involvement, while the friendships of boys are more structured and more directed toward common tasks in learning, sports, formation of vocational identity or social activity.

White *et al.* (1983) found a significant difference between the sexes in relations with parents during the transition to adulthood. Young women aged 24-26 reached a more advanced stage of social perspective, they perceived their mothers as separate individuals, whereas the average young man related to his mother in terms of her behavior toward him, even though he had also progressed in that direction relative to his adolescent period. It was also found that for young men at the above ages, relations still focused around the problem of individuation from parents, and not from separate entities. In the group of 26 year old women, as contrasted with the 22 year olds, some described their mothers as recognizing their maturity and their separateness, indicating how each one could understand the other side's differing point of view.

The picture of the transition from adolescence to the early adulthood stage growing out of our interviews does not really differ from that described above. Most of the young women were involved with their mothers' needs, and sometimes even to a certain small degree in their fathers' needs, despite their limited communication with them. In the interviews there was a variation in the patterns of relating to the mother, of identifying with her, in complaints about her and expectations of her. However, the interviews express the struggle of one woman against another, whereas there is less communication with the father, less conflict, and even a lesser degree of attempting to understand his mode of functioning as a person.

By contrast, young men are more focused on themselves and their functioning, less involved in the family, and show less empathy for the needs of mother and father, even though they admit that the mother is involved in their needs. We see here in various respects that young women achieve integration between the identity formation process and the process of preparing themselves for intimacy (Gilligan, 1982). In other words, young men are involved with social activity and forming a vocational identity and desire autonomy from their parents and usually from their girlfriends as well. Young women, though, desire autonomy, but are involved in communication and coping with their mothers and with a boyfriend or husband. Within the marriage configuration, they sometimes also maintain a dual communication with the husband's mother: as a woman and as a mother-in-law who interferes in the couple's lives.

Communication Patterns with the Mother as Compared with the Father

During the process of adolescence, interpersonal communication develops, but in most instances it is communication between the mother and her children. Communication with the father generally remains of an authoritarian type, being limited to the cognitive and behavioral areas of development.

During childhood parents appear as authority figures. As we described in the previous chapter by means of the of social perspectives scale of development designed by Selman (1980), adolescence means the ability to perceive a significant other, either friend or parent, as an individual with a unique personality, and to establish mutual communication with him. Data gathered from our interviews and by others (Bell & Bell, 1983; Youniss & Smaller, 1985) show that this transition to interpersonal, mutually shared communication develops to a much greater extent between mothers and their children, and is in most cases not characteristic of father-son or father-daughter relations.

Most mothers gradually develop more egalitarian communication patterns with daughters and sons, over the broad front of needs and problems of that particular developmental period, instead of the hierarchical, linear pattern which typified communication during childhood. But for most fathers communication remains primarily unidirectional and judgmental, from father to son or daughter, limited in extent, and focused particularly on values and behavior problems of cognitive development, deportment at school and planning for the future. It might have been assumed that the democratization of relations within the family which has developed in the past two decades would contribute to a change, but Youniss & Smaller (1985) found a picture similar to what we have presented, and they generalize in the same way. They add two explanatory generalizations which also fit our data: during the adolescent period parents maintain their authority by a pedagogic and tactical shift in communication pattern according to the area involved; they suggest, discuss and compromise. In other words, communication is more democratic and shared.

Other investigators (Krosnik & Judd, 1982; Bell & Bell, 1983; Cooper, Grotevant & Condon, 1983) describe a similar situation in which parents are careful to preserve their authority in a few areas, but in other areas they act in a more cooperative fashion. There are even some areas in which parents practically renounce any involvement or from which they are removed. A remarkable example of such an area is the sexual development of the girl or boy, or in most cases all the aspects of boys' social activity in peer and friendship groups. They also found that since the adolescents' center of interest is their current emotional and social development rather than planning for the future, which are the things that are usually more significant to the mother than to the father, a clear picture of maternal activity, involvement and coping is created. The father intervenes only in special cases when difficulties arise which the mother cannot deal with alone, or when she herself is at the core of a difficult conflict with one of the adolescents.

Most fathers are more distant and judgmental, are involved in limited areas only, understand less and are less flexible than the mothers. This generalization presents a situation which most adolescents and most psychologists view unfavorably, which they suggest that "modern" fathers change. However, it is also worth examining other aspects of this situation. The behavioral variation between mothers and fathers actually expresses a difference between womens' and mens' development and between their fulfillment of sex roles in society and the family. Each of us, in accordance with his values and needs, can and in our view must aspire to change in these areas. But despite the many changes which have occurred since the adolescence of the fathers' and mothers' generation, it appears that the classic description of Parsons & Bales (1955) of role distribution in the family basically still applies: for men/fathers the focus is instrumental, for women/mothers it is affective. Existence of a certain balance between perception of the sex role and its fulfillment affects adolescent development. Perhaps some change in the future that will influence creation of a different balance is likely to bring about a positive development. But just as we have no doubt, in terms of children's and adolescents' developmental needs, that the family is an essential institution, each parent's role is also essential. Adolescents and parents must be supported so that through their efforts to adapt the role to the other's needs they will clearly see the significance of all its dimensions both for the one fulfilling the parental role and for the one who is learning and being formed during his adolescence.

The descriptions appearing in our interviews as well as those of others also permit us to discern the positive contribution of the differential functioning of each parent. This difference teaches children that their parents do not appear to have an unbreachable compact. The adolescents relate that for some things they turn to the mother and for others to the father; they struggle with the mother over certain behaviors and are supported by the father, or vice versa. Even when they are struggling with the outside world they are sometimes aided by the mother, and at other times by the father. In this way they make a tactical gain. But more importantly, this differentiation makes an important contribution to forming a sexual identity and developing coping ability preparatory to building a family and to a mature struggle with the differing expectations of women and men in their family and social roles.

Relations between Adolescent Girls and Their Mothers and Fathers

Until now we have been describing generalizations. Now we will begin a more detailed description. We have chosen to present a discussion of the relations of adolescent girls with their parents, assuming that the majority of our readers are women educators, advisors, psychologists and that this path of communication is important to them. Also, a considerable portion of the examples and inferences is appropriate to parent-son relations as well. The differences will be discussed in a special section.

Findings

A major finding in our interviews is that 80%, the great majority of adolescent girls feel close to at least one of their parents, primarily the mother, but in half of the cases to the father as well. Contrary to clinical descriptions or stereotypes presented in the mass media in which the period is depicted as filled with clashes and accompanied by feelings of anger, rage and hostility toward their parents, our interviewed painted a very different picture. Adolescents girls do indeed tell of conflicts in various areas, but most also indicate that they view these instances as normal phenomena, tending to discount their centrality without intensifying them. Most parents fill an important and central role in the lives of adolescents. Though the girls do attribute importance to the peer group and to girlfriends or close boyfriends, they still indicate, sometimes explicitly, that "parents and friends are two different things, neither of which substitutes for the other." Apparently, adolescent girls are interested in involving parents in their lives, each one in the area and manner appropriate to the girls within each unique family context.

It is important to understand two main qualifications in order to properly evaluate this generalization:
1. our interviews were conducted in families whose adolescents were aged 16-21; i.e., during the period in which the biological transformation crisis is waning, social perspective is developing a capacity for differentiating between conflict and the need for relations, and a perception of the parent as a person rather than just a role player is growing. Influence of the peer group at this age is also declining in certain senses, while the need for significant communication with parents develops along with a need for ties to a close friend. The latter ties are required for the sake of forming personal identity and coping ability. The social skill of coping with a parent develops during this period, as well as with a friend, teacher or counsellor, according to the adolescent's perception of who he is and how it would be possible to establish the desired relations with him.

2. the 150 families interviewed were intact (mother, father, boy or girl) and not exceptional. Only 20 families had adolescents living outside the home in a residential school.[1]

Furthermore, these were families which responded to a request from the advisor or another interviewer we had sent, asking for a free, in-depth interview with each parent and adolescent and who were, therefore, prepared for the self-exposure required. It may be assumed that a sample more representative of the overall population would contain a higher incidence of cases of hostility, alienation and crisis; such results could be assumed to be characteristic of about 20-25% of adolescents, as found in studies conducted in the United States, with different samples and instruments (Offer, 1969; Youniss & Smaller, 1985).

The following examples from the interviews describe the nature of the relationship and represent the various nuances of perception:

"We have very close relations. We talk about almost everything, actually I was always able to tell her everything" (adolescent girl, family 2).

"The relationship with my parents is very close. There is advice and help. I am with them a lot" (adolescent girl, family 3).

"She often consults with me, beyond what I expect; actually, she shares practically every decision with me, and I try as much as possible to make her decide by herself; because it is hard for me and isn't good for her, either" (father, family 3).

"I am very close to my parents. I can talk with them and consult. It's not possible to tell them about everything, because there are things which remain in the realm of boyfriends and girlfriends; but my parents are quite understanding" (adolescent girl, family 35).

"I don't recall any serious quarrels during recent years" (adolescent girl, family 80).

"I feel free to talk with Mother about nearly everything, aside from things connected with my relations with my boyfriend. About this I simply told her that it is my private matter, just as I accept that she has things which she doesn't tell me. She sometimes tries to touch on this, too, and I say 'stop'. Then she looks at me, eyes wide with surprise, embraces me and says nothing . . ." (adolescent girl, family 30).

"I tell my parents what I feel the need to. There are things they ask about and I answer, and there are things which I say are my private

---

[1]Data and previous generalizations cited about residential schools were derived from another study and were based on questionnaires.

business . . . they don't always agree, but things work out; because Mother says that she loves me and is concerned about me, and I respond saying that I love her, but it's my life . . ." (adolescent girl, family 25).

In our opinion as well as that of all who read the entire 150 interviews we may generalize as follows:

Parents did not escape their responsibility

Unlike what may be found in descriptions and generalizations originating in the United States during the seventies, parents are involved in various ways in the adolescent girl's life, and she wants this involvement, although she expects her privacy to be respected and her autonomy preserved in certain areas. These excerpts also attest to existence of relations on a very different level of readiness for exposure and parental involvement, as well as existence of varying communication patterns.

Mother-daughter relationships differ from father-daughter relationships

In response to a general question in the interview concerning the nature of relations with their parents, many adolescent girls (about one third) indicated that they are close to both mother and father. However, when we attempted to focus more on the meaning of these relations, it became clear to us that the dominant tendency in emotional issues is to open up to the mother. This is likely to come about since the overwhelming majority of mothers want to be involved, including themselves in all areas of their daughter's emotional and practical life, whether or not she desires it. Moreover, mothers are accustomed to doing so, since they are concerned or feel responsibility for their daughters or because they are meeting their own emotional needs. As we read the interviews and held discussions with adolescent girls we felt that today's mothers are no less involved or anxious than their own mothers had been. On the other hand, most fathers are only involved in specifically defined areas of their daughter's life. Generally speaking, those areas are school, planning for the future or supporting the mother, at her request. In the great majority of cases there is a considerable difference between the man/father's as opposed to the woman/mother's personality structure and/or role conception. In about 20% of the cases adolescent girls attest that the father is a remote, authoritarian or even domineering person, as opposed to an involved, warm and expressive mother. According to various adolescent girls, it appears in these cases that in the absence of an open, emotional connection with the father, they feel a need to maintain good relations with the mother at all costs, and tend to share all areas of their lives with her. They even accede to her pressures to expose areas in which they would rather she not be involved.

Generally speaking, there appear to be 5 points which may be cited to explain the nearly diametric opposition of the nature of the relationship with the mother as opposed that with the father in most families (about ⅔):

- Although about 75% of the women in the families interviewed work full time or fulfill another function outside their homes, mothers devote a great deal of time to child care. According to a criterion of an absolute weekly schedule, and relative to fathers, women are more available. This situation constitutes a natural source for a relationship and support.

- Mothers desire a relationship and create it. They demand their daughter's involvement and involve themselves in her life, even when she is not prepared to accede. They demand normative behavior and create conflicts; defend and attack the daughter; and a considerable portion of them even expose themselves as a person/woman, expecting the daughter to expose herself in turn. Frequently, they even make the daughter's individuation process more difficult due to a feeling that they need to protect her or because of their own personal needs.

- It appears from descriptions by daughters and mothers that in most cases the mother tries to show understanding, is prepared to comply and to hear, initiates contact, is close and flexible. She also frequently acts as a "shock absorber" and support against demands made upon the daughter by teachers, friends or the father. Due to their anxiousness and over-involvement it often happens that mothers invade their daughter's privacy, preventing her autonomy and creating a conflict which affects both of them and thereby their relationship. It is important to add that in most cases mothers and daughters compromise quickly, successfully showing mutual flexibility, thanks to their deep connection and their great dependence on its continuity.

In about 20% of the families interviewed, according to the daughter's or mother's description, the father may be defined by one or more of the following epithets: rigid, strict, suspicious, etc. Such an authoritarian character makes all communication between him and his daughter difficult or confines it to limited, instrumental areas. In most of these cases the mother is described by the daughter as warm, lenient, helpful and supportive. A strong contrast is created regarding the nature of relations between the adolescent daughter and her mother as opposed to the daughter's relations with her father. In such families we also find parallel testimony from mother and daughter, that social relations have developed between them, a sort of mutual defense treaty which, at least partially, ensures the quality of family life.

- Most fathers do not view themselves responsible for socialization of daughters, except for defined areas, entrusting the primary relationship with the adolescent daughter to the wife/mother. It also seems that a considerable portion of the fathers do not know how to establish a significant relationship with their daughters in various emotional areas. All those involved prefer that relations in these areas remain between daughter and mother. In many instances the mother mediates information and evaluations for additional discussion between herself and the father and he thereby undergoes what might be defined as indirect experiencing of the emotional areas through her transmissions.

To illustrate perceptions of relational patterns, we will cite excerpts from several interviews:

"We talk together a lot, try not to argue. And if we fight, I try to stop immediately, because it is important for me to have good relations with her. She is like my "Wailing Wall." A really good friend; she is torn between me and my father" (adolescent girl, family 106).

"I am freer with my mother, I tell her everything, just like to my friend; she not only listens but also advises and shows openness. With my father there is a brick wall" (adolescent girl, family 94).

"All in all we are terribly close. We talk and tell about ourselves. I really love to hear her and share what is happening to her; it's very important for me, because we are close and are alike . . . you understand, Mother touches more on the little things which influence me, and she's closer to me. Father is more remote" (adolescent girl, family 121).

"I talk openly with my mother about social relationships with my girlfriends; more than once my mother has recommended whom I should go with and with whom to develop close relations . . ." (adolescent girl, family 130).

"I have a stronger relationship with my mother than with my father. Possibly because of sexual identification. Also, Mother has more time . . ." (adolescent girl, family 1).

"I'm very close to my mother, I have no connection with my father, just a desire to do the opposite of what he thinks" (adolescent girl, family 22).

A father's reaction to such a situation is likely to be very significant here: "My daughter tells my wife everything. It angers me that I am not in the picture. How come, aren't I the father?" (father, family 22).

We found an example of the opposite situation, representing a small minority of cases, in family 34; the 21 year old daughter states: "Father is involved in my studies and social experiences; he appears authoritative but he's sensitive; his relationship with us—the girls—is very important to him, and he also helps my mother to get ahead . . . he provides me with real emotional support . . . he's open to expression of feelings, and isn't afraid to reveal the weak aspects of his character." The same daughter says about her mother that she is "career oriented, dominant, domineering and ambitious. . . . Mother only shares her professional concerns, but not loving concerns. She is afraid to expose her weaknesses. She wants to present a perfect image." It is important to add that in other cases the daughter claims (as in family 129) that "Father only decides about basic issues and doesn't get into little details, leaving the decisions to me; as opposed to Mother, who gets involved with the details and wants to know afterwards."

Four points are clearly demonstrated by examination of a table comparing the daughter's, mother's and father's perception of the nature of relations with the mother and the father:

- Although we had not posed a specific question on this subject, the great majority of adolescents girls spoke about the difference between relational patterns with the mother and with the father, defining the quality of their relations with one of them as contrasted with the other. In other words, adolescents construct perceptions of their father and mother by comparing one to the other.
- Adolescents are aware of this difference and clarify for themselves the causes of its development and nature. Thus, we think it would be meaningful, through use of appropriate exercises in a peer group, to discuss their perspectives and their estimation of their parents' perspective, whether any change is needed in this area, etc.
- Definitions of these adolescents, the great majority of whom are aged 16-21, reflect individual and age-related variations in development of social perspective.

- In the 20% of cases where a disparity is expressed between the adolescent's and the parent's perception of their relations, some of them provide interesting explanations. For example, the parents state that the relationship is normal but the daughter claims that she wants more honest relations, explaining that "she doesn't disagree with them because there would be no point to it, and it would just hurt them." Another interview shows the daughter identifying more with her father and being closer to him, but both parents have developed a defense mechanism to try to cover that up. The father feels that discussing this area would hurt the mother, while the mother feels that denial is a desirable option for her. In another case the father struggles with considerable difficulty over his position of authority in the family. He expresses extreme denial that his daughter has grown apart from him, while she articulates this very clearly, explaining the coalition which has been created between herself and her mother by her need to defend herself against his authoritarian behavior.

Most fathers encourage their daughters' intellectual development and are more active than the mothers in this regard.

This hypothesis was tested by examining fathers' expectations of their daughters as compared with the mothers' expectations, as well as by examining the daughter's perception of paternal and maternal involvement. It seems that in about ⅔ of the interviews the area of studies appears as a center of activity dominated by the father, and that only about ⅓ of the mothers are also involved in this area. Only in a small proportion of cases do we find a father who does not concern himself with his daughter's studies. It is clear from the interviews that this is not just supervision of homework but a clear message concerning the importance of academic studies for the future.

We find the extent of this generalization very interesting, since it stands in opposition to the message previously conveyed by the psychological and sociological literature. In particular it contradicts the claims of feminist literature from the sixties and seventies, as though fathers want their daughters to be amiable housewives and mothers while supporting career development for their sons.

Examples from the interviews show that daughters appear to affirm their parents' evaluations. Thus, for example, one father states about himself:

"I am a dominant factor in her drive to succeed academically. In the past year and one half she has understood that success in her studies has importance beyond social conventions" (family 150). The daughter affirms her father's words: "I quarrel with my father over grades. He wants me to bring home higher grades, that I should be the very best and not less than that" (adolescent girl, family 150).

"My mother, her aspiration is that I get married and have a house and family. My father wants me to continue with academic studies" (adolescent girl, family 70). "I try to have an influence on her studies and on vocational orientation for the future. If she sometimes has difficulty in preparing lessons in a subject that I can help with, I help her (father, family 70). We may add that in the separate interview the daughter from that family formulated it this way: "It's very important to Father that I succeed in my studies and complete high school successfully."

"They are very concerned with my studies. Neither of them were very good students, so perhaps they have concluded that I need to study more" (adolescent girl, family 129).

An exceptional example is a case where the mother was described by the daughter as a strong, career-oriented woman who pressures for academic achievement, but the father says: "I try to guide her in a more domestic direction. I am somewhat bothered that she, like her mother, is leaning towards an exaggerated career. All her energies are put into learning, while she invests less energy in other areas of life" (father, family 34).

In a table contrasting the father's perception of his functions as parent with the daughter's perception of them, a uniform picture results. For example:

Family 108—The father: "I help her with math and science." The daughter: "I ask him for help with mathematics, he wants to see me as a university student."

Family 115—The father: "I am involved in academic matters but not in social matters." The daughter: "If you have problems you go to Mother. Father is involved in academic matters."

Family 134—The father: "I try to have an influence in the direction of values." The daughter: "Dad encourages academic achievements . . . I go to him about work issues, money, apartment."

Family 4—The father: "I am involved in the area of studies . . ." The daughter: "My dad is ambitious about my studies . . . and generally he is the one who makes important decisions about my future life."

Family 107—The father: Did not respond to the question. The daughter: "My father wants me to be a physician, and he repeats that in various ways."

Family 70—The father: "I influence her concerning religious values and want her to study in the university." The daughter: "I want to study . . . my studies are important to him, and I tell him about them. Not about social matters."

In the interviews we found the dominant phenomenon was fathers concentrating on their daughters' studies, either alone or with the mother's support. Participants in training sessions, group leaders and adolescent peer groups came up with five trends of interpretation which could explain this phenomenon:

1) The fact that learning is a dominant value in all sectors of Israeli society. Both traditional and modern fathers look upon insuring the scholastic progress of their sons and daughters as their instrumental role in the family. This is true for both culturally deprived families and for more established populations (supporting evidence also appears in Smilansky, Fisher and Shefatiya, 1987).

2) Many fathers as well as mothers were not fortunate enough to study on a university level, and some of them not even on a high school level, due to the social reality in which they grew up. Three clearly defined groups of parents are included in this category: those of European origin who spent their childhood during the war and Holocaust period, when schools and study opportunities were closed to Jews; Israelis who spent their childhood during the period when the dominant values were agricultural pioneering, kibbutz and defending the Homeland, and university studies were not part of the adolescent "dream" or were impossible even in cases where they were desired; and those from Middle Eastern and North African countries, in which countries this had not been a viable option for their parents, or, who, upon arriving in Israel, encountered absorption difficulties, low-level education, poverty in a dependent family, etc. This phenomenon is prominent to such an extent in all groups that it would seem that fathers and mothers not only see to their children's future, but also try to achieve status or realize a personal dream through indirect achievement.

3) The message of all the media is the expectation that in the future everyone will need to study in the university, that without completing post-secondary education people will be cast by the wayside. In addition the message currently appearing is that only marginal children don't study, and thus, whoever does not see to his studies, detracts from the family's status. This message has been received in one form or another by most of the families we interviewed and is also transmitted to those children who lack motivation to study or who lack the ability to continue at the university level.

It is generally accepted by both parents and adolescents that if women wish to work outside the home or must do so, it is preferable that they be employed as white collar workers and/or professionals in order to be assured of high status and an appropriate standard of living

As we discuss in greater detail in a later volume, Israeli vocational education offers a wide variety of vocations currently considered high-status to the boys, which carry an implicit promise of a high income for the future. For girls, nonetheless, nearly all the vocational schools offer training in low-status occupations with expectations of concomitantly low compensation. Therefore, girls make up approximately 60% of the total enrollment in academic schools. Fathers, regardless of ethnic origin or extent of education, push their daughters to remain in high school, even if they are of average or low ability. They make every effort to see that their daughters are accepted in white collar employment (office clerk, bank clerk), at a preschool teachers' or general teachers' normal school, or "at least in nursing school."

The fifth approach relates to the father's importance in terms of his daughter's development. We have already noted previously that for most adolescent girls in the midst of the individuation process daily contact means mother-daughter interaction. About two-thirds of the fathers interviewed noted increased distance between themselves and their daughters and increased closeness between their wives and their daughters during the adolescent period.

Various theoreticians and clinicians have attempted to explain this distancing. The psychoanalytic approach explains this phenomenon as a reaction to awakening sexual drives and a regression to the oedipal stage of father-daughter relations. Social learning and cognitive approaches explain that the daughter views the mother as a potential model for imitation and identity. Sociological approaches point to sex-role differentiation within the family and the adolescent daughter's entry into the fray in terms of attaining her psycho-social maturation tasks.

Comments in different sections of this work indicate clearly our own approach to the family as a socio-psychological system in which the father and mother seek out ways of fulfilling their needs through balanced role division and through the formation of unique relational systems with each of their children. Thus, in fact, both parents contribute actively to the distancing phenomenon. The mother's contribution grows out of her need to be connected with her daughter, her multifaceted role in the daughter's socialization, her deep involvement in the daughter's day-by-day functioning and emotional life, and her readiness to be attentive and provide for the daughter's needs. Thus, the mother, consciously or not, dominates the relationship with her daughter. At the same time most fathers are preoccupied with tasks outside the family and they appear remote to adolescents including their daughters. The father as an individual is not free himself and therefore is not involved in the daughter's emotional life; ties with daughters focus on instrumental areas such as social behavioral norms, academic achievement and career planning.

The problem of physical distance between father and daughter was raised in the workshops, a subject to which the interviews did not relate. Responses indicated that most fathers were wary of physical expressions of love to their daughters, recognizing the danger of awakening sexual drives. Some had experienced a negative, distancing reaction from their daughters, and others feared a negative reaction from the mothers.

Nevertheless, this is only a partial picture of father-daughter relations. Fathers fulfill an essential role in shaping their daughters' identity and coping ability, both in theoretical terms and in the perception of adolescents and parents. Therefore, the father should be supported and enabled to fulfill the role to the best of his ability.

The essential nature of the father's role in the daughter's adolescent process may be summarized thus:

The Israeli family has remained a traditional family in which father and mother divide roles so that the father is responsible for instrumental areas and the mother responsible for affective areas. This accords with the classical formulation of Parsons & Bales (1955). Although 75% of the mothers interviewed in our study worked outside the home, the father and daughter (and in most cases the mother, as well) viewed the father as the "foreign minister" and representative of the outside world. He is also involved, for the most part, in family issues involving outside behavior: studying and preparation for the future. These are the things he knows best and in which he is generally interested. According to his wife's testimony and his children's perception, these areas do not demand personal exposure or emotional communication from him, for which he has not been prepared by his own socialization process.

It would appear that there is less conflict between fathers and mothers in such a role division. Despite women's entrance into the working world, in nearly all cases the home remains the woman's domain, and she feels and acts accordingly. It would seem that, whether it is objectively true or not, in many cases they are afraid of offending the mother, who is a sort of minister of the interior, a feeling which is shared by the family's children as well. This perception is reinforced, because mothers are, in fact, more successful in this role.

Many daughters express the feeling that "a man would not understand this" when referring to her relations with a girl- or boyfriend or when dealing with her intimate feelings and needs as a developing woman.

Sexual stereotypes prevail among all members of the family. Even in many families claiming to be ideologically liberated from stereotypes, daughters and fathers consider the father's greater activity in intellectual or business spheres and lesser activity in interpersonal relationships as a "natural" phenomenon. The father *qua* man, displaying either one image or another, serves to shape his daughter's sexual identity. His model of masculinity is the one with which she must cope, including advantages, limitations and problems, just as there were advantages, limitations and problems with the mother's model. Individuation, the process of shaping a girl as she emerges toward womanhood, develops out of the struggle with these models.

The father, because of his relatively greater remoteness as compared with the mother and because of his focus on the maintenance of defined behavioral norms—concern for the future in the areas of studies and work, clearly symbolizes the meaning of individuation for his adolescent daughter. The father facilitates faster individuation for her than does the mother, since he does not bind her in an emotional sense. He even spurs her on to accept personal responsibility at earlier stages.

Furthermore, the father's presence and activity advance the daughter's psychological differentiation from her mother, both directly and indirectly. The father provides a balances to the mother's influence, enabling the daughter to complain about her, compelling the daughter to fulfill the mother's expectations or compromising between her and the daughter. In many cases he struggles with the mother, openly or discreetly, over power and authority in the family. Sometimes the daughter identifies with the father, earning his steady support in emotional terms as well. One way or the other, support for role and boundary definition aids the daughter's separation from her mother, which, in turn, advances the daughter's individuation process.

Portraits of the father as remote and lacking contact are correct in some senses, but are incomplete. Observations and in-depth conversations with girls have revealed evidence of an active interpersonal game between two "cautious lovers:" the daughter who had been Daddy's girl becomes his princess; a father's reactions to the biological changes emerging in the daughter, circumspect hints, and even cautious contacts which he makes relay the message that she has become a woman. In many instances these things occur when she is at a stage when the boys with whom she interacts are too immature to fulfill her expectations and needs or communicate appropriately with her.

Views of parents and daughters on the need to complete school and expectations of life as a working woman, who is also responsible for a home and children, are similar in the overwhelming majority of families interviewed

Formulation of a desirable balance between the different roles vary from one family to another; however, the interviews affirm that practically no young Israeli woman is consciously willing to forgo family life. Acceptance of a daughter's integration into the working world is usually willingly or out of necessity. Therefore, seeing that building a family has to be combined with work, the question of coping with the need for an appropriate balance is imperative. Quantitatively speaking, when asked about dreams for their daughter's future, only about 20% of the fathers or mothers described it solely in terms of marriage, raising children and emotional-familial quality of life. The remaining parents spoke of combining studies and career successfully with marriage and parenthood. Most of the fathers emphasized the issue of studies and career, making supplementary remarks about the importance of family life; a minority emphasized the quality of family life, noting the existence of studies and work.

These examples of the parents' dream for their daughter in terms of the working world illustrate our findings:

"It seems to me that we will be proud of her in the future. Now I am proud of her will to learn" (father, family 141).

"I want her to succeed in the area she applies herself to, and she will be . . . successful in her studies, work and future" (father, family 149).

"I want her to study and then get married and be happy with family life— she should have a good husband and a good profession. She should do well in her studies. And I don't want her to engage in anything not respectable. I want her to study in the university" (mother, family 149).

"I would like her to be an independent woman. I wouldn't want to see her like I am, waiting for her wedding day . . . I wouldn't want to see her like that, and that's not the way she is . . . That's what I think. I would like her to shape her personality first and only afterwards get married" (mother, family 109).

"I expect my daughter to succeed in school and in life. She should be independent in order to develop her personality and not be a dependent character. At the moment it's important to me that she succeed in her studies; later on, in the future, it's important to me that she establish a happy family. Even so, I would want her to continue developing" (father, family 1).

Parental conflicts mentioned by adolescent girls have developed for the most part with their mothers

Responses relating to quarrels between adolescent girls and their parents indicate that about 70% of the conflicts are with the mother; less than a third of the conflicts are with the father or with father and mother together. Only about 20% of the interviews reported conflicts as a problem in adolescent-parent relations. A full analysis of conflict patterns will be covered in the section on adolescent-parent relations. Therefore, the following examples will illustrate the general pattern described above:

"My messiness makes my mother angry. She is afraid that my husband will run away from me shortly after getting married due to my lack of order. . . . We quarrel very little because I am quite reticent with my mother, since I know I won't be able to convince her. If she thinks she's right, she always manages to raise guilt feelings when we quarrel" (adolescent girl, family 34).

"Usually there are no quarrels with father, because we barely talk. . . . I quarrel with my mother when she interferes too much in my life. And she usually gets angry at me because I don't help her and my room is not neat" (adolescent girl, family 141).

"I don't quarrel with my parents. Even if there is a little argument, it's possible to compromise. . . . I have a feeling that my father doesn't understand social matters or clothing. People used to dress differently than they do now. He doesn't always understand that things have changed and, anyway, a man doesn't understand girls' fashion issues at all" (adolescent girl, family 10).

"I had many problems with my mother, because we are very similar, both of us are aggressive. We had fights and my father was the mediator" (interview with the mother about her own adolescence, family 14).

"My father was very good. I got along with him more than with my mother. He was nicer, he carried less of the burden of childrearing. Mother was the one who always said 'no.' As an adolescent I had lots of criticism and complaints about her" (interview with the mother about her adolescence, family 150).

"Quarrels break out frequently. And if this happens, it's with mother, regarding simple things: she doesn't want me to continue watching television until late or to visit my friends late at night" (adolescent girl, family 70).

"She doesn't listen to me; she isn't prepared to obey; she thinks she is old enough" (interview with the mother, family 17).

"She doesn't help me and I am her maid. I have failed to educate her in that sense . . ." (interview with mother, family 4).

"It's hard for my parents to understand what has happened to me. . . . They also didn't understand my need for privacy" (adolescent girl, family 81).

It is clear, then, that adolescence is not simply a period of conflict, and that the struggle is difficult for both mothers and daughters.

A combination of factors are involved in the tendency for more conflicts between mothers and daughters; the most important of these are:

In general girls are tied more closely to their mothers, consciously and unconsciously; mothers constitute an identity source for them; their interrelationship is deeper, more equal and more symmetrical than that with the father. Thus, daughters are more open to take offence and react more directly and frankly toward the mother.

Despite the fact that the mother in 75% of the cases interviewed worked outside the home, the mother was more available. She is the one who deals with organizing the home and controlling the children's behavior. As described above, mothers are active in all areas, whereas the fathers' sphere is prescribed to areas with clear norms basically acceptable to the adolescents (fulfillment of academic obligations and planning for the future).

Democratization within families and the fact of women working outside the home have not broken women's domination of the home. The woman feels that the home is hers and, by virtue of this feeling, she instructs her young woman how to act within its walls, expecting her to dress, eat, talk on the phone or host friends according to her regulations. In many instances the father finds his position is marginal in this alignment of relations. Sometimes he wants it this way since it is easy for him, and sometimes he discovers that it is an immutable, established fact. He often finds himself involved only when a precinct policeman is needed to defend the mother or to mediate a conflict between mother and daughter. There are also situations in which the mother is perceived as a punishing and restrictive figure while the father, who is less involved, is perceived as pleasant and kind.

The vast majority of daughters/women, looking back, admire their mothers' involvement and are not angry about her behavior. Only a minority continue to define her negatively in terms of dominating for the sake of realizing egotistical needs.

During adolescence the balance between mother and daughter in terms of health, beauty, power and authority changes. Since both are women, in many instances it seems that this change brings about competition with its potential for hurt and offence. One or both may be aware of this situation; such awareness may or may not be expressed by one or both of them. The expression of this competition may take on certain behavioral patterns which are difficult for both of them. For example, when the mother attempts to play adolescent (in dress, manner of speech, interaction with her own or her daughter's friends, etc.), or when she exercises her authority to withhold legitimate autonomy from her daughter, who seems to her to be proceeding at an undesirably fast pace or even as permissive.

In contrast, the daughter does not view herself as competing with her father. He maintains distance and status and has defined points of intervention. Thus, he can try to convince or even impose norms without arousing the feelings of deep hurt awakened by the mother.

Adolescent girls who grow up in an authoritarian family achieve differentiation earlier than those who grow up in a democratic family system

We compared reports from parents of families which would be considered authoritarian, according to specific criteria, with respect to the differentiation of their adolescent daughters to those parents of families which would be considered democratic. In general, adolescent girls reached differentiation earlier in nearly every family which could be categorized as severely authoritarian. However, early differentiation could be identified in less than a third of the girls from families which would be considered democratic.

This contrast is reflected in these quotations from interviews with authoritarian families:

"One problem was that Mother plagued me so much, telling me what to do until it became very important for me to be independent quickly and decide by myself" (interview with the mother about her adolescence, family 150).

"I wished to break away at an early age due to the difficulty of life in my parents' house" (interview with the mother, family 94).

"Being geographically distant along with leaving home early also effected separation from dependency and becoming independent" (interview with the mother about her adolescence, family 106).

Contrast the slow process which occurred in democratic families in which differentiation progressed in slow, positive terms or was even delayed:

"It was a natural process achieved only after I married" (interview with the mother, family 130).

"Mother dominated me, and it was hard for me to decide important things in my life without asking myself what she would say, and whether my decision would not be contrary to her view. It may be hard for you to understand, but she was so interwoven in my life that only under my husband's pressure did I begin to understand that I am no longer my mother's little girl . . ." (interview with the mother, family 110).

"I had already left twice to live by myself, but I knew my connection with my mother and my father determines every one of my decisions. They love me, they live my life and are a model for me of what a good family is. So how can I decide anything crucial which wouldn't be fitting for them. However, I gradually became more independent, daring more to proceed along a particular path without asking how my mother would feel . . ." (26 year old female student in university seminar).

Adolescent-parent relations in general, and father-daughter relations in particular, are, to a great extent, more positive in the present generation as compared with the parents' generation

A large proportion of the parents who were of European origin rebelled and deserted their parents. At first glance, it might be supposed that this came about as the result of the influence of natural rebelliousness plus ideologies which were proponents of rebellion, such as anti-religiousness, Zionism or a combination of Zionism and socialism. However, in the interviews it becomes clear that in a number of these "abandoned" families the father ruled without giving his children autonomy, basing his authority on religious norms or another source acceptable to his environment. Most of these rebels *cum* "deserters" lived and went through their adolescence, at least in part, on a kibbutz, moshav or residential school, resulting in a very weak tie with their families. A larger proportion of parents born in the Middle East underwent a similar experience, but most did not consider the possibility of rebellion. A considerable portion of the latter group, boys and girls, described rigid fathers who were unaware of their children's needs in general and of their daughters' needs in particular.

Approximately half of the parents interviewed grew up in conditions of poverty and deprivation as a result of the socio-political situation in the home countries of Europe, the Middle East and North Africa or as a result of the socioeconomic situation in Israel at the time of their emigration. Most of the descriptions of their adolescence include memories and emotions reflecting extremely difficult situations. Often families from the Middle East included many children and elderly and/or sick fathers. Many of these fathers died, so that the child was forced to support himself, and sometimes his family as well, from early adolescence. They describe how, as parents, they attempted to compensate their own children by providing them with as much as possible materially and by encouraging them to continue studying.

The father of family 143 describes how he was constantly engaged in seeking housing and food after his father had died. The father in family 134 relates a similar tale of going out to work after his own father had died. The father in family 148 expresses the feeling of deprivation and exploitation by his parents, as he worked and his father took the money he earned in order to buy drink. He discusses at length the extremely negative relationships within the family and his decision as a young man that when he would become a father, he would make a far better life for his children. The father of family 140 describes how his father abandoned his mother and that she later sent him as an adolescent away to a residential school when she wanted to get married. The parents of the father in family 108 separated resulting in his developing a feeling of extreme antipathy toward his father. He became so embittered that he felt that it was difficult for him to provide his own children with what he did not receive. He claims that he is different from his father, but his daughter indicates that he is a difficult man with whom it is hard to communicate.

The various descriptions in the interviews show how the parent's personal biography shapes his character, his expectations of parenthood and his relations with his children. We will deal further with this subject below. This contextual background to the problem may be raised in conducting exercises on this subject in peer groups. We feel it important to develop adolescents' perspective regarding the effect of the total environment on personal development including the intergenerational difference in the conditions of adolescence, so that they will understand their parents better as people and as parents. Such exercises may be supplemented by the adolescents interviewing their parents regarding their own "growing up." Experiments in this direction in adolescent peer groups were very successful and most of the adolescents indicated that they had gained a great deal of understanding.

Although early entrance into the work world promoted adolescent independence and, in most cases, also advanced the individuation process, in some cases it distorted parental role perception, causing inappropriate expectations for the socialization of their adolescent sons. The interviews reveal parents who are prepared to give the adolescent everything unconditionally and without an expectation of a symmetrical response. There are other parents who express the feeling that when they were their son's age they had worked, taken care of younger siblings, understood their parents and cared for them, etc. Such descriptions are openings for exercises concerning judging and interpretation in peer groups.

Changes occur in adolescent-parent relations as the maturational process progresses

The first chapter discussed this subject on the theoretical level by presenting the developmental theories of Blos (1962) and Selman

(1980). The material from the interviews suggests several generalizations to supplement these observations.

It appears that early adolescence is a period accompanied by many conflicts over certain behavioral issues: adolescents reported that quarrels with their mothers focused on straightening up their territory, dress and maintaining privacy; quarrels with their fathers related to setting limits on social issues, bedtime, time for returning home, etc. Parents complained primarily about lack of neatness, moodiness, lack of punctuality and the use of harsh verbal responses to parents' demands and requests.

At mid-adolescence, around ages 16-17, a partial decline is reported in the extent of quarrels and in the intensity of such clashes. The focus of these conflicts has moved to the adolescents' demand for recognition. They claim that their parents do not recognize that they are no longer children, that they want their autonomy respected. This demand is aimed primarily at the mother. A demand for greater involvement and intercommunication is addressed to the father.

A lull occurs in conflicts between both groups during late adolescence (18-23). There are fewer conflicts and greater understanding is evident between parents and adolescents. Discussions occur at a level of "principles" and limits and autonomy are negotiated. In most cases the change is mutual: the daughter notes that a shift has occurred in the mother's and father's attitude toward recognizing that she is no longer a child, but a person, and the parents also indicate that their daughter is beginning to understand that they are people. There is also an indication of developing social perspective in terms of viewing the family as a system. The daughter understands that her relations with her parents and the relationship between the parents and other children in the family are interconnected. The intergenerational influence also is recognized. Adolescents girls describe their mothers in comparison with their grandmothers and themselves; they analyze patterns of similarity and variation and refer to them in trying to explain their identification with certain values and personality patterns.

The perception of parents undergoes a qualitative change as well. In early adolescence the mother and father are viewed as the entity "parents": "my parents don't let me . . ."; "they don't listen" and "they feel . . ."; the expression considers them as a unit, with no place to relate separately to either the father or the mother. This is a common phenomenon even when mother and father are described in the interviews as different types, specifying differences in the quality of the conflict with each one and citing different expectations for each parent.

Furthermore, parental descriptions tend to be dichotomous, black and white, without distinguishing between the relative seriousness of issues or between the intervening shades of human diversity. For example: "They don't understand anything"; "they limit me in everything"; "they don't permit anything."

Thus, formulations reported in the interviews indicate that most adolescent girls still find it hard to make the necessary differentiation between father and mother, between her own parent and other parents, and between herself and other adolescent girls. At this stage the various parties involved are perceived as though they can be altered and are examined from a relative perspective. When making comparisons, they relate to the specific instance and the person in question without dealing with the complexity of relationships and problems. Moreover, there is no perception of a link between the adolescent girl's behavior and the parent's reaction or between the parent's behavior and the daughter's response. It is perceived as though it were a case of "that's the way they are" and "what can you expect from them" rather than as a complex interpersonal transaction conditioned by mutual patterns of communication, as emotions accompanied by reactions, etc.

Gradually, with growing maturity, during late adolescence, differentiation appears more and more in all areas as the complexity of events and their relative nature is perceived. The adolescent girl now distinguishes clearly between father and mother as well as between her own parent and those of her friends; moreover, she relates to the traits of the particular parent involved in the conflict. At this point, girls may explain the father's or mother's behavior and even justify it with biographical and psychological explanations, perceiving it as part of a specific family constellation. They are also able to examine one relational situation and compare it with another situation, generalizing from it to the overall context.

Thus, an adolescent girl (age 15½, family 148) speaks of her relations with her father, focusing on a specific trait (apparently dominance) of the father—he is "stubborn." All of her descriptions move around this concept, as though she does not perceive the existence of other characteristics. His character and behavior are presented in negative terms: "He doesn't open up his heart, doesn't explain his decisions and is not prepared to change them." She does not relate to the question of why he is like this. The parental interview makes it clear that there are difficulties in the relationship between the father and mother. However, the mother adds the fact that "he is good-hearted, he is prepared to help anyone" to her negative assessment, attributing his behavior to the difficult relationships prevailing in his family of origin during his adolescence.

The adolescent girl (age 15) in family 115 describes her father: "Dad is very sharp, very quiet, very concerned about what happens in the economy, and he gets irritated very fast." Everything is perceived in extremes. There are no intermediate qualities in her description or behavior which could be interpreted in relative terms, such as in comparison with other events, in a different family context, at a different time, in a conflict of a different nature, etc.

Family 134, in which the daughter is nearly 19, presents evidence of the process of developing perspective. This girl's relationship with her parents, especially with her father, was characterized by deep conflicts including expressions of extreme physical and verbal violence. Currently, she says: ". . . the truth is that whoever heard these things from me would say: 'What an unfortunate girl; she has such terrible parents.' But deep down inside I am grateful to my parents. If it weren't for this education who knows how far I might have fallen?" This young woman evinces the ability to see a positive dimension in an extremely difficult, negative relationship. Such a possibility appears with the capability of achieving high level social perspective and of discussing the complexity and/or logic of interpersonal relationships within the family as though observing it from the outside. At this point the individual is capable of seeing the other person as an entity with a biography which includes past and present reality and future paths; of relating to motivation and patterns of expressing needs through behavior; of judging others by means of a dialectical working through of processes, factors and results to the point of being able to justify even that which seems painful and insulting.

A 22 year old woman (family 126) describes her experience: "My mother neither wanted nor was capable of seeing her daughter as a mature person, making her own decisions, who had the right to maintain her privacy and did not need to account for her actions." After describing the specific instance, she concludes: "The relationship with each of my parents is now generally good. It was less so in grades 11 and 12. There are no overall conflicts with my parents now, just small quarrels. . . ."

It is possible to see, even in the above two brief excerpts, that there is an evident ability to distinguish between what is common to mothers as human beings and parents and what is unique to the particular family constellation, to distinguish between a basic conflict and a quarrel about something specific.

Notwithstanding the generalizations made about group development, there is marked variability in individual development.

A seventeen-year old from family 145 divides her maturation process into periods: "When growing up there was a very good relationship during childhood, a bad period began in early adolescence—there were many conflicts accompanied with bitterness, particularly in relations with Dad. Now relations are much better."

Another young woman of the same age (family 118) restricts her generalization in time, distinguishing between developmental stages: "Like other girls, up to a certain age I used to view my father as God's assistant. . . ." At this point she gives a description of her father's positive and negative traits, depicting him as a complex man. However, another adolescent girl, also aged 17, differentiates between her father and her mother, presenting an absolutely good father contrasted with an absolutely bad mother. A 20 year old adolescent (family 2), who is in the middle of the transition to adulthood, has still not formed an initial identity. Regarding most of the things which relate to her, she responds that: "I haven't thought about that yet and I still haven't decided about the other." Indeed, when speaking about her parents she says explicitly: "I think of them together—as parents," and her goals: "they need to be changed to fit into the kibbutz."

There is a connection between interpersonal relationships within the family and the adolescent girl's perception of choosing a mate and building a family

We will limit ourselves to describing just a few findings which affirm that there is indeed a connection between the family's interpersonal relationships and the adolescent's perception of her future mate. These findings emphasize the importance of the father's role in the family alongside the mother's role and clarify the systems approach to the family as essential for understanding adolescent development.

Undoubtedly, most women are conscious of a direct connection between the character of their fathers and mothers and the nature of the relationships which developed in their families. Furthermore, most seem to be aware, as well, of the relationship between the latter and their choice of a man with whom to build a family and form a relationship. Such an observation reinforces our estimate of the importance of peer group work using the unit dealing with adolescent-parent relations. We expect that initial coping will develop out of that unit, concomitant to adolescents' perception of their parents and the interrelationships between them. For grades 11-12 in the units devoted to choosing a spouse and building a family, there will be another confrontation with the subject. These units will focus on analyzing the factors which influence this choice, dealing in depth with the connection between experience in the family of origin and experiences in heterosexual social relations: attraction, love, sexual experience, involvement of beaux and friends, etc.

Nearly all the 18-23 year old adolescent girls we interviewed regarded choosing an appropriate husband and building a family as an opportunity to emulate parental qualities which they viewed as positive and to replicate that part of the family pattern in their parents' home which seemed good and proper. At the same time they regarded this as an opportunity to correct, improve and change those things which did not seem positive to them.

To a certain extent these adolescents do not differentiate between the potential mate's personality and the model of family relationships which they wish to build in the future. Based on their perception of the experiences in their own families, they view the family pattern as being a direct result of the spouse's characteristics. Therefore, they try to be aware of their own personalities and behavior and emphasize those traits of a prospective husband which will enable him meet their expectations and fill their requirements.

The great majority of adolescent girls regard their father as a model of masculinity, either positively or negatively, and their definitions and array of expectations of their spouse accrue from that model . They select such requirements by constructing a profile which compares the father's "positive" and "negative" characteristics. If the father seems "wise" to them, the daughter would also like her husband to be wise; however, if he is also perceived of as "stubborn," she might indicate that she wants a "wise and compliant" husband.

At the same time, the daughters define and mirror themselves according to the mother's profile. Thus, for example, one daughter might say: "I have a 'domineering' mother, and she has turned Dad into a 'dish rag.'" To this she may add: "And I'm also domineering by nature," inferring either implicitly or explicitly that she supposes it will be difficult to make any fundamental change. Her conclusion is therefore, "I wouldn't choose a weak husband who would allow me to do to him what my mother did to my father."

In sum, in most cases a young woman builds a profile of her ideal mate for building a family and for establishing a desired relationship at the end of the adolescent stage of her development. There may be a direct relation between these two factors and the degree of satisfaction with her father's functioning in the family of origin and with the relationship that developed between her parents. The more favorable her view of her father's role and the better the perception of her parents' relationship, relative to her values and personality, the more likely it is that she will choose a personality similar to her father's and

seek to build a relationship with her husband in the future which is
similar to that which existed between her parents.

An adolescent describes her father from family 107: "Quiet, shy, stubborn,
passive, doesn't talk much and uninterested in going out, uninvolved in the
outside world and doesn't want innovations." Her requirements for a spouse
and relationship: "An intelligent, involved husband, with whom it will be
possible to discuss everything, who will be interested in going out."

A similar description of an adolescent from family 148: "Dad is a solid
wall, . . . suspicious, stubborn, inflexible, it's important to him that people
respect him, not receptive to changes, impatient, pessimistic, a worrier."
She describes the relationships within the family as negative to the point
that she doesn't view her parents as a couple. Her description of the type
of spouse and relationship she wishes: "A husband who will be smart,
understanding, considerate and compliant. . . . establish a family which has
true partnership, equality and responsibility and joint action by both partners."

The adolescent from Family 4's perception of her father is "Reticent,
introverted, stubborn, very critical, unsociable, doesn't express feelings,
honest, reliable." She describes the relationships within the family: "Barely
speak with each other, no relating of experiences, she and her mother do
not tell things to the father because he is so critical. The father is the one
who makes decisions about important issues." Her description of the type
of spouse and relationship she wants: "To establish a family in which there
is love and understanding, members will talk with each other, and in which
relations will be different than those between my parents."

The perception of the father of the adolescent in family 108 is: "A difficult
type, rigid, smart, suspicious, wants everything to be done the way he
wants; has mastered mathematics and scientific subjects and thinks he is
the only one who is smart." She describes the relationships within the
family: ". . . parents are not open, mother and father argue, the father
threatens to leave, but can't do anything without the mother; the daughter
is angry that her mother does not rebel." Her description of the type of
spouse and relationship desired: "Do not want a husband like her father;
she will not be afraid of her husband; will look for a smart but easy going
husband, rather than a hard, irritable one like her father."

In family 109, the adolescent perceives her father as: "Emotional, warms
up easily, always in a good mood, jokes, irritable, quick-tempered; pedantic
and expects everything to be perfect; aggressive, rigid; concerned about
people and teaches good citizenship." Her relationships within the family
are: ". . . good. The mother is closed and the father open; the father is
emotional, giving and urging; they get along through compromise rather
than after submission." Her definition of a spouse and relationship:

"Many things in Dad's and Mom's relationship are similar to the relations
between me and my boyfriend. I will look for a quiet but self-confident
husband; not a noisy, empty sort; a smart person, one that you can rely on
and feel good and comfortable in his company. I don't want a domineering
person, I will search for someone who will enable sharing with him on an
equal basis (according to her, she is a great deal like her mother)."

In family 134 the adolescent's perception of her father: "A good but stub-

born man, very domineering, not permissive, knowledgeable and understanding." The relationships in this family are perceived: "The father
respects the mother, but does not show signs of love and indulgence. They
don't talk about feelings, and each person is closed off by himself. The
parents get along together despite the difficulties." Her desires for the type
of spouse and relationship: "Dad and Mom together are my model. . . . a
warm, supportive husband. . . . A house where people talk about inner
feelings. . . . I will be open and free in my relations with my children. I will
look beyond the surface, into their thoughts, I will be their friend, not just
a plain father and mother. I wouldn't want a domineering father and a
mother like that."

The adolescent in family 70 perceived her father: "A traditional father,
old-fashioned ideas, stubborn, active in the home." Her view of the relationships within the family: "Relationships are determined by Tradition—
each one knows his place. It covers up the real situation and that's not
honest . . ." The type of spouse and relationship desired is described: "An
educated husband who knows his way in the modern world. Not slovenly,
someone who understands others. . . . I will see to it that sincere relationships develop with everyone. . . . I want to build a family like theirs, but
with more freedom and more independence."

The seven cases cited above illustrate the evident connection
between the adolescent's perception of her father and the family's
relationships and her definition of the ideal character of a husband
and the family relationships to be established.

*There seems to be an intergenerational, historical perspective for women and
mothers in the patterns of the connection between experiencing a particular
transaction during adolescence and choosing a spouse and building a family*

The excerpts from the family interviews in the table on the next two
pages indicate how today's mothers perceive father-daughter relationships during the girls' adolescence, from the psycho-historical perspective of a wife and mother.

This table shows clearly that the father influences his daughter, now
a mother, in practically every family. This influence is reflected in
terms of choosing a husband and establishing relations with him and
in the relationships with the children. This influence may express itself
as a choice of a husband who resembles the father directly: he is like
the father was as a husband, cares for the children like he did; or it
may express itself as a choice of someone who is different from the
father. For example, there is an obvious similarity between the father
and the husband in family 148; in family 126, as well, the mother was
quite aware of the similarity between her husband and her father; in
family 109 egocentric traits, like searching for convenience and lack of
involvement with the children, are shared by the father and second
husband. In contrast, the mother in family 4 sought a calm man, who

Family	The father and relationships with him	Choice of mate and relationship with him	Relationships with my children
148	The father didn't love his children, sought quiet and comfort for himself. Secluded himself, died when she was 14.	Her first marriage was immature; divorce and difficult second marriage. "Difficult type," "loves himself," "thinks of himself," difficult relations to the point of physical violence.	"I live for the children, unlike my father." Loves to care for others.
34	The father, an economist-accountant, is submissive . The mother died during her adolescence. The father yielded to the stepmother, so she was treated harshly. He married her off quickly to get rid of her.	She was married young, divorced and married again. Studied economics like her father.	She was afraid that her husband, too, would not treat her children nicely, but relaxed with her second husband. Relations with the children are good, but parenting reawakens criticism toward her father.
126	Very decent, a believer, soft and gentle. She grew up without a mother, with a stepmother; remains close to her father to this day.	Honest, good-hearted, believes people, scholarly, "my husband is like my father."	This is a different generation "and we can't imitate the past."
4	The father is industrious, loves women but yells and is a nervous type. He hit the children. The parents were always quarreling. "I didn't love him," "I was afraid of him," "I hate him . . ." Relations with the mother are also disturbed. "The parents were a bad example and I'm not like them."	I looked for a man who was not irritable, didn't yell, gentle, not violent —and I found all that in my husband. In addition, he's honest, trustworthy, sensitive, takes care of the family. "He has difficulty expressing the warmth and love in him." When she was young she feared members of the opposite sex because "I had a feeling that each one was like him" (the father).	"Unlike my parents, my children are the center of my life . . ." "relations with the children are warm."

did not yell, was not violent, traits which this woman ascribes to her husband.

It is clear that the death and absence of a father affects the course of the daughter's life. This is true not only in terms of a deteriorating economic situation in the absence of the primary wage earner, which in and of itself is extremely significant, but it is true in terms of psychological influences and implications.

The painful, prolonged, unresolved loss of the father, the development of symbiotic relations with the mother and the concomitant dif-

Family	The father and relationships with him	Choice of mate and relationship with him	Relationships with my children
134	She grew up in an open home, good relationship with her parents. The father was sick so she went out to work early. He loved her the best of all his children. She respected him but it was hard for her. She developed such a close relationship with her mother that it was hard for her to leave when she went to the army. Admires her parents very much	Dependable and devoted. She chose him because of his warm attitude toward his mother. He loves work, helps others, is tough, consistent and stubborn.	She mediates between the children. "I am the one who is soft with them. I have not had any serious conflicts with them, unlike my husband."
133	Her father died when she was six. People say he was handsome, educated and generous and that he had fine relations with the mother. She still suffers from his absence even now.	Marriage constituted a difficult separation from her mother. Her husband is a charming, loving, reliable man, and she is proud of him.	Positive relationship of dependency and mutual responsibility; the son is harder for her than the daughters.
109	The father is egocentric, closed up, does not express feelings; he claimed she wasn't talented and suppressed any ambition in her. The mother died when she was 13. She had serious quarrels with her father who did not allow her autonomy. She left the house at an early age. Grew up lonely. "I resemble him in his compulsiveness, which I can't overcome."	There is something of my father in my husband: this meticulousness and occupation with detail . . . this fastidiousness." Marriage turned her into a mature person, and had a good influence, even though the husband is conservative and difficult to change. He helps her. She chose her vocation following in his footsteps and is dependent on him.	She functions as a good mother to her children "as opposed to my father," but maintains a certain distance. She is disappointed to discover egotism in her children, as it is important to her that they not be egotists. Regards problems in relations between the children as "something natural."

ficulty in separating from her are evident in family 133. The unresolved negative relationship with the father of family 4 prevented the adolescent girl (now a mother) from participating in proper social joining with members of the opposite sex and contributed to her developing an anxiety toward men. She also failed to choose a husband who would be different from her father.

Family 34 presents a reversal: loss of the mother figure during adolescence which, in turn, brings about a loss of a significant part of the support received from the father, resulting in premature marriage and divorce. In her second marriage the woman finds warmth and support, but she reports that anxiety still accompanies her. Also, she is the one who is career-oriented in the family and the husband is the domestic person, a switch of roles which she claims to have needed.

The mother in family 109 also died in her daughter's early adolescence, and she describes loneliness and quarreling with her father, who suppressed her personality. Despite her claim that her husband is "a wonderful father and a wonderful husband," she is aware that his traits are similar to those of her father.

Father-daughter relations have an influence on the daughter/ mother's behavior toward her children. Most of the mothers in the study indicate explicitly, without having been asked, the correlation between their relationship with their own children and the relationships they recall from their own homes during their own adolescence; they express a sense of the influence behavior in their parents' home had on their own behavior. Connection patterns vary from families in which the mother indicates explicitly that she is emulating her mother's behavior toward the father; to those in which the mother copies an overall pattern of relations from her family of origin rather than a particular parental characteristic; to those in which the mother claims that she consciously acts toward her children in a way which is different and even contrary to the relationship with her own mother or father.

The study has shown, generally, that when the relationship between the father and mother is good and reliable and adolescent- mother relations are positive, there is a chance of positive relations in the daughter's relationship with her own children, where the mediating factor is the husband. We think that the most significant finding of our study of families is the great importance of mate selection for the development of each family member, even where there was conspicuous deprivation in childhood and adolescence. When we discuss mate selection and building a family, we will discuss this subject in detail. (Smilansky, 1991)

The Relationship between Sons and their Parents

Until now we have focused our discussion more on the relationship between daughters and their parents. Now, we will complete the picture by noting several aspects in which boys' perception and behavior vary from that of girls.

There is less communication, less involvement and less conflict in parent-son relationships. A study of the interviews and of material from peer group discussions suggests several explanations for this phenomenon.

Adolescent boys, like men, are generally less involved in what happens in the family

They disclose less of themselves, expect less self disclosure on the part of their parents, and are less offended by such limited disclosure and communication. They are more occupied with the world beyond the family or with their own hobbies or projects, such as sports, youth movement, computer, boat, motorcycle. They usually seek parental intervention when they need advice or support in crisis situations, such as with a teacher, counselor or regarding relations with a girl friend.

Father-son communication, when it exists, generally focuses on three areas: information and exchange of views on subjects or projects outside the family, inquiries with regard to academic progress and plans for future study, and/or complaints about difficulties in mother-son relations

Even in these areas, however, only about half of the adolescents indicated that they would choose the father as a preferred partner for such discussions; others chose mothers or friends. In the United States the preference rate for ties with the father is even lower (Younis & Smaller, 1985).

When adolescents wish to disclose things about themselves or to consult with a parent about personal social problems, 80% initiate a connection with the mother

Adolescents in Israel, as in other countries, do not communicate with their fathers about sexual topics; figures show only about 7% of the boys and 2% of the girls turn to their fathers. However, in fact, only a minority consult with their mothers either in this connection (about 15% of the boys and 30% of the girls). This points once again to the importance of systematic peer support group activity specifically concerning this area.

Although the vast majority of boys perceive their fathers and mothers as interested in their development, they vary as to their perception of the nature of the father's involvement as regards that of the mother. Fathers are generally viewed as direct socializing agents in the areas of studies, vocation and appropriate behavior. They try to explain their stands to their sons, but in about one third of the cases are prepared to listen to their sons' views as well. A small minority of fathers appear unconcerned or permissive. Compare this to the portrait of the mother as someone who tries to understand and help with the son's problems in school issues, friendship and relations with the father, which is described in 60% of the cases. There are practically no reports of a disinterested mother, and a small minority of instances describing a permissive mother.

Furthermore, when the situation occurs, both mothers and sons interviewed express their appreciation of the significance of the fact that the father knows how to listen to his son and to communicate with him openly and mutually. Interviews indicate repeated instances in which sons talk to their mothers and freely discuss immediate or extended family affairs. However, a parallel connection with the father is described in only a few cases. Interestingly, the lack of many expressions of disappointment may indicate that boys accept this variation between their parents as a natural fact of life.

Generally, sons love shared activities with their fathers, especially in early adolescence. About 25% of the adolescents mentioned relishing the fact that they had gone on excursions, attended sports events, or worked on a project such as building in the yard or collecting stamps or coins with their fathers in their early adolescence. Such activities almost never occur with regard to the relationships with their mothers. About 50% noted watching television together with the father, joining him for supper when he returned from work, reading a newspaper article suggested by the father and discussing its significance. Only a handful of cases mentioned such activity with the mother.

About 60% of the adolescents mention their fathers helping with homework; in most cases this is described positively and in a few negatively. The mother helping with homework is mentioned by about one-third of the boys. In some of these cases the same boys who indicated their father as filling this role mention their mother as well; others seem to be those who do not enjoy their father's help. In only about one third of all cases does parental involvement in homework preparation fail to appear altogether.

Many boys mention appreciatively the interest, involvement and relatively free communication with their mothers. About 60% of the boys note that the mother was always ready to listen, expressed interest, and was less judgmental than the father; they felt the mother understood the son better than his father. Even those adolescents who claimed later on in the interview that their mothers annoyed them with their demands regarding dress, keeping their room orderly, nutrition, homework preparation, etc., added that she did this as an expression of concern, anxiety about their development or sincere love, etc.

The greater autonomy accorded to the boys is very conspicuous. Only the tiniest minority of boys complained that the mother interfered with their privacy, and almost no such complaints were voiced about fathers. Nearly all of the boys relate that pressure on them is focused on conduct at school, preparation of homework, and, in a few cases, on the areas of dress, behavior at home and returning home late without notification. If we recall the description of the girls' difficulties, particularly those with regard to relations with the mother but often including the fathers as well, the difference is very noticeable. In a majority of cases the boys describe how the autonomy they earned fulfilled their expectations, mentioning conflicts only with regard to meeting the school's expectations, homework preparation and conduct toward the teacher.

The greatest problem boys report regarding fathers is the feeling that they have not met their fathers' expectations.

The interviews clearly indicate that sons are more distant from their fathers than from their mothers. It is more common for a son to complain about his father's remoteness than for a daughter. Sons mention their expectation that their fathers will some day express their love, recognition and confidence in their present or future success more frequently. Others also refer to their fathers' seeming imperviousness to their feelings, but these remarks are not different from those of girls with regard to their fathers. Girls emphasize more the fact that the father does not disclose himself or communicate with them symmetrically, whereas the boys express concern that they don't meet his expectations. Even boys who attain open relations and regular, clear support from their mothers do not find that sufficient. It seems as though the father's recognition and esteem is more important to them.

There is a minority of cases wherein sons describe their fathers' encouragement and support with great admiration, but, for the most part, it was clear that support groups aimed at improving father-children relations could provide an essential service. The fact that many mothers explain the fathers' behavior to their sons or even defend him in various ways is not an adequate substitute for the sons' expectation of receiving appropriate reward and acknowledgment from their fathers.

The extent of communication between fathers and the current generation of adolescents and the degree of involvement, in comparison with the previous generation, has improved markedly. This is especially evident from the descriptions of today's parents of their own relations with their fathers. It would seem that the greater education of the present generation of fathers and the democratization within the families is responsible for the change which has occurred in their perception, behavior and greater readiness for involvement in their children's needs. The fathers of today's parents were more patriarchal, more remote or more alienated, and less communicative.

Patterns in Adolescent Perception of Relationship Development from Adolescence to Adulthood

Reports of parents and adolescents indicate quite clearly the wide variation of relationship development patterns between families. Generally speaking, six clear patterns emerged in the testimony of the approximately 150 families which were interviewed.

The following is a concise presentation of each pattern, using only a few of the possible examples. To these examples may be added examples already cited in various contexts and further examples in the next chapter, which deals with conflicts.

The slow, tranquil, extended individuation pattern

This heading includes various sub-patterns connected with the parents' educational and socioeconomic status, personality, and overall family relationships. For example, the son in family 5 relates, and the parents confirm, that he grew up in an educated, liberal family. Both parents were involved in their work, loved their children but interfered with their behavior only at times of crisis: when problems arose at school or when they returned home very late at night. Even when they did intervene, the parents' reaction was characterized by gentle words. His active socialization took place from the outset of his adolescence within peer groups, at school and in a youth movement. An occasional conflict with the parents arose regarding marginal issues, but according to both their perceptions, he attained recognition and autonomy from an early age. This autonomy developed gradually and the process was completed once he had left home for the long period of army service at the completion of which he got married.

Family 60 represents another example of this classification. The parents' background is very similar to that of the previous example, but in this case the parents are very involved in their children's lives. The adolescent boy says that as a youth he enjoyed warmth and felt autonomous within the family constellation, but felt not ready for social involvement in a peer group or youth movement or for an intimate relationship with a girl. His separation process continued until his late twenties and only achieved with the onset of a family crisis brought on by his choice of a bride.

A third example is the boy from family 51, a family of laborers. He relates that at the age of 14-15 he felt he had no autonomy, insisted that he was not a child, and argued for the right to be responsible for his own behavior, like his brother who was two years older. He describes negotiating behavioral norms with general success. Confrontations occurred a few times about different things, but he always felt his parents understood him. He was a good student and helped his parents. He concludes: "I didn't feel different from them, or that I wanted to be different. I only wanted for them to give me more freedom to go out with friends." He sees himself as similar to his father in many ways and wants to develop according to his father's guidance. He says his father is a wise, understanding person even though uneducated.

This comprehensive pattern seems to include about 35% of the adolescents participating in our study.

The "storm and stress" pattern

This pattern refers to adolescents who, by their own account, their parents' account or according to both sides, appear to have undergone adolescence in the format described in psychoanalytical literature. The following three examples will illustrate different subcategories of this pattern.

"Sometime around the beginning of seventh grade I felt that my parents were not all right; they were not like I thought they were. My father talks about everything in fancy language and preaches to me. Mother is the kind who tries to dominate everyone and interferes in everything. She didn't understand me and claimed that I didn't understand her. I also felt strange inside: one day I would think I knew more than everybody and the next day I would be in such a state that nothing would come out of me at all. When I think about that whole period until the army, I had plenty of problems. I quarreled with teachers, quarreled with my older sister who also argued with Mother and Father, and quarreled with the youth movement counselors. . . . But at the youth movement I felt good. There I had friends and eventually there was a counselor who understood me and whom I respected, and we got along. He knew how to approach me about things . . . the change in me began only in the army, ..." (family 69).

"My problems began when we moved to another apartment and I entered junior high in Ramat Aviv. Both my parents were occupied with my brother

. . . I used to quarrel with my older brother to the point of exchanging blows, and school just wasn't good for me. First of all, it was boring; then, the teachers used to pick on me and claim that I couldn't sit still, as though I had ants in my pants, and that I didn't do homework. I skipped entire days. I would leave home and go to the sea or the woods or I would skip out early. My homeroom teacher invited [my parents] several times and told them that I would never amount to anything. She said that she and the guidance counselor suggested I be sent to a residential school. When Mother told Dad and they asked what I thought, I shouted at them that I know they want to get rid of me. . . . that they are like everyone else and don't care about me. . . ." (family 36).

"Things weren't good for me even before adolescence, because I always felt that Mother didn't respect me; anything that happened she would blame on me. . . . later I understood that she simply didn't want me when I was born. In seventh or eighth grade things were really bad. I saw that I was not pretty; I was afraid that boys wouldn't want me; and so I kept away from them. I was only good at sports. . . . There in HaPo'el [a professional sports club] I disgorged all my hate together with all my energy . . . I married early—during the army, to the first fellow who loved me . . . I've already told you about the problems with him . . ." (family 65).

This category seems to account for about 15% of the cases in our study. It may be assumed that this proportion is higher in the general population, since we included only intact families (father, mother, adolescent) in the interviews and did not deal with single parent families or separated families. Our adolescent sample does not include any from the categories of special education, emotionally disturbed, neglected or delinquent.

Quick separation model

This pattern includes a combination of two groups, which will have to be separated in the final analysis. First, there is a small group whose members reached an overall level of social development such that by age 14-16 they were able to define themselves to their parents, cope positively with developing significant ties with friends and attain a stable relationship with a mate. This group is represented by the following woman's story.

"Around the age of 15 I had figured out clearly for myself who my father was and who my mother was. I knew their strengths and shortcomings; I could tell myself what sort of permanent mate I wanted, in the sense that he shouldn't be passive like my father, that he should be active and involved politically in society, that he should be intellectual, that I should be able to talk to him about everything. I didn't want a situation like I saw at home, where my mother was dominant and domineering . . . and I already knew then that I loved them, needed to and wanted to help them at home and in their joint business . . . and I also knew how to establish ties and choose a friend . . . and was prepared to marry that same friend. . . ." (family 45).

The proportion of girls to boys in this group is very high.

The second group consists primarily of adolescents who grew up in families of minor tradesmen and laborers. These adolescents describe how it was clear to them that as long as they were living in their parents' home and studying, the parents would be the ones to decide. On the other hand, their parents gradually gave them more freedom to go out, to bring home friends and to express opinions.

Indeed, their freedom increased when they began to work part-time, since they no longer needed their parents' money. When they began to work after leaving school at age 16 or 17, their parents' supervision and intercession ceased. This situation is especially common for boys. Girls report that their involvement with the family, as well as parental intervention regarding the boys they dated and the time they returned home, continued until their induction into the army and even until marriage.

The following remarks of an adolescent boy from this group reflects the prevalent attitude.

". . . I have two older brothers and I'm like them. I'm not like my Dad, because he's in the old generation: somewhat religious, unsociable, doesn't talk . . . he finishes work, seats and reads the paper, then he eats supper and watches television until he falls asleep. I'm like my brothers. I used to ask permission and obey everything my mother said, or even my father, and they told me: 'Do it this way . . . don't go out until you've done your homework . . . bring this or that from the store.' That's how it was until I was just about fed up with school, and I said to my father: 'Look, you are taking the fun out of my life and I'm making Mother angry. I'll go to work in a garage, like [my brother] Yaakov and then I can be a grown-up and also help Mother.' We talked it over. . . . at first they said 'No,' especially my brothers, who even now try to run my life and interfere with everything, as if they were my father . . . But then my grades dropped and they called in my mother, and then they hit me . . . The end of it was that when the year was over, I left school and went to work in a garage where a friend of my brother's works.

Ever since then I have felt good and it's been good for everyone. Mother prepares food for everyone in the morning . . . I return from work, and then they ask me: 'Yitzhak, how are you doing? How was it? . . .' By the time I've showered, Mother has already set out my slippers—just like for Dad and my brother Yaakov . . . and I know that I'm a man. . . . I give her half the money, since I also eat at home and all that, and I take half for all my things . . . What can I tell you, it's like a new life for me . . . and I'm not like a 17½ year old, it's like I'm going on 20, like Yaakov—I think what I want, do what I want, I just show them respect, since they are now like old people for me. . . ." (family 71).

These two groups account for about 15% of the study sample, but it would seem that since the number of working youth included in the sample was so small, it is likely that the pattern represents a larger amount of the general population.

Personal leadership activity pattern

This group also includes adolescents who belong to various subcategories. They share the factor that due to events in the family and unique aspects of personality development, they have taken on the responsibility of shaping their identity earlier than usual, developing a pattern of coping with the environment, investing great effort and paying the price to be able to declare: "I have created myself; they have not raised me—I have. They have not built me, but I have built myself." The various factors mediating such development are poverty, a family crisis, a strong life theme requiring the ability to prove oneself, etc. Individuation patterns differ among these cases, but members of this category seem to share an exceptional capacity for activity and a sense of one's ability to fashion oneself, to become a "self-made" person. Nearly all the examples we have are men, but this should not be interpreted that there are no women in this category. They have developed through three main paths to social mobility: early entry into a vocation, military service and residential or kibbutz education.

The following three examples, each of which represents one of the above paths, illustrate the various factors included in this pattern.

"I didn't find any meaning in classes at school, but I was active in the Labor Party's youth organization. I decided that I didn't want to continue studying at age 16. My parents were against it; they yelled, threatened, but nothing was of any use to them. I already knew what I wanted from an early age, and I always did what I wanted. I looked for work during summer vacation, and a friend arranged a job for me at his uncle's business. I began to travel with his brother, distributing merchandise in stores in Arab villages, moshavim and kibbutzim. We would leave very early every morning, deliver merchandise, get an order and go on. The more you travel and sell, the more you make. He would drive and make out invoices and I would load, unload and arrange things on the vehicle. On the way we had a great time. This man was a nice fellow, we used to talk and tell stories all the time, stop to get a drink, and we always ate at one of the kibbutzim. After a number of months, maybe a year, I already had a driver's licence and I drove part of the time. . . . Later, he stopped working for the company; I was put in charge of the van and I had a helper. What can I tell you, I became a man very quickly. . . . I would read the paper, tell my mother and father things in the evening and they listened and respected me. I began to study a bit at night because I had promised them, but nothing came out of it, since I came home late all the time, tired and all that, actually excuses . . . I was already doing what I wanted, and they didn't say anything to me, and when I returned from the army I went straight to a distributor like this one and suggested that I work for him on commission. My father put up money for a vehicle and I was a regular guy like everyone. . . ." (family 90).

"I came from Poland with my parents. . . . both my father and my mother, all of their families were killed, and they got married after the war in a refugee camp. It was extremely difficult for them to manage, and they sent me to a kibbutz, through Youth Aliyah. It was very hard for me there. The children didn't like me, since I came along in the middle—a stranger, when they had already been together for a long time; also, I didn't know Hebrew well, and I wasn't sociable. It really was hard, and I asked my parents several times to take me home. But things were not good at home, because they weren't managing, and I don't want to tell you what was going on there . . . There was no choice, until I adjusted a bit. In other words, I learned to ignore the children, and there was also one girl with whom I established a tie—it was a real tie, because she was lonely like me . . . Then it was time for the army. I was very afraid, I didn't know if I would get along in the army, but there was no choice. I told myself, you must do what you must do—there is no one in the world who will do it for you; and if you don't succeed, you will end up all the way down at the bottom. And this girlfriend from the kibbutz also helped, because I would meet her at her base when I was on leave. She was good to me, she encouraged me, and we felt good together . . . She also wanted to get married, but given my situation then, how could I have married anyone? To make a long story short, I was accepted into an officers' training course. . . . I worked myself almost to the breaking point, but I had to prove to myself and everybody that I could do it. I was also very proud that a Pole like myself had commanded native Israelis; how many of them were unfortunate like me? As for my parents, whom you're asking about, I didn't have much contact with them—they remained what they are and I was a new person. . . . to be successful, I worked day and night and seven days a week. . . . because of that, I also didn't have much contact with girls, until one decided that she wanted me on my terms . . . and even that didn't always last very long . . . because I was like a horse running straight ahead, or like a painter painting his pictures . . . to tell you the truth, even now—when I have a wife and two children—they're by themselves and I'm by myself, even though I love them very much . . . because for me my life is in the army, and I'm already working on what I'll do after the army . . . that's how I am, like they say . . . a lone wolf . . . not part of the flock . . . even though I also studied in the university, and I also know how to get along with people—but not being together . . . like they say, I'm on my own . . ." (family 105).

"If you're asking about my adolescence, then I think I had three stops: the first stop was at an agricultural school at the age of 14. Though I arrived there with my mother, I had decided that I wanted to leave home and be independent. There were lots of children in our house and there was little space and less income; I already told you about what happened at home and also at school. My mother left and they put me in a room with three other children. I remember that it was sad the first night. I was alone and wanted to cry. I thought about maybe changing my mind, because they said it was possible to pull out until Sukkot. I didn't sleep all night, but not because I didn't know what to do; I already knew then that you have to fight so that you can have a little space. I told myself not to give up and to be strong. Then they would say: 'Stubborn like a Moroccan,' and later they said: 'like a Casablancan.' What can I tell you, our counselor would say: 'I'm going to make human beings of you . . .,'' but I'm telling you that I made myself into a human being. I learned to take blows . . . real blows, and blows to my feelings; but to accept what you have coming or even if you don't have it coming . . . You ask if my parents influenced me? What did they have to do with me! I didn't think much then about . . . no, I thought about Mom—how hard she works, like an ox, and carries everybody and everything on her shoulders . . . I won't forget that about her . . . she also came to visit me, and would bring all kinds of dishes and cookies that I shared with the guys in the room . . . she was special . . . but like a mother and not someone who built me . . . The second stop was the army; I went to the Golani Brigade where they worked our butts off and squeezed us dry, but they made us strong. I was made a sergeant and was already running others around, not just them running me around . . . The third stop was when we left the army. No, actually that's not right, I was already thinking in the army what I wanted to do to be a man and also to help my mother out with my brothers who were younger than me. I found this Moroccan like me in the army, and we went together to work in construction. We found a small contractor, this Pole who builds a house and then takes a break until the lot he purchased is desirable, and then he builds again. An old man, he doesn't want much anymore. I was both mechanic and driver, and also did all sorts of things, until I learned from him . . . I decided after quite a few years that I already knew how to work alone, and then when he took a break I went to look for work doing repairs—that's how I came to be a renovation contractor . . . I didn't tell you that I rented an apartment not far from my mother together with my friend from the army. At first my friend and I would eat with her in the evening and give her money. And I also gave her a key, so that my brothers could do homework in a room of my apartment . . . as long as they didn't bring other children there . . . This ended later because we moved from Jaffa to Ra'anana, and then to Lod and again to Bat Yam where I had already bought an apartment . . .'' (family 85).

The incidence of this separation pattern is higher than expected in the material revealed by the study, particularly in the parents' accounts of their own adolescence. It appears that they are articulating the special situation of Jews and Israelis growing up during that era who are now parents of adolescents. This category includes about 15% of the men and only a few women at this point in the study.

Conflicts emerging out of personality and expectation differences pattern

This category includes adolescents whose basic personality characteristics were very different from those of their parents and who did not respond to parental flexibility or attempts to compromise. The adolescent's unwillingness to accommodate led to recurring conflicts and to becoming psychologically or even physically remote. This simultaneously brought about a relatively fast separation including various emotional and behavioral expressions, as the following five excerpts describe.

"My father and I are very different in all sorts of things, and each time we end up in a confrontation. You were asking about examples, I'll tell you: He is a died-in-the-wool, old-time Mapai [labor-socialist political party] supporter while I live in today's world . . . even when we read the same newspaper, or see the same movie, he sees white and I see black" (family 111).

"My mother is stubborn and I'm stubborn . . . It isn't important what we are doing together, so others will say that we are alike, but I have decided that we have different taste, and I have a different orientation in life . . . it was good for her to have a husband that she turned into a dish rag, and that drove me crazy . . . I know now, at the age of 16, that I will look for a husband who will be strong like me and good like me, who will know how to get along with me, or he won't be . . ." (family 139).

"Each time my mother and father quarreled, which happened lots of times, I found myself forced to take his side or her side . . . I learned quickly—what I want to be, and what I don't want to be . . . I knew that I didn't want to be like her, but I also don't want a husband like him . . . and I'm constantly racking my brains about how I want to be and what sort of husband I want, how I will act, and all sorts of other things I told you when we spoke about my dream when you asked me . . ." (family 131).

"I'm telling you that I do love my mother and father, each one differently, despite what they did to me . . . and what I've learned from them is not to make myself a family like this one. They're simply not compatible together, like I'm not compatible with them—it just doesn't hold together . . ." (family 142).

"My father is so difficult that it's impossible to get along with him. I learned to run away from him . . . when he comes from work, I have my homework, or Scouts activity . . . I figured out how not to clash with him . . . I can't wait to start my army service in order to be far from home. After the army I won't have to be at home—I'll go to study in Jerusalem . . . so things will be good for them . . . I told you my sister is not like that . . . she gets along with my father. But that's because she is so sweet and I'm sour or like a prickly pear . . ." (family 6).

This group contains more boys than girls, who, in turn, report clashing with their fathers. Girls seem to clash with one parent, either the mother or father. About 10% of the cases in the study seem to belong to this category.

Immediate or gradual severance pattern

This category includes cases in which an ideological, psychological or physical separation occurs between the adolescent and one or both of his parents.

Among those who are currently parents of adolescence, there is a prominent subgroup who separated from their parents and left home as the result of a onetime rebellion or an evolving conflict growing out of an ideological stance such as anti-religiousness, Zionism, pioneering, going to a kibbutz, etc. Sometimes this conflict was an expression of intergenerational rebellion, and sometimes it was simply the next step within the ideational context of the parents' beliefs. Either way, the conditions of severance led to fast, clear separation and individuation.

There is, in Israeli society, considerable testimony of young people who have turned their backs on their parents' life-style and have chosen a new path, either with parental consent or despite their active or passive opposition. Such accounts appear in the annals of each wave of immigration, in the collective history of political (youth) movements and in their founding members' personal biographies. Although this phenomenon is less common for the parents of today's adolescents, we still found representatives of nearly every political-ideological pattern typical of Jewish/Zionist life in the late 19th and early 20th centuries.

One pattern was the family was religiously Orthodox, from Poland or Hungary, and the son or daughter joined a world-order revising (revolutionary) political youth movement: Communist or Socialist or Revisionist or Liberal Zionist. They went to training camps or traveled with a group to Israel, either to a work camp or to a kibbutz. Some told of total severance from their family after the trip and others maintained contact through correspondence with one of the parents. The parents in some families were exterminated in the war, while in other families the parents came to Israel later on and the family was reunited in Israel. Physical severance brought about the psychological separation of adolescence for all these individuals.

Another pattern is that of prominent conservative, bourgeois or liberal families. Most of these children effected their separation through emigration to Israel and came from Germany and Austria, Iraq and Egypt.

The third pattern is that of native-born Israelis from various backgrounds who joined pioneering youth movements, with or without parental support or even despite their opposition, and went to a kibbutz while adolescents. In many cases physical contact was maintained, but life in a different social system created a psychological separation at the point when their identity was being shaped. The identity of these adolescents was shaped initially through the youth movement, then in the settlement group and finally on the kibbutz.

Even if there was little or no ideological gap between this second generation and their parents and they evinced no complaints against their parents, their maturation process did not develop subject to parental influence, but rather through the values and activity patterns of the peer group. This factor does not negate the effect of parental influence in various personal areas discussed in other contexts.

Such a category accounts for about 10% of our cases.

To summarize, it is important to add that the categorization structure we have implemented is quite crude. Often the nature of the data makes it difficult to ascertain affiliation with a particular pattern and certain instances may fit more than one pattern. Our forthcoming book, *Three Generations of Israeli Families* will enter into additional, more complete analyses.

Chapter Three

Conflicts and Areas of Struggle in Adolescent-Parent Relations

Potential causes of conflict

CONFLICTS IN INTERPERSONAL RELATIONS ARE UNAVOIDABLE, NATURAL, and a primarily structural phenomenon. This no less true in parent-adolescent relations than it is in more general relationships. These conflicts originate from both conscious and unconscious factors: differences in basic personality characteristics; variation in the socialization processes experienced by the parents; unresolved feelings internalized in childhood, unknown to the child or parent; variance in individual needs according to the person's sex and age; difference in social roles, social status and power. Moreover, certain conflicts aroused are typical of a specific developmental period in the lives of all involved in family transactions.

Beyond the "natural" structural factors, there are factors unique to specific periods in which, for example, social change occurs quickly, to conditions in a particular society, or to a defined social ecological constellation.

It is important that group leaders, adolescents and parents be aware of the existence of factors that are either universal or unique to a society and/or a specific group. Thus they can appreciate that the conflict generating factors are not necessarily a function of negative traits of the young person or his parent(s). By understanding the causes of conflict, it is possible to cope better with its overall significance and search more usefully for appropriate ways of communication. Such communicative interchange enables conducting positive negotiations, the purpose of which is to arrive at possible alternative solutions. In order to design effective support for adolescents participating in peer groups, areas and topics of structural conflict unique to the present era were selected. The assumption in each of these areas is that it is possible to identify and then define potential foci of significant conflict for discussion in peer groups. The order in which these areas are presented does not attest to their importance, since a phenomenon which may be central to one particular family or person, may very well have marginal importance for others.

Biological change in adolescence

From the beginning of the century (Hall, 1905; Freud, 1905) until the 1960's the conception that adolescence is a universal period of "storm and stress," expressed through negative feelings toward parents, almost daily mood swings, developmental regression, etc. was accepted by almost all theoreticians. We now know that this generalization describes the experience of a minority and that it should not be considered characteristic of most adolescent development.

However, most investigators agree that the pace (slower or faster than everyone else) of biological changes can arouse anxieties, doubts about sexual identity and basic problems in self-image. As a consequence of these reactions, there are concomitant changes in family relationships. Some of these and other resulting difficulties have been dealt with in earlier chapters. The deep emotional interdependency of adolescents and their parents is as much a factor as problems arising from the transition from childhood to adulthood. The previous chapter pointed out that adolescents expect understanding and support from their parents, both because they have internalized the parents' images since childhood and are immersed in an internal struggle with them, and also because they lack confidence about everything connected with their own image, identity, way of life and future.

Changes in family equilibrium

Changes occur in family equilibrium as a result of changes the adolescents are undergoing in contrast to the aging, either actual or psychological, of parents.

Transition from equilibrium to disequilibrium is universal; however, it is even more significant in a fast-changing society and, particularly in cases of immigrant transition from traditional to modern society. Extreme changes in conceptions of appropriate sex-roles, swings in economic patterns and conditions of employment and pressure of mass media-induced expectations contribute to adolescents' feeling (often echoed by their parents as well) that "parents can't understand," and therefore cannot fulfil the traditional role of socializing their children. And in fact, in certain cases, parents look to evade their responsibility.

Psychologists add further that adolescent sexual development, which often occurs concomitantly with the parents' biological aging process, arouses conscious or subconscious feelings of envy and, in some cases, even provokes competitiveness from a defensive parent toward his son or daughter. The mass media emphasis on the appearance of a young body build and on external beauty and sexuality strengthens such a potential reaction, especially but not exclusively for women.

The influence of an adolescent's prolonged economic and legal dependence on their parents

The fact that until age 18 youth are legally considered minors and need their parents' consent in order to participate within the social system creates a feeling of dependency. Prolonging their period of studies reinforces this dependence on their parents. In the more affluent segments of the population economic dependence often continues through the period of post-secondary and higher education at least for some of the families. There may be expectations that parents will continue to support their children financially even after they have gotten married "to help them get on their feet."

Although a young person may say to himself and others that he wants to shape his own way of life and establish himself as he wishes, both he and his parents are aware that continued parental assistance can assure him of a higher standard of living.

The universal phenomenon of unequal power and authority

During adolescence parents are in charge of the property: the house, the car, the money. As a result of such control and the acceptance of social responsibility for their children's development many parents feel they have the right, within certain limits, to determine norms about inviting people to the house, determining standards of conduct and exercising power toward their children. Patterns of utilizing the privileges of power and authority differ among various ethnic groups and social classes and even among families within the same social group. Certain phenomena recur in families from very different backgrounds and they may therefore be defined as universal. An example of such universal usage of power is a mother who proclaims to her adolescent child: "in my house you will do what I say!" either in the wake of a conflict arising from irregular behavior at school or in response to an impertinent response.

The different stages of parents and children each struggling with self-actualization in a complex, unstable society

Parents and adolescents are at different stages of shaping their life patterns, but each of them is struggling with problems of self actualization in a society which is complex and changing in terms of opportunities and expectations. In the past in a traditional society it was customary to assume that chronologically mature people, who had become parents, had already formed their personal identity and were prepared to fulfil the same, defined social-sexual roles throughout their life-span. It was assumed that adolescents would struggle to find their way in terms of adjusting to their parents' and the community's expectations.

Accelerated social changes as a result of the modernization process have spawned new phenomena. The most prominent of these, particularly since the early 1970's, is the legitimation of searching for and experimenting in identity and self-actualization throughout various periods of a mature individual's life. Thus an adolescent girl may be struggling with forming her personal identity and developing her coping ability within the context of an abundance of alternative possibilities for self-fulfillment at the very time her father and mother are also immersed in struggling with their present identity and may even be engaged in attempts to change their future life pattern. Parents of adolescents, then, having new legitimation to explore alternative possibilities for self-actualization in their forties and fifties, may also be in a transitional period, commonly referred to as the "mid-life crisis" (Levinson, 1978; Gould, 1978).

Parents and adolescents were shaped in different historical eras

Parents and adolescents have been influenced in differing ecological formations or what sociologists and psychologists refer to as the "age cohort effect" (Elder, 1974). The fund of value norms and personal experiences significant for human and social development during the historical period of the parents' generation is the source influences of which they may even be unaware. The Depression of the 1930's, the Vietnam War crisis and the youth rebellion during the 1960's, etc. were watersheds in the United States; in Europe the economic crisis in the 1920's, the rise of Hitlerism in the 1930's and the Nazi conquest of the 1940's, postwar liberation, rehabilitation and economic expansion in the 1950's, the student rebellion in the 1960's, etc. In Israel there were many influences including the waves of immigration and pioneering settlement in the 1920's; the rise of Nazism resulting in emigration from Germany and Austria, the political awakening of the pre-state settlement in favor of immigration, the riots of 1936 and service in the Haganah, the underground or civil guard duty in the 1930's; World War II with conscription into the British Army or the Palmach, influences of the Holocaust and the beginnings of the struggle for independence in the 1940's; the War of Independence, mass immigration from Middle Eastern and North African countries and from the refugee camps in Europe and the economic crisis in the 1950's; rapid industrialization and the Six Day War in the 1960's; the Yom Kippur War and the ascendance of the opposition party, peace with Egypt, establishment of West Bank settlements in the 1970's; the Lebanon War, the national "unity" coalition government and events in the occupied territories in the 1980's.

Today's adolescents have opportunities available as well as experience pressures which their parents' generation did not know. The effects of mass media (radio, tape cassettes, television, video, comic books), the potential of being able to tour throughout the world, sexual permissiveness, the decrease in family stability, new developments in science and technology, politic changes, etc. all influence the way people live, creating expectations, problems and demands which pose a challenge to the values and behavior patterns of the adult generation in general and especially to parents of adolescents.

Parents of adolescents frequently occupy the center link of three generations

Parents have obligations toward their own aging parents, in addition to their responsibility to their children. Meeting these obligations often involves spending the parent's precious free time, financial and/or emotional resources. This frequently clashes with meeting his own personal needs, influenced both by the demands of an achievement-oriented, competitive society and by the new expectations of middle-age self-actualization. In many instances adolescents see their parents as indifferent or insensitive toward their own aging parents. In such a case parental behavior serves as a negative model and an example of hypocrisy for adolescents. Parents demand understanding and empathy from their children for themselves while they themselves demonstrate the very behavior they preach against when relating to their own parents.

Ambivalence toward the change in situation and roles of parents and adolescents

When the children were small, the parents were big, strong and wise. The parents knew the cultural heritage and saw themselves responsible for shaping their children and transmitting values and behavior defined as "good" and "correct." In most cases they themselves, their children and the demands of developing situations responded to their control, according to expectations. But now with their children's entry into adolescence, it is clear that their offspring have grown up and the system of expectations has changed. They are aware that in theory they ought to allow the adolescent autonomy and to transfer certain areas of responsibility to him. However, often parents do not know how to pass on responsibility. They may fear what new things mean, shying away from the effects giving autonomy may have on their children. One minute they declare: "You're not a child, take responsibility for your actions!" and another minute they assert: "You still don't understand; that's not how to behave!" as though he were still a child.

The adolescent is also in an ambivalent situation: one minute he wants autonomy and responsibility and the next he wants his parents to worry about and take care of him as they did in the past. Furthermore, Halpern describes (1977) how parents and children hold onto expectations and communication patterns formed in childhood: the "music and dance numbers" composed in previous developmental stages persist in emotional terms, and often also in behavioral terms, into later stages despite the changes in status all those involved in family transactions have undergone.

Exhibition of undesired traits, both of parents and adolescents

In modern, secular society it is possible to choose one's friends, to live with a member of the opposite sex or to marry them, and to separate either informally or legally when things don't go well for them together. However, the same is not true for the tie between children and parents. They are bound to each other, legally, economically, socially and emotionally, from childhood throughout their lives. Therefore, all family members are in a constant state of trying to cope with the lack of congruency between traits and needs.

In certain families such incompatibility exists from birth. The mother or father expected a girl and got a boy or vice versa. Another familiar example is that of the vigilant mother prepared to turn the world upside down, who claims that she "found" a child with a slow temperament, "passive" according to her, who often reflects the intolerable character trait of her husband, father, or mother. During adolescence such a problematic reality is reaffirmed or rediscovered with an additional aggravating factor: the very development from childhood to adulthood has deepened differentiation of basic character traits, evoking feelings of the past and the need to accept what appears to be an accomplished fact.

Rapid sociocultural change creates intergenerational gaps

In a certain sense the gaps between generations are similar to gaps between people who grew up in different cultures and societies. Thus in Israel, for example, there are great gaps between those parents who came from traditional, religious, patriarchal and agrarian cultures and adolescents in a modern, secular, urban, industrial, democratic and permissive society. It is important to note at this juncture that frequently the parents' generation adjusts to the new environment quickly despite the huge gap in cultural patterns. As a result, even though these parents are unable or unwilling to change their behavior and values, they are prepared to understand their children's behavior and to adjust their expectations and decisions.

Another phenomenon should be discussed: the rapid changes in technology, society and the educational system have made many parents unable to understand their adolescent children. In a traditional and relatively stable society age signified proprietorship of a rich accumulation of cultural contributions and personal experiences: "I've seen more, learned more, and therefore I, the parent, know more and understand more than you, the teenager." However a society characterized by an accelerated process of change and modernization challenges the significance and advantage of parents' past experience, insofar as judging the present and future are concerned. Adolescents and young people may feel they know more and are smarter than their parents, and thus are unprepared to accept their judgment, denying their right to guide them. There are also parents, feeling unable to cope with the changes, who have waived the responsibility of educating their children.

Although this phenomenon has special significance for parents from "culturally deprived" economic strata, whose confidence has been greatly shaken and who are unprepared to struggle over their status, it must be noted, nevertheless, that certain forms of evasion of responsibility are part of a universal phenomenon to be discussed further below.

Both parents and adolescents socialized in an historical period termed the "Century of the Child"

Today we cultivate basic assumptions about the importance of the early years in human development and about parental responsibility to assure the optimal development of each child. Since the 1970's, influenced by factors described in the chapter on the challenge of modernization, the premise of "it's coming to me" has emerged among many adults as well. Adults feel that they are entitled to

self-actualization, to act according to their needs and emotions and to enjoy the present. This feeling is supported and confirmed in the mass media and by mental health experts. If confrontation between assumptions of a patriarchal, traditional society cultivating the privileges of the side of power and authority as opposed to the weak, characterized the past, conflicts have appeared in the present which seem to originate in the tension between demands of adolescents' egocentrism and demands of a similar phenomenon on the part of one or both parents. In such a situation questions of priorities arise, requiring mutually considerate communication, recognizing that both parties feel "it's coming to me . . . right now."

Internal and interpersonal conflicts arising from the increase in parental roles and heightened expectations of everyone in the nuclear family

There are so many society-imposed roles and often dissonant demands and expectations devolving on the nuclear family that it would be hard for conflicts and feelings of frustration not to arise. Division of roles and norms in the community as well as in the extended and nuclear family was clearly defined in traditional society. Such a clear division extended into the family system itself.

Today the nuclear family unit is the major unit to be dealt with; this unit consists of parents and children who have extremely high expectations of understanding, emotional involvement, care and responsibility. This means that, within this small, half-closed entity, we expect the father and mother, who in most instances work long hours outside the home earning a living, working in community roles, and, in addition, often also supporting their own parents, to meet all their children's expectations. In the often not so distant past considerable portion of these expectations were met by the extended family and the community. Furthermore, with expanding knowledge of general and particular psychological theories parents expect themselves to be able to fill the role of first-rate psychologists and educators for their children. Inability to fulfill these high expectations quickly disabuses adolescents of the belief that their parents are omnipotent. Although this is desirable in terms of the adolescent's individuation, it also arouses the parents' feelings of disappointment (because of unmet expectations) together with frustration and anger. Comparing the parents' descriptions of their adolescence and adolescents' descriptions of their current feelings toward their parents in the interviews, it is amazing how the vast majority of adolescents view their family as a very meaningful, primarily positive system; negative descriptions occur in only a small percentage of cases. Similar findings, showing a positive perception of the family by adolescents, have been obtained from other studies based on interviews with adolescents (Offer, 1969; Lasch, 1977; Youniss & Smaller, 1985).

The effect of entry into "middle age" on adolescent-parent relations

A considerable or possibly even decisive portion of parents of adolescents have reached the developmental stage termed "middle age" (Levinson, 1978; Gould, 1978; Vaillant, 1977). The marked interaction between the parents' developmental stage with that of their children is quite significant in the interviews with family members in the present study. Therefore, it is appropriate to note the issues among the theories and concepts associated with this stage of parental development which have meaning for our discussion. Most parents have reached the peak of their development and some of them are standing at a crossroads in their development and social mobility. For many these achievements have been the result of a supreme effort, both in terms of how they feel and also according to objective criteria. Thus, they have invested themselves deeply in the tasks of acquiring a profession and developing a career, building a family, filling the roles of parenthood and seeking community status as part of shaping their identity and life style. They have learned to cope and feel that they know and are capable.

However, many reach this stage only to find themselves at a crossroads, often referred to as "the mid-life crisis." Some middle aged parents feel they are facing a crisis regarding their status and their future. For a minority this crisis can mean the actual destruction of the family structure, the changing of a profession and/or place of employment, a change in life style, etc. (described by Vaillant, 1977; Rubin, 1976; Levinson, 1978; Sheehey, 1979).

Most of the parents interviewed claimed they felt self-confident and had faith in their ability to control the realizing of their present and future expectations. However, when facing their adolescent child, who is himself at a crucial point in his transition from childhood to maturity, when his need to be differentiated from his parents and to shape his identity and life style is the sharpest, these parents admit that they no longer feel confident. As in interviews from other studies, there are conspicuous expressions of a feeling of lack of confidence and even helplessness toward the adolescent, such as in this example: "Where I was concerned, I knew that if I would make the effort and be willing to pay the price, I would overcome and succeed . . . but where my child is concerned, I don't know how to help him, or how to relate to him, as he is so different from what he used to be."

Men's vs. women's problems

A discussion of the psychological differences between the sexes, in a separate volume, deals extensively with the variation between women's and men's problems. For example, one subject which arises in different ways with the men and women interviewed is the discussion of the difficulties unique to the father's role and to the mother's role. In his adolescence today's father had undergone the same phenomena characteristic of his child's adolescent years. He worked to separate from his parents, particularly from his father, and progressed toward fashioning a personal identity and a personal and family life style. He acquired power and authority through his economic and social activities. When faced with his adolescent child's expectations and demands for autonomy, power and authority, he finds himself confronted with areas in which he may commit mistakes of judgment, he may show weakness in terms of intervention, he may be faced with having to support his wife against his adolescent children or to support them against her.

To this kind of problem-pattern is added the issue of women's status. For the purposes of this discussion, we will use the classification by Stewart (1977), O'Connel (1976) and others; they identified two main groups of women: those who married and bore children in their early twenties, their sexual identity and life style having focused ever since on building the family and being a mother; and those others who deferred motherhood by about ten years, focusing on this task in their thirties. The respondents in our study include mainly mothers from the first group. These women expected that when their children reached adolescence they would reach partial emancipation from household burdens and be able to seek opportunities to expand their career or social activities. Thus, their children's adolescent problems appear to many of them as renewed, unexpected pressure. As one of the respondents articulated: "When they were small, they had first priority. I gave them everything and couldn't expect them to understand that I have needs, too, since I am also a human being. Now that they have matured, I anticipated a new stage in which I could allow myself things that I hadn't allowed previously, especially when our economic situation had become more established. But that's not how things were. Once again, their needs and concerns deprive me of the enjoyment and development I had expected . . ."

Particularly poignant is the complaint of women who put off a professional career in order to bear several children in their early twenties and who anticipated "emancipation" and self-actualization at this stage of their development. Many of them describe themselves as "dried up" or even psychologically "shrunken," because they had lived with and for children for such a long period of their lives. At this point, many of them express a lack of adequate social legitimation in their expectation of changing their lives. This is echoed by husbands saying in the interviews: "I agree that she should get out, that she should study or work as she wishes, provided that she doesn't hurt the children."

Although the above list of 14 causes for potential conflict between adolescents and parents is only sketched in briefly, it is sufficient to grasp the dimensions and complexity of the problem. Therefore, it is particularly important to recognize that parents and adolescents must learn to have meaningful communication so that each will understand the other's needs and expectations and will be able to relate to them even if unable to fully respond to what is expected.

We have selected 27 patterns of conflict from the hundreds of conflicts mentioned by adolescents and parents in the interviews and in the peer group discussions.[1] These findings seem to represent different areas and patterns of conflict, some which are dominant in early adolescence, and others in the ensuing developmental process. Some of them have already been integrated into the exercises proposed for Part II of this volume, and others may be added and developed.

---

[1] From interviews of students in US Department of Labor Job Corps Centers and from peer group discussion in the U.S. and Israel's secondary education system.

Although the curriculum is structured, it should be remembered that it is essentially experiential and therefore open-ended. Counselors and other group leaders should add exercises originating from things that they and the adolescents view as unique and meaningful and as stemming from the needs of that particular peer group.

The random order of presentation is intentional, to stress the fact that there is no objective criterion for the conflict's severity. The factor precipitating conflict may be marginal or meaningless to one person, yet arouse and agitate another violently. What is perceived by one adolescent or parent as impinging on his set of values, rights, needs or feelings may be incomprehensible or even meaningless to someone else. Moreover, there are clashes which begin in a particular situation, termed a "given ecological context," but which also serves as the basis for developing into a conflict about the right to autonomy and individuation. Therefore, although the examples are cited randomly, they will be classified according to certain criteria into components and indices of basic needs at the end of the chapter.

If a mother or a father is selected for illustration, it indicates, according to the evidence available, that this behavior is more characteristic of either the mother or the father, but may also appear in the other.

The Focus of Conflict

Conflict No. 1: Struggle over territory and territorial autonomy

Parents are responsible for their home and socialization of their children, at least until their majority. They want the adolescent to straighten his room within the bounds of agreed norms, and to meet certain behavioral expectations in the family home. The problem begins when parents, primarily mothers, struggle with the adolescent over the image of the room defined as the young person's room. This focus of conflict is typical of early adolescence, when the adolescent feels and argues that this is "his room"—an autonomous territory into which the parent may not impose his norms. The mother, however, views the room as part of the more general territory of the home and thereby within her jurisdiction. Also, she is not prepared to accept the adolescent's assumption of territorial autonomy, since she feels responsible for her children's socialization.

Patterns of this same struggle showed up in various interviews. The depth of feeling, sharpness of reactions, and the similarity of events occurring in families that were otherwise very different came as a surprise. Four girls and their mothers, who were prepared to reveal themselves in front of the video camera, participated in a matching exercise. All the participants were surprised to find out how similar their communication patterns were. The following case illustrates conflict and the reaction: "The mess in my room makes my mother angry. She is afraid that my husband will run away from me shortly after the wedding because of my disorderliness. . . . We used to quarrel, but now I don't say anything, because I know I won't be able to convince her when she thinks she's right. Also, she always succeeds in making me feel guilty when we fight" (family 34).

Conflict No. 2: Treating the adolescent like a child

Parents are ambivalent about the adolescent's move from childhood into adulthood and it is particularly difficult for them to alter their treatment of him during this transition period. Many parents, mothers in particular, continue to relive the initial childhood period, characterized by its symbiotic, emotional state and associated idealization, when they molded each step of their child's development. The mother repeats with great pleasure, dozens of times, either consciously or unconsciously, stories of how the child was little, how cute he was, how he wet his pants. She even does this when guests are present. Many adolescents describe their reaction as feeling that parents are trying to remind them of their littleness and that the parents are big, and they feel that parents ignore the fact of their real growth by making them become children again.

Various mothers were asked for their reaction to these complaints. We discovered that many mothers are unaware of the fact they hurt the adolescent's feelings when discussing him in potentially embarrassing or uncomfortable situations. However, some of the mothers confirmed the more serious complaint that that they do indeed express, albeit unconsciously, the need to remind the adolescent of the family hierarchy and historical symbiosis.

"When my mother keeps the shoes I wore when I was a baby and my hair from that same period, I like it, because it expresses her feelings toward me in the past. However, when guests come and she begins to relate how I used to wet my pants . . . that I didn't want to eat, and how they didn't sleep at night because of me, she is applying emotional blackmail. Sometimes I am not sure if these are just stories or if this is a score presented for settlement in the present" (17 year old girl, adolescent 301).

Conflict No. 3: Continual correction of behavior

A clear majority of adolescents accept parental authority in principle and even expect parental intervention and support in various areas. However, a considerable portion of adolescents claims that their mother or father "get on their nerves" by their systematic attempt to correct the adolescent's behavior; their actions seem to aim at proving their own omniscience and perfection as opposed to the adolescent's lack of proper perception, knowledge or social skill.

There are different patterns of this parental behavior. For example: "My mother knew exactly what I need to be and she feels that her role is to train me—what to wear, how to sit, and what to say to the teacher. However, what makes me even madder is that she also expected me to report to her what has happened, as if she were the driver and I were only an instrument or means" (student 202).

"My father is always correcting my style . . . at first I would get mad and tell him to stop, but later on I decided that I would simply ignore him. I told him—that's how I think, this comes from my heart and this is my mouth speaking . . . I don't correct things that you say, and I'm not a child who needs to be corrected . . ." (adolescent 389).

"What I or my sister say, my father corrects. If I say that it happened this way, my father will immediately say that it was a bit different. Apparently, it's important for him to be right or at least the one who knows more than I do . . ." (adolescent 305).

"I know that however I do it, my mother will prove to me that she knew it had to be otherwise, 'I told you it shouldn't be done that way'—that's her fixed recording. She simply tries to control me by repeating that she knows better than I do what one needs to do" (adolescent 335).

"My father and my mother acted like an army master sergeant: 'Yitzhak, you didn't wash up this morning, you can see it . . .' 'Look how you're sitting . . .' 'use your napkin . . .'; 'how slouched you're standing'; 'behave like you ought to . . .' Those are just examples that I remember from the time we moved to the city and I began junior high school. They really crowded my life . . . I didn't want to eat with them although I always loved them. They simply irritated me, and when I would answer back they would get offended: 'You know I am only saying it for your own good . . . what will others say when you're together with them socially, when I won't be with you . . .'" (student 201).

The focus of this conflict has been introduced in exercises with parent groups of varying ethnic and educational background. The feeling was shared by many parents that adolescents were like children, that they needed to be trained and taught, otherwise they would not end up as desired. It would seem that many parents are sure that they are the ones who know how one should behave and that they are responsible for their children's behavior. Therefore, they feel the need to be on guard and active all the time; they must not delay, must correct every error and shortcoming. It seemed that they were not particularly aware that they were using constant behavior correction in order to maintain power and authority and not only out of a need to modify their children's behavior. A considerable portion of the parents were unaware that they were themselves continuing their own parents' behavior towards them, even though it was clear to them that today's world differs from the one in which their grandfather or grandmother were active.

It is important for parents to realize and remember that the central task of adolescence is taking responsibility for shaping his identity and developing his own methods of coping. He needs to learn to give autonomy and he must receive autonomy in order to progress in the individuation process. The parents' task is to prove to the adolescent that he is capable and to support him in developing his sense of capability, not to repeatedly point out his shortcomings or to prove that the father or mother are the truly capable ones while he never seems to live up to their expectations.

Conflict No. 4: Mothers who try to be friends

Although many mothers succeed in creating a relationship of openness and mutual understanding with their daughters during adolescence, for many others a situation develops which contains the seeds of conflict. Some mothers exceed the bounds of their role in an attempt to force their daughters to view them as friends. One adolescent girl said it all:

"I don't need another friend, I need a mother." She relates how "my mother wants to hear intimate details of what happened between me and a boyfriend when I return from a movie"; or, "she expects me to consult with her about things that I want to think about and do alone."

Other girls echoed similar plaints: "Sometimes I feel that my mother is competing with me, or competing with my girlfriends, to be a friend: she wants to know what happens among the girls, she tells Deborah, my closest friend, things that she suddenly felt Deborah needs to know . . . She simply cooks things up like the girls do . . . this makes me mad . . . Yes, I told her, but it doesn't help, because she is immediately insulted: What, aren't I your mother, don't I love you? Sure she's my mother, but she isn't my friend . . ."

Another girl presented the same problem in a different form: "I know that my mother really cares about me, but I can't have her entering into my social life. I want to hear things about her when she wants to tell me, and I want to tell her when I feel something is important for me to tell . . . even good friends learn that it's not good to intrude into someone else's private thoughts when they don't wish it . . . but a mother is not a friend! A mother is something else . . ." (adolescent 330).

Mothers must be able to create a distance from their daughters and allow them to maintain it. That is the initial significance of separation in the individuation process. It is important for daughters to know that when they wish to disclose themselves, to consult or to gain support, their mothers are available to them. However, they have a right to maintain their privacy in different areas of their emotional and social lives, as long as it does not impinge on their safety or health or that of their parents. Even then, parental intervention should take the form of communication and negotiation.

It is difficult to determine the extent of possible or desirable disclosure between mothers and daughters or sons during adolescence, both because of great adolescent sensitivity to infringement on their autonomy and because mothers and fathers have their own needs to be involved and autonomous. Therefore, the degree and areas of disclosure in parent-child relations ought to be determined by personal insight as well as by mutual sensitivity and empathy. The basic assumption is that the parents' role is different from that of friends. When parents are isolated, they deserve their adolescent's empathy and support and they may need professional help as well which, among other things, can help them to remain their child's parents rather than attempt to become a substitute girlfriend or boyfriend.

Conflict No. 5: Mothers and fathers who preach

Adolescents expect parents to acknowledge them as partners in a dialogue which is as open and relaxed as possible, in which each may express himself freely and get feedback from the other. Many democratic families achieve this, primarily in mother-daughter relations and to some extent with sons, too. However, many conflicts seem to originate in the tendency of fathers, and sometimes mothers, to lecture instead of discussing and to preach instead of explaining.

Adolescents present this as follows: "My father begins: 'When I was your age I already knew how to work. I knew that my mother was a human being and that I had to help her . . .' He continues, and my ears are already blocked up . . . Instead of asking: 'What happened between you and your mother? . . . Why did you quarrel? . . . How did she offend you and how did you offend her . . .' Instead of wanting to listen, instead of talking with me, he closes up my heart so that I can't open up to him in a situation like this" (adolescent 331).

"My father doesn't know how to talk, he only lectures. I say one sentence and he immediately lectures. He has answers for everything. I just wait for him to stop or make a mistake, so that I will feel that he is a human being and not a computer." (family 9).

"When my father begins to talk and explain, he isn't aware of anything, even when we are no longer listening. He is our history teacher, who speaks like someone reading aloud from a book, and has no audience . . . I don't know how to stop him without offending him . . . since I love him, and afterwards I feel bad that I didn't want to listen to him" (adolescent 309).

Adolescents are especially sensitive to lectures and preaching, since they are exposed to it several hours a day in the school environment and also because they understand it as the father invoking hierarchical authority.

Many adolescents relate that the nicest days they remember in the family were days of shared activities with the father: on an excursion, in a shared project of home renovations, etc. Yet, many fathers unconsciously use the lecture style in order to maintain distance and to defend themselves against such involvement and exposure. Some fathers speak judgmentally and make generalizations, thus preventing themselves and the adolescent from discussing and clarifying feelings and opinions related to the specific instance. Other fathers use sarcasm or cynicism, hurting the adolescent's feelings and not effectively preventing him from tolerating proper criticism and perhaps even rendering him deaf to approval.

Conflict No. 6: Manipulation and emotional blackmail

Adolescents admire sincerity and reliability very much, asking for these traits both verbally and through emotional expression. However, many parents are used to assuming that their child is too young to understand, too sensitive to withstand hurt and not open to direct communication. They ensure his acceptable behavior by manipulating facts, over-interpretation, playing with feelings, etc. Many adults act in this manner in their own environment, with other adults: couples acting out, one against the other, or colleagues dealing with each other or with officials in society. Employing such a behavior pattern with adolescents is both dangerous and problematic. Adolescents claim that they lose faith in the parent who acts this way. The following examples of adolescent reactions illustrate this point:

"My mother constantly declares that she lives only for me . . . I don't want to hear that. As a teacher, she quarrels with teachers and students at school, and that's not for my sake; and she argues with my father, not for me . . . then what's this story that she lives only for me. It's her right to do whatever she feels, but not to transfer it onto me" (adolescent 316).

"My mother isn't prepared to recognize that I'm a person with feelings, too. She begins to carry on with emotions and tears until she nearly faints. She makes me feel that either I surrender and do what she wants, or I'm killing her . . ." (adolescent 370).

"My father can talk and talk around about, and I sit and think— what number is he doing on me. I want him to talk with me like a person. I need to feel that I can talk with my father and not with a salesman who is going to prettify things for me, or turn them into something that you have to accept" (adolescent 336).

Conflict No. 7: "Talking from both sides of the mouth"

Adolescence is a transition period in which ambivalence appears in the behavior of both parents and adolescents. One of the results of such ambivalence is the simultaneous transmission of double messages by both parents and adolescent. These may have the effect of keeping the adolescent from knowing what to understand from what the parent has said; it may also become clear to him that he is being purposefully cornered so that he will accede to the parent's views or feelings.

"Mother says that I can go to the party, but at the same time also says to me that she won't sleep. And when I return, she says she didn't sleep and cried out of her great concern. And all sorts of things like these . . . I am certain that she doesn't rely on me to know how to behave, although I'm not a little girl . . . and I can't stand hearing that I'm killing her every time I go out with someone . . ." (adolescent 302).

"I don't know anything about my father. He doesn't tell about what happens with him at work. And when I read the newspaper or listen to the radio and hear about something bad happening to someone,

I'm worried about Dad. Once I tried to ask him, and he began to tell me meaningless things, until I decided that I wouldn't ask anymore. Why can't he say things to me simply and directly, like my friends and I talk, straight and to the point. I agree that it's possible not to tell me things. But I don't agree with people talking to me dishonestly" (adolescent 369).

"My mother simply talks from both sides of her mouth . . . she does not realize that she is saying yes and no at the same time. She wants to seem as though she is in favor and against as well . . . I'm not a fool. I try to understand, but I close up inside when she gets on my nerves that way, not being honest" (adolescent 350).

Conflict No 8: I hate it when they talk about me . . .

In their encounters with the nuclear and extended family, at work, in the army, among companions and with friends, adults converse and relate things about themselves and about significant others. Adolescents do this as well, but many adolescents indicate sensitivity to the fact that they become the topic of a parent's conversation with his friends, whether socially or as part of work, whether they are present or not, whether they learn about this by chance or are told.

The adolescent demands that his right to privacy be acknowledged and is unwilling for others to be entertained stories about "my child." The sensitivity displayed by adolescents during this period is explained as egocentrism. Adolescents feel as though they are the center of the world, that everyone is looking at them, talking about them and judging them. Complicating this feeling, a lack of normative confidence is also typical of this stage, stemming from the rapdidity of developmental change. This lack of self-confidence seems to cause adolescents to suspect that people are picking on them, looking for their faults and judging them.

"My mother can talk about me with the teacher as though I'm not there . . . as though I'm not a person who also has feelings" (from a peer group discussion).

"I suddenly heard from my friend Deborah that I was the topic of their conversation at home. She went into the kitchen and heard how my mother was telling all sorts of things that I don't want to say here . . . it was a good thing that Deborah told me, because I already made such a scene with my mother—with crying and yelling . . . both mine and hers—that I am embarrassed to tell you" (conversation with guidance counselor).

Conflict No. 9: Expressing a lack of faith in the adolescent's capacity for future responsibility

Many parents, filling their role of socializing their children, assume the appropriate way to stimulate motivation for change and achievement is to point out the adolescent's weaknesses and cite the connection between his lack of preparedness and/or capability and future behavioral tasks. Parents' declarations that if a child doesn't learn to behave properly, he will fail in his future life, are frequent. Adolescents may react to such parental pressures as did the adolescents quoted in the following examples:

"My father tries to knock it into my head that I won't amount to anything . . ."

"My mother yells that I won't ever learn . . ."

"Nothing drives me crazy more than my mother's declarations: You will never understand . . ."

"My father repeatedly declares that no workplace will ever employ anyone like me . . ."

"My mother constantly repeats that my husband will run away when he sees the mess that I make . . ."

Parents need to understand that comments like these anger the adolescent and make him unwilling to listen to any real advice or unable to cope with the significance of the message they wished to transmit. Phrasing their criticism in this way damages the adolescent's self-image by labeling him negatively and opens the way for behavior which becomes a self-fulfilling prophecy. Adolescent behavior and problems tend to focus on the present; therefore, there is generally no point in relating to the distant future.

Conflict No. 10: Negating the adolescent's views and feelings

Many parents do not distinguish between their perceptions and feelings about certain situations and the adolescent's personal view and autonomous feelings. One need not accept the opinion, approach or behavior of an adolescent, whether his judgment be objectively correct or not; however, as with any other autonomous human being, he is entitled to his view and his personal taste and is ultimately responsible for his choices. As such one may not negate an adolescent's views or feelings.

The many expressions of adolescents' feelings in this area recorded attest to its common occurrence and depth of feeling in reaction.

"My mother knows not only what I should eat or wear, but also how I ought to feel . . ."

"I tell my father I saw it, and he argues that I didn't see . . ."

"I tell my mother that I think it's pretty, and she says that can't be, as though my view and hers were the same thing . . ."

Adult guidance and influence may not be accomplished by direct confrontation including the denial of an adolescent's right or ability to judge for himself. Influence may be tendered only by means of discussion which includes the presentation of alternate possible views of the situation and clear delineation of the consequences of making certain decisions or engaging in specific behavior. It is important any adult judgment be rendered in terms of norms, values and feelings and that the adolescent's right to a view based on different values and feelings be recognized.

Conflict No. 11: Ideological-political conflict

We have noted previously that in most cases we did not find any noticeable gap between the political views of adolescents and parents in Israel, the United States or in other countries. Parents undoubtedly have the right to influence the political socialization of their children. This is also seems to be one of the areas in which most parents are successful to a great extent, especially fathers. However, in situations where a gap is evident between parents' attitudes and those of the adolescent and the conflict is acute, the parent's problem is primarily one of how to maintain mutual communication instead of blocking it by being hierarchically judgmental. The father and mother are responsible for developing an adult who has a socio-political perspective and for preventing the adolescent's negative emotional reaction as a result of their efforts to silence him or to deny his ability to understand, their evident unwillingness to listen to him or their preaching that their's is the only right way.

The following situations are illustrations of what could happen.

The role of the Soviet Union in the war in Afghanistan became the topic of discussion in an extended family gathering with friends. Uri began to express an opinion and his father interrupted with a correction: once, twice, three times. Uri was offended, stopped and left the room. The father continued to lecture in order to prove that he knew the facts better and understood the situation better.

The son in a family with very left-wing political views began to talk about the "nobility" and beauty of the lives of the poor as contrasted with the "crudity" and emptiness of the rich. His father, a scientist, corrected him and explained that the poor are not at all noble, that most are unfortunate and their lives are devoid of beauty, and also that many of them beat their wives, abuse their children, get drunk, etc. A discussion began in which most of the family took part. The son tried again to defend his idealistic thesis, and the father instructed him in socio-political realism.

The discussion in another family focused on the arms shipment to Iran. The entire family is extremely right-wing and nationalist and they usually agree with each other. The son began to expound about Iran's success in exploiting the issue of American hostages in Lebanon for the purpose of cancelling the arms embargo. The father interrupted and accompanied what he said with cynical remarks that he (the son) did not know the facts, that he was making unbased generalizations, that he did not understand the geopolitical needs of Israel, etc. The son tried to defend himself without success. He stopped and remained silent and the father continued to present the "true picture" according to his own view.

These three examples were from situations in which there were no basic political disagreements between father and son. In the first family, the son wanted to show off his political knowledge and the father countered, using his superior knowledge in order to prove his authority, until the son capitulated. In the second family the son expressed an idealistic stance characteristic of many adolescents flirting with "salon communism," and the father tried systematically to teach him realism. In the third family, the son presented his thesis confidently, but earned a cynical reaction by means of which the father preserved his power and authority. The son capitulated, but the father felt it necessary to continue proving his superiority.

In each example the adult must consider how to act so as to acknowledge the son's right to a personal opinion, to support his political development, to help him improve his critical thinking on a level appropriate to the complexity and intricacy of such problems, and, at the same time, to avoid creating conflicts over power and authority.

Conflict No. 12: Adolescent idealism and parental realism

Characteristic of many adolescents is their belief in change, their idealism in perceiving a situation, and their readiness to man ideological barricades in intellectual debate or in their behavior. Many parents trained during adolescence in ideological values—of religion, socialism or liberalism, have had these ideologies smashed, blurred or distorted by their own life experience. Parents from some families, especially fathers, try to spoil the idealistic innocence of their children as early as possible, to present the implications of their own experience as the "real" truth, and to direct the young people toward the pragmatism which, in their view, is necessary for the current reality.

This is not the forum to deal with the broader question of socialization through education for shaping a political identity; that deserves a thorough, systematic investigation in another context. In a discussion of conflict, it is important to note three things:

- Belief in basic values and belief in possibilities for progress, change and development are essential for support of adolescent individuation. Faith is the foundation for shaping a "dream" and pattern of living and assures positive coping with present and future difficulties.

- There is no great danger in the innocence and idealism of the transition period from adolescence to adulthood. Cynicism, which negates belief in change and development, is far more dangerous. Life experience limits all adults and will eventually limit youth in their future. They don't need the help of their parents or teachers in order to reach that limitation. As their social perspective develops, they will learn about the complexity and intricacy of problems. What is important for them is the basic sense of assurance that there are alternatives, that there are nice people and that there are favorable possibilities. A person can and should believe that he, his family, his ethnic group, his state and the whole world have the alternative to be good and do good things; a person should have the opportunity and guidance to develop social skills for taking on personal and social responsibility while striving toward realization of that dream.

- Just as there is no justification for imposing nostalgia and presenting yesteryear's world as though it was beneficial, there is likewise no basis for viewing the future in negative, gloomy terms. There is certainly no reason to examine the future in stereotypically negative or positive terms. In peer groups, adolescents should be supported so that they will be able to understand the development of mankind: their own, their family's, their society's and that of the world at large. Their understanding should be differential and develop out of high level critical thought and broad, profound social perspective. They should be able to view things in their complexity, not simplistically, because things are not simple. However, it is important that they believe in people, so they will believe in themselves and in their significant others; that they see that possibilities exist for improving people, so they will accept personal and social responsibility in order to act for the sake of this change.

Conflict No. 13: Expectation of parental understanding and support

Adolescents at any age and in any social setting expect their parents' involvement and support. Their reports reflect their feelings even in conflict situations, as is seen in these examples of comments made during peer group learning experiences. It seems clear that there is a need to fashion peer group learning experiences through which the adolescent who has not managed to achieve positive fulfillment of parental expectations can learn to cope with his parents' reactions. Concomitantly, there is a need for appropriate supportive learning experiences for parents which can help them to learn to provide more effective guidance to their children.

"I expected that my Dad would try to understand me and not just the teacher . . . even if I wasn't right, perhaps, like you say. He should listen to me, he should say he understands what I felt, before beginning to preach to me . . ."

"What I admired when this happened with the teacher was that my father didn't immediately become a judge. He began by saying: 'I understand, Mark, what you felt; I would also certainly have gone crazy from so much anger' . . . and only afterwards did he sit down with me to talk about what happened. And what I could have done."

"That's the difference between my mother and my father. She is immediately prepared to listen, and I know she is with me. What happens with my father is that he appears like a lawyer and a judge, or like a teacher . . ."

Conflict No. 14: Full scale attack

Even when planning battle strategies it is considered advisable to study the options before acting: should you destroy the enemy or take a chance on a future, more favorable development of the relationship? In adolescent-parent like adolescent-teacher relationships, it is clear that the desired end-result need not be a total response, with its destructive potential, but is rather a search for ways to cope with specific problems and relatively unique situations. Therefore, It is most important to constantly deal with differentiations in each of the various situations; questions such as "what is (really) involved?" "how serious is it (the matter)?" and "what can we (adults and adolescents) learn from this behavior?" or, particularly as adults, parents, guides, questions such as "how can we help the youngster learn without hurting him so much that it would block the ability to communicate?" "to what extent will he be open for further learning following this kind of confrontation?" are essential.

Assessment criteria may be proposed to help bring various incidents and ways of expressing oneself into proportion.

For example, it can be highlighted that it is impossible to present each incident in the most extreme form, such as stated by several adolescent girls: "With my mother each thing was a total disaster. . . ." *or* "My mother 'dies' from everything. . . ."

Aside from the need to learn that things may be seen in proportion and how to judge "figures of speech" vs. reality, they also need to learn that there is a way out of every situation, even if justice is not done in every instance. Value-based and emotional criteria involved in judgment may be suggested as a topic for thought and discussion for the adolescent, parent or teacher, together or separately. Parents, facilitators and adolescents can strive to deal with conflicts and emotions in a given situation by conducting negotiations, seeking compromises, settling for partial "victories" and returning later to the bargaining table.

Applying personality labels will scuttle any chance of creating a favorable change in behavior. A parent or teacher who says: "You are simply lazy," or "You are incapable of understanding," or "You'll never be a decent human being"—effectively shuts the door on the adolescent's willingness to listen, to discuss the problem in a positive manner or to try changing his behavior. Even objectively speaking it is difficult to change basic personality traits. This is all the more true in an emotional situation such as that in which the conflict develops, since a subjective situation has been created which prevents listening, seeking ways to continue communication and making an effort toward change.

The tactic of focusing reactions on specific behavior in a specific context is always more useful and agrees with various psychological and pedagogical assumptions as well. If a generalization, such as: "You are always like that," or "It doesn't matter to you that I could die," is used instead of dealing with the incident, the adolescent will be unwilling to examine what has actually happened in the particular case. Only when the adult includes inquiring how the adolescent feels about the incident as part of his effort to uncover the various causes is there any chance that the two will be able to succeed identifying alternative paths which would be available in future, similar situations.

Conflict No. 15: Esteem and constant criticism

The need for both positive and negative appraisal and criticism is universal; therefore, only conflicts originating in the heightened sensitivity of adolescents who are subjected to constant supervision are included in this category. Adolescents at home and at school feel as though an appraising, critical eye is following them; they express feeling as if adults do not trust them to act like responsible people.

"I can't stand it when my mother constantly checks what I put into my book bag, whether I changed my underwear or brushed my teeth —can't she understand that I'm no longer a child? . . ."

When my father begins to praise my progress in English, I already know what's coming next: 'Why didn't you progress in mathematics? it's impossible to complete your matriculation exams without mathematics . . ."

"I feel that Dad's problem is to prove that his thinking is more correct than mine. He analyzes everything logically—comparing, formulating, correcting and laboring to defeat me in debate, instead of trying to sense what is happening to me and how ready I am to escape from this lesson that he gives . . ."

When this problem was presented for discussion in parents' groups there were various reactions. The following proposals for changing parental approaches are based on these reactions.

- The adolescent should gradually assume responsibility for evaluation and criticism in various areas; it may be suggested that he keep track of various activities, such as preparing homework, going to the doctor, repairing things, etc., in a manner and at a time interval suitable to him without parental pressure or supervision.

- When you intend to criticize, don't begin with praise. Adolescents consider this as an indication of insincerity and unreliability. Everyone likes to receive praise when he feels he deserves it, but when it is not deserved he feels he is being manipulated. People tend to react to manipulation with anger and do not know what to expect afterwards.

- Criticism should be aimed at something specific and not be expressed in generalizations. Saying: "You are lazy, irresponsible, not a decent person," etc. will not produce the desired action, because most people cannot tolerate such accusations and will react accordingly. It is best to describe the problematic situation which has developed and to avoid evaluating the individual. The adolescent knows that he had a part in creating the situation; a discussion conducted about his characteristics as a person will not enlighten him further about his role; however, a discussion about options in coping with the new situation and how the adult could be of help to him will not only enable him to resolve the present problem but reinforce his ability to cope with similar situations in the future.

• It is permissible to request that requirements be met within the framework of a mutual relationship between two people who are prepared to support each other's needs.

Conflict No. 16: Anxiety about disappointing father or mother

A positive assessment from one's parents is very important for nearly every adolescent. Any adolescent who truly no longer wishes his parents' approval, is most likely in need of professional help. Many adolescents feel that their parents, especially their fathers, have developed clear expectations of them and will express disappointment if the adolescent fails to meet these expectations or behaves unexpectedly.

Parents have expressed the awareness of the adolescent's right to autonomy and individuation in private conversation and/or parent groups; however, it seems that they still feel they know better and are more responsible than their children, and are, thus, disappointed when their children act in unexpected ways. Some parents express their disappointment in the form of public pronouncements; but the adolescent feels their disappointment no less keenly with the more common indirect expression of expectations:

"I know that my father is disappointed in me. He doesn't say it, but I feel it . . ."

"My father has a plan for exactly what I should be. If there were a registry office like the land registry, he would certainly register there. Instead of this, he regularly repeats: 'Jerry, you can become what you wish, as long as you're happy with it . . .'"

"My father never told me directly, but I know that if I don't become a doctor like him, it would be a sign that I failed in life."

"Mother always repeats that she wants me to be happy. But when she repeats that, I know immediately that I have in fact disappointed her because I haven't done what she wants me to do . . ."

Conflict No. 17: Parents who push

One of the central problems of a period of rapid modernization is the stress resulting from the fast pace of change, the need for adjustment to such rapid change and the necessity of "moving ahead" in a competitive society. Beyond such "objective" conditions is the fact that a considerable portion of adolescents' parents grew up in economic and/or educational conditions which have encouraged them to search for a shortcut to success in the development of their children.

Children and adolescents feel they must measure up to parental expectations in terms of social mobility along with other areas. Many adolescents feel that parents push them by confronting them with future expectations and measuring their daily progress toward the goals of interest. In some of the families there is a sort of natural division of roles: the mother pushes her daughter so she will mature into an acceptable woman and the father pushes her to develop intellectually and professionally. Despite the concomitant declaration that "it is your life and you will decide what is good for you," the undertone is "Run!," accompanied by warnings about falling on her face.

The interviews and peer group discussions revealed many examples of such situations. The following statements represent various types of adolescent feelings:

"Korey, you don't work enough. At your age I was already a full-fledged car mechanic . . ."

"Other children are already dating girls, and you seclude yourself with some pictures or coins . . ."

"I would like to go to my room with a friend or go with him to the movies, but I know my mother feels this is not proper, that I should be like all the boys."

"When my mother sees that I don't have a boyfriend, she tries to arrange something, through the mothers of my girlfriends."

"Even when I try hard I know that it's not enough for my father; at my age he was setting the world on fire and I'm just studying . . ."

"My father is only happy when he is accomplishing—he builds, he organizes, he feels he got where he was going without education and I am standing still . . ."

Conflict No. 18: Parents' concern for daughters

Concern for a daughter's physical vulnerability and sexuality has undoubtedly existed as long as there have been daughters. Today's sexual permissiveness makes the situation even more complicated. Conflicts over this issue develop in nearly every family in which girls grow up. How can family members learn to live with this phenomenon without engaging in mutual destruction?

Expressions of the problem vary among different families; the first examples presented below represent extremely adverse, atypical situations:

A girl: "My father doesn't care much for my friend. He thinks that I deserve someone better and gives all sorts of reasons. But they don't pressure me to stop because they're sure that he will protect me when we go out socially . . ."

Mother: "I'm worried sick and my husband makes me shut up. I know that he is no less worried than I am. He maintains a facade. I spy on her through her girlfriends, and always take care not to hurt her . . ."

The following present favorable views as perceived by adolescents and parents:

Father: "We have reached an agreement with our daughter. There is a fixed time for coming back home. She suggests it by writing it down on a slip of paper, since this situation of striking a bargain and of fears was hard for her and for us, because we are ruining her evening out in advance."

Daughter: "We agreed that if I want to stay out a bit longer, I phone. I also accepted that they are permitted to worry."

Daughter: "We divided the responsibility: they won't bother me about how I behave and don't require me to report what happened. They agree that I am responsible for my behavior. But I need to think how not to destroy them with worry."

Father: "I told our daughter straight out: it is unacceptable that you should enjoy yourself while we sit at home and suffer on your account. You suggest a formula by which you can help reduce our worry and we will be calm."

Mother: "We sat down with our daughter several times, in order to help her distinguish between her right to these or to other feelings. But we insisted on our right and our responsibility for basic values of behavior. As long as she has not reached the age of 18, she lives at home, and there must be agreement about certain values.

Father: "In an open, not so simple conversation, she also understood that there's no way we will be policemen or detectives. She is responsible for her own conduct. But at this age we share norms which are basic to a family like ours."

Mother: "My feeling is that there is a time which you have to know how to get through. My daughter is also scared—for her reputation, for her body. She just wants to feel it is hers and that we help her in this. I wasn't different from her at the same age."

Daughter: "It is important to me that they understand that I also have feelings; and that they shouldn't impose rules and prohibitions on me, as though I were a child or a prisoner. If they understand me

I can try to understand them. I also have a need to set limits for myself, but I need to feel that it is my life."

Mother: "One of the things I learn all the time is how not to be my daughter's teacher. My mother was always being a teacher—both at school and at home, and it used to drive me crazy. Every time I catch myself acting like my mother, I tell myself: 'No more! Hear her, listen to her, discuss with her, it's her life—you won't be together with her and the boys, and she will be responsible there . . . Help her to be responsible.' It's not simple, like I said, but I am sure that this is correct in principle."

Conflict No. 19: Maternal anxieties impairing the need to feel autonomous

All mothers (and many fathers, too) worry about the normal or even optimal development of their children. However, evidence from studies, clinical and personal contacts attest to the variations from one person or group to another. Modern society provides unprecedented opportunities to create stress and anxiety: the mass media communicates every disaster across the nation instantaneously, the intense pace of the race for achievement and the emphasis on being healthy cultivated by society. Furthermore, and unique to this historical period are anxieties due to the decrease in the number of children and the increase in single-child families, due to delayed marriage or childbearing which places the child in a situation of being the sole link with immortality for his parents, due to the effects of disasters in different families—Holocaust survivor families, war widows, widows due to traffic or work accidents, post-divorce families and single parent families, etc.

Understanding causes does not change the fact that adolescents may feel pressured and sometimes even smothered in the face of their mothers' concern. As noted above, adolescent sensitivity about autonomy plays an important role and must be taken into account.

When the following example was articulated in a peer group, it elicited other examples from the participants, all of which involved accusations, in varying degrees of anger, addressed to the mothers.

Johnny, 16 years old: "From the moment she wakes me up in the morning until I shut myself in my room to sleep at night, her refrain continues: 'How did you sleep last night?' . . . 'Did you eat the sandwich I gave you for school? . . .' 'Why are you clearing your throat?' 'Why do you have a tick? . . .' 'Why did you come home late? . . .'

'Why didn't you phone? . . .' 'Why didn't you wash your hands? . . .'
And so forth, why this and why that, as though I were still my mother's baby and not a 16 year old guy. And when I burst out and yell:
'Don't tell me what to do. I'm not sick and not a child, leave me in
peace,' she is terribly insulted . . . I'll tell you that I don't want to hurt
her. She loves me an awful lot and cares an awful lot. I love her. But I
can't stand this . . .''

Conflict No. 20: Adolescents' need for verbal expression of the father's love

There is no doubt that, aside from pathological cases, fathers love
their children, take care of them, and are prepared to do what seems
necessary for their development. However, at the same time there are
undoubtedly many adolescents who yearn for a direct and sincere
verbal expression of that love.

Adolescents repeated in practically the same terms in all the forums
of this study the complaint that father did not speak, father did not
say and father did not confirm his recognition, his love or the support
he provided during the adolescent's development process.

It would appear that many fathers are unaware of this fact. They
are surprised by such a plaint even at a later stage, when family
therapy is being conducted or when they are confronted with an
advisor or some other person treating the young man caught up in a
problematic situation.

Josh, age 22, tells: "I always knew that my father loves me, but he
never said it to me . . ."

Herbie, age 16: "My father never told me that he loves me. Mother
says too much that she loves me, that she likes me, that I am hand-
some, and other such things which sometimes sound like nagging . . .
I know that my father would be willing to kill himself for me, or to kill
anyone who touches me, but he doesn't know how to express what
he feels . . . You ask why that is so important to me? I don't know.
Perhaps it is a kind of affirmation. I need to hear from the teacher that
I'm okay, and from the counselor that I'm all right, but it's even more
important to me to hear that from my father . . ."

There are four possible explanations for the need for verbal affirmation of what is already known:

- During formation of his individuation, the adolescent needs the
  father's recognition and his affirmation. He needs support during
  his struggle to differentiate, while facing alternatives and difficult
  decisions. The father, in his role as the model of masculinity needs

to recognize that his support is part and parcel of his role in the family of providing a balance to the mother's function.

Furthermore, the adolescent, ever egocentric in this period, feels that he is at the focal point of family and society, while at the same time unsure about his preparedness, the direction of his functioning and his dreams. He naturally turns to the person whose judgment, in the vast majority of cases, is one of the basic elements of consolidating his ego for support.

- Most fathers are both judgmental and do not talk or disclose themselves, a confusing and sometimes tragic situation. The adolescent knows that his father has things to say, that he expects things of him, and that he keeps track of him; when his father does not follow through as he expects, he is disappointed and has no opportunity to engage in mutually clarifying, remedial, compromising and supportive communication to determine the reasons for the silence.

- The contrast with the mother's behavior emphasizes the severity of the problem. Most mothers reveal themselves, provide support and give compliments. Their expression in words, embraces, kisses and other ways points up the contrast between their feelings and expectations and those represented by the father's image and functioning.

Of course, the father, as well as the mother, must be perceived as sincere and credible when expressing his feelings; it is insufficient to express such feelings as would be expected while filling a role; adolescents seek affirmation that the parent means what he expresses. A lack of confidence in their identity and status is expressed by adolescents' intolerance of a parent giving out praise of doubtful or questionable truthfulness.

Conflict No. 21: Mothers acting as though they were adolescents

One thing which agitates and arouses the ire of adolescent girls (and boys as well, although they express it less, perhaps they pay it less attention) the most is the mother acting as if she were an adolescent in public, particularly in the presence of the adolescents' friends.

Deborah, age 16½: "My mother tries to compete with me. She wears mini or leather skirts, and when friends come over, she serves good stuff, sits with us, and begins to talk slang as though she belonged to the group . . . The kids didn't offend her, but I was bursting inside. I am sure they talk about her behind my back, but they are afraid to say anything to me . . ." (adolescent 368).

Elly, age 17: "I'm embarrassed to tell you, but if you ask what I don't like about my mother, it's that she sometimes acts as if she were my age. She takes a skirt or dress of mine, puts on too many rings, and joins the conversation with a boy who comes to visit me . . . I once saw her flirt with one of the boys, and then I waited until he left and said to her—sorting holding back, half in jest and half for real— 'Mother, were you competing with me when Jack came over?' She turned red as a tomato, and burst out like a crazy person: 'How could you think that, you know how I love you, you are my whole world . . . I do everything for you!' . . ." (adolescent 303).

Mona, age 16½: "The most maddening thing about my mother is that she acts as though she were one of the girls . . . I need a mother and not another girlfriend. I can't stand this act, since it's phony. I can't stand phoniness even in the girls, but in my mother it kills me . . . " (adolescent 334).

Several explanations suggest themselves:

- Some mothers, unaware of the meaning of their behavior, feel a need to appear like young girls and they act out of this need even in the company of their daughters. The processes behind such a need might be: the transitional stage of Middle Age; the contrast between the adolescent girls' blooming, nascent sexuality and the mothers' fear of withering; a problematic, unsatisfactory relationship with the husband; a carry-over of behavior intended to create a certain impression in another social group—at work or in a leisure time social setting, the implications of which are revealed at home, in the daughter's presence.

- In some cases the problem is not the mother's but rather the daughter's. Lack of confidence in her identity, competition for a place in peer society, or difficulties in her relations with the mother or father can inspire images in her mind lacking any factual basis in the mother's behavior. But one way or the other, it is clear that a problem exists in which the daughter needs to be supported in improving her relationship with her mother.

- Sometimes there actually is competition, conscious or unconscious, between daughter and mother, especially when one of them contributes more in one area and the other projects things into another area. This dynamic configuration is one in which the two of them can only be helped by professional, family therapists.

- There is a certain potential confusion in the value accorded to modern mothers' preserving their youthfulness and the early maturation of most adolescent girls today. The absence of role norms in "liberal" families may also contribute such a feeling in the girls. Clarifying communication would go a long way in preventing uncomfortable feelings, confusion and conflict.

Conflict No. 22: Mothers meddling in the adolescent's private life

Very few things were confidential in the life of family members in traditional society. Modernization, the isolation of the nuclear family from other family members by the move to apartments or individual homes, the decrease in number of children per family, and a commitment to the individual's rights to autonomy and self-realization have evolved a particular expectation of autonomy in middle or upper class families which is gradually filtering down into other families as well. The thrust of this expectation is primarily as regards maintaining one's privacy. Adolescents expect that their letters will not be opened, their phones not be monitored, and their drawers not be searched, etc.

Mary, age 16: "My mother is always being a detective. I've already caught her eavesdropping several times on the second phone when I was talking with a boyfriend or girlfriend. She also snoops in my drawer and I'm sure that she's read my letters . . ." (adolescent 324).

Rachel, age 15½: "Mother opened a letter which came to me from a friend and apologized for not seeing that it was for me and not for her. Since I have already caught her several times reading my diary and my letters, I saw red when she opened my boyfriend's letter, and I yelled at her: 'You're a liar, you're always snooping in my private things. I'm a person too, not a dishrag!' . . . I burst into tears and ran off to my room. She tried to come in, screamed and cried, but I didn't open up for her. Afterwards I was terribly sorry for insulting her, but I couldn't stand it anymore. The next morning we didn't exchange a word, and only when she came from school and my father wasn't home yet, she came to make up . . . and we talked until a girlfriend came . . . The thing is that she doesn't change, although there was a time that she had stopped . . ." (adolescent 308).

It is fairly clear that the background to conflicts like those described above is deeper than the behavior might indicate. In general, one or more of the five motives described below probably produces parental behavior such as discussed. Although the mother is cited most often, there are occasions on which the father is involved as well.

- Parents are anxious about their children's development, particularly about a daughter's sexual behavior. They employ a tactic of "the detective" in order to keep "in touch" with what is happening to their children. The belief is that if they know more about their daughters' conduct, they will be able to intervene either to prevent undesirable behavior or to supply necessary support at the appropriate time.

- Many parents, especially mothers, use the "detective tactic to maintain authority, power and control over the adolescent. Women seem to resort to this more often than men out of their perception of their particular responsibility for the affective sphere in the family. Sometimes this perception stems from their relative weakness, and sometimes from their personal experience with similar conduct as an adolescent in their own family of origin.

- Certain parents experience sexual memories or fantasies from their adolescence and youth by invading the adolescent's privacy, either consciously or unconsciously.

- Certain adolescent behavior reinforces the mother's urge to "play detective." Their actions are replete with hints; they disclose something and hide something, leave open letters on the table or elsewhere, and complain when they are read "by mistake;" they give the mother messages to tell someone they don't wish to speak with that they aren't home or something similar and involve her in their sexual-social games.

- Mothers who lack satisfaction in other relationships and whose life may be filled with frustration may look to fulfill certain needs indirectly through involvement in their daughters' relations.

It is noteworthy that although some fathers are involved in these processes, the evidence indicates that it almost always occurs in mother-daughter relations. It is possible that although the mother nearly always performs the sleuthing activities, the father participates in the process by playing the role of a secondary participant, benefiting from information reaching him indirectly through the mother.

Conflict No. 23: Maternal domination in the family

In the section on adolescent perceptions of their parents, it was noted that more than half of the adolescents, especially the girls, perceived their mothers as dominant in the family. The descriptions of the mother's dominance were clearly drawn. The adolescents offered very interesting and lively explanations for this phenomenon and attempted to deal with its significance for family life generally and for adolescents in particular.

"My mother is the dominant one at home. My dad does threaten, but without Mother he is incapable of doing anything" (family 22).

"Who's dominant? My mother, and that's all. My mother is the one who decides what we do, where we go, and that's that—my father follows her lead" (family 144).

In a considerable portion of the cases concerned, the description takes on an increasingly negative tone. The dominant mother is often accused of being domineering and, in many instances, of humiliating the father. Such cases clearly reflect a severe, ongoing conflict between the adolescent and the mother. The following three examples have been arranged according to the degree of the problem's severity.

"My mother's the one who dominates and influences the direction of development in the family. The truth is that I am critical of this; however, when I say this, my mother lets me have it, so I prefer to do what I think best and not to declare my feelings" (family 130).

"My mother is domineering and humiliates my father with her behavior. She gives him orders, as though he were one of the children she teaches in school . . . I couldn't stand this at first and now it riles me" (family 137).

"My mother is so domineering that she makes a dishrag out of my father. She engineers all sorts of manipulation in order to make sure things go the way she wants them to. My father tries to defend himself, but he immediately closes up and is silent . . . like a stone . . . that eats me up. I quarrel with her about this, and I can't forgive . . . that doesn't mean I don't love her. She takes care of everyone, Dad, too; she arranges and fights for each one, and she is reliable . . . but that isn't relevant . . ." (family 72).

It is interesting that while domineering mothers were mentioned by about one-third of the women's interviews (including both parents and adolescents looking at their mothers), less than 10% of the men mentioned it. Clearly men as well as women encountered such a phenomenon in their families; the following three hypotheses could account for the difference and peer group facilitators could work to enable adolescents to express their feelings about the subject.

- According to historical, clinical and literary evidence, Jewish culture includes a higher proportion of weak fathers and strong, even domineering women.
- The greater involvement of the mother in all areas of their children's lives as compared with the limited involvement of the father, creates an image of the mother wielding greater control in the family than in actuality.

- The formation of the adolescent daughter's identity is influenced by her mother's dominance, especially the domineering quality of that influence. This probably explains the fact that more than twice the number of girls raised the problem as did the boys. It can also explain the girls' greater sensitivity to interpersonal relations in the family, and to the significance of the problematic aspect of the situation in the daughter's life. Such influence can be seen in the previous chapter's accounts of present-day's mothers' perception of their own mothers as compared with that of today's adolescent girls. This clearly has implications, as well, for choice of spouse and for future parenting style.

Conflict No. 24: The father's segregation from exposure and communication

This is slightly different from the adolescent perception of their fathers, discussed previously. In this instance, a negative perception becomes the source of an emotional conflict for the adolescent and may be sometimes converted into a negative behavior reaction against him.

"He doesn't show his feelings. He doesn't explain his decisions, and is unwilling to change . . ." (family 37, girl aged 15½).

"He comes from work and reads the paper while eating, and afterwards sits next to the TV. Then, 'Yaakov, why aren't you preparing homework?' in the evening, shut up in his room, he reads and works. It is forbidden to disturb him . . ." (family 58, boy aged 17).

"When I was at home, before going to agricultural school, I couldn't stand his silence. I am so sociable that I can talk freely with other kids. Only with him it is impossible to talk. He says nothing about himself, neither to me nor to my mother. The last time I was supposed to come home for vacation I suggested to him by phone: 'Dad, I want to get to know you; I want to talk with you; let's meet at Nissim's Coffee House—just the two of us, we'll sit in a corner and talk . . .'" (family 42, son aged 17).

"I love to do things together with my Dad: to go on excursions, to build things in the yard. He has things to talk about and likes to hear jokes. But I know that he doesn't know to talk openly about what is happening to him" (family 87, boy aged 15½).

"Mother, grandfather and the guidance counselor tell me that Dad had a difficult childhood . . . I understand this . . . but I need father to act differently: to speak with me, to relate to me like a person . . ." (family 63, son aged 15½).

"My father is a simple man, doesn't think deeply; it is impossible to get him to analyze things or to tell about himself like I would have wanted. But he is a very honest man. He cares about things and he works very hard so that things will turn out good. I know that he loves me, but I would like more from him" (adolescent 313, girl aged 16).

My father says everything so many times that he makes me angry. He's like a stone wall inside, you can't get in to know what he feels. Mother gets along with him nicely—by compromising and doing things herself. He makes me mad and drives me crazy . . ." (adolescent 333, girl aged 16).

"I'm freer with Mother. I tell her everything, she's really my friend. Not just attentive but she is open and also gives advice. In contrast, it's hard to talk with my father, he's like a stone wall" (family 94, girl aged 17).

"My father loves us. He's prepared to do anything for everyone; he talks about politics, sees that we study and that we behave properly. One thing irks me with him, that I don't know anything about his personal life . . ." (adolescents, boy aged 17).

There are several general comments which arise from these descriptions.

Adolescents need to accept the fact that their fathers have a particular personality structure, that it is hard for them to change, and that there is no point in expecting a basic change to occur. When choosing a friend, it is possible to ask what type of person would be nice; but parents, like children, cannot be chosen. It is, however, possible to change the quality, the significance of the tie with a parent. To do that, the trick is to think about the parent's positive aspects, not only about his limitations. Disappointment arising from a lack of response by the father, according to one's internal father image, must be exchanged for learning to enjoy his favorable aspects and looking for gratification from other things with other people.

Understanding the parent by knowing his biography is important for the adolescent; however, it is insufficient to resolve the problem of a father who does not fulfill his son's needs. In cases of extremely problematic relationships, the adolescent can be helped to find gratification in other ways—in relations with a boyfriend or girlfriend, in satisfying peer group activity, by focusing attention on satisfying projects, etc.

The inability of a father to disclose himself arises, for the most part, from personality structure and socialization, not from a lack of love or wish to be involved in his children's lives. Counselors can help fathers by organizing support groups or through personal discussions. They can aid adolescents learn how to establish communication with the father and to negotiate a middle ground with him without deluding themselves that they will really succeed in changing his basic personality characteristics.

Some fathers maintain an image which is the antithesis of the mother's image: she is involved, reveals her feelings, intervenes, supports, etc. Just as it is both impossible and unnecessary to change the mother's style of relating, there is no necessity to change the father's behavior. All that is necessary is to help the adolescent and the father, separately and together, to provide mutual support as they work towards greater involvement in areas appropriate to their personalities.

Conflict No. 25: Parents using their past as the basis for criticism of the adolescent and his contemporaries

Many adolescents wish to be involved in their parents' lives and to hear about their past, their adolescence and their problems. However, the appropriate time for discussing such a topic and the degree of revelation appropriate must depend on each individual. They do not want parents to force their past on them, especially in certain forms.

- A parent's history rewritten: it is usually the father, who recites regularly a nostalgic description of the beautiful world in which he grew up—a world of pioneers, idealists, people who were workers, ambitious, concerned, etc.—not like today.
- Personalized, comparative historical research: "At your age I worked hard"; "I studied mornings and I was active in the [political] movement and in the 'Haganah' in the afternoons"; "I helped my mother and made the effort to understand her and . . ." etc.
- Forecasting the future contrasted with nostalgic history: "You won't grasp what awaits you in the future without mathematics . . .,"; "When I was your age I knew that if I didn't work hard there wouldn't be any bread . . ."; "You will have to live in a world where people struggle for a job, and only someone whose profession is in demand will have a chance . . ."; "I knew how to work day and night, and you are given everything; you aren't ready to make the tiniest effort . . ."

These three forms of reconstructing the past share the parental view, either stated outright or implied, that the parent and his contemporaries were good, responsible, believed in values, etc. The inescapable conclusion is that the adolescent and his friends represent a negative image of all which the parent considers desirable.

There are three perspectives to this type of parent-adolescent conflict which should be considered:

- The era and ecological context of the parent is different from that of his child. Just as drawing comparisons between themselves and their parents had no meaning, no advantage accrues from their expecting their child to be as they were. Fathers tend to employ inaccurate, stereotypical generalizations; but even if an objective comparison were made, it would be worthless. Each person shapes his own identity, determines his dreams, and fashions his life style during the individuation process within the ecological environment in which he develops. He develops as a totality according to his perceptions of his needs, his values and his experiences.

- Since comparisons of the sort described above, by their very nature, are aimed at negating the adolescent and his friends and substituting an idealization of something undesirable or insignificant for the reality he knows, they cannot help but be an insult and affront.

- Such a comparison brings to bear pressure inappropriate to the individuation process itself. The adolescent should be informed that: it is your life, you are responsible for formulating a consequential viewpoint, acquiring important skills and evolving a unique coping ability which will enable you to develop yourself and within the society of which you are a part. Such comparisons, though, deny him responsibility, bind him to things over which he has no control, and arouse feelings of denial and isolation instead of involvement and adjustment.

Conflict No. 26: Permissive parents who evade their responsibility

Most parents fulfill their obligations toward their children, taking on responsibility according to their various personalities, values, ethnic origins and the character of their offspring. However, there is a small group of adolescents who describe a different picture of their parents. These parents are mainly from the middle and upper classes and mostly businessmen, although some of them engage in professions. They evince permissiveness regarding their children's behavior: they do not interfere and allow the adolescent to do whatever he wishes in various areas. They may extend their permissive style even in their marital relations. Sometimes they posit an ideology that their nonintervention approach is correct, and at other times their neglect seems to originate in their personal egocentrism. There seems to be three types of this type of conflict.

It appears as if the mother finds no meaning in raising children although she claims she loves them, just as she claims that she loves her husband. She clearly wants to be on the outside—to devote herself to her business, to engage in a lot of social activity. The house is maintained by a housekeeper who keeps things proceeding normally. One adolescent expressed: "I could do whatever I wished, as long as I didn't get into trouble and arrived to eat and sleep . . . that nothing negative has developed from me is only by chance . . ."; or: "I have no doubt that if Mother and Father had been actively involved, if they had believed that I could learn, if they had intervened and pushed— I would certainly not be in such a situation . . ."

The permissive ideology of these parents is couched in the argument: "Who knows what's best?" The adolescent feels that his parents do not define any limits, and he or she must integrate into a hedonistic peer group or suffer from isolation. In either case adolescents blame the parents, particularly the mother, since they assume the father is busy with important work and it is the mother who is obligated to provide for her children's well being.

When relations between the parents are disturbed or the adolescent lives with his mother after separation or divorce, the mother is focused on herself, her present needs, or seeking solutions for the future. The adolescent finds himself abandoned or free in the sense of disconnected, since he is caught between the father and mother.

Conflict No. 27: Physically abusive parents

Some parents express their concern and anger with physical reactions. Such punishments produce conflicts in the adolescents. However, the interviews revealed few comments about this subject, and it was not certain that the problem was extensive enough to justify inclusion in this chapter. Studies conducted abroad (Kitwood, 1980) and consultations with parents, adolescents and guidance counselors indicated clearly that such a problem does exist and needs to be discussed. It appears that few adolescents report it because of a fear of labelling the family as pathological.

The paucity of data in the interviews makes it difficult to make generalizations. Questions must be asked: Who is doing the hitting? When does it happen? How does it happen and what do those

involved feel afterwards? Evidence available from other sources seems
to indicate:

- Physical abusiveness exists in certain families, as a kind of child-
  rearing pattern; and it is impossible to say that the parents are
  problematic. Mothers or fathers whose families of origin did not
  follow such a child-rearing pattern avail themselves less of this
  method than those from families who did. However, those coming
  from the same family which resorted to such a child-rearing pattern act differently with their children, each explaining his differing behavior in his own way.
- Hitting occurs in all ethnic groups and classes, although families
  with poorly educated parents report a higher rate of use of this
  method.
- Although both fathers and mothers do the hitting, the proportion
  of fathers who hit is much higher.
- Reasons given for hitting adolescents include in response to worry
  about a boy or girl returning home late despite a promise to the
  contrary, girls dating undesirable boys or against the parent's
  express wishes, in response to being tricked by lies about where
  the youths are going or what they are doing away from home.
  Corporal punishment has also been reported in cases of involvement with deviant behavior such as driving without a license,
  drunkenness, drugs, etc.—phenomena which arouse parental
  concern and/or hurt the parents' reputation or authority.
- In most cases adolescents accepted hitting as a legitimate punishment for their behavior. It did not seem to impair the quality of
  the adolescent-parent relationship. However, sometimes it elicited
  deep anger, a sense of humiliation, a desire to rebel and even a
  decision to leave home as soon as feasible. Although adolescents
  who were hit often report swearing they would never do likewise
  to their children, the evidence indicates continuing recurrence
  over as long as three generations, even in families of teachers,
  counselors and psychologists.

Summary and General Conclusions

Initially we defined the foci of conflicts between adolescents and
parents based on interviews included in our study of families and on
interviews with adolescents in peer groups. We then chose 27 conflicts
which seemed representative of the foci of conflicts as described above
and examined them according to different families and different ages.

Table 3-A: Frequency of 20 conflict subjects of conflict by sex (descending order), ages 15-18 only*

Girls	Boys
1. Preparing homework (the process of preparing and the pressure for achievement).	1. Preparing homework (the process of preparing and the pressure for achievement).
2. Protection against sexual involvement—premature or problematic (curfew, dating a particular boy, dating boys), sexual activity, sleeping away from home.	2. Intervening in daily behavior (time for rising or sleeping, manner of speech, sitting, eating, standing, dress).
3. Intervening about external appearance (dress, make-up).	3. Intervening about behavior outside the home.
4. Intervening in manner of behavior (mode of speech, sitting, eating, standing, time for rising, bedtime).	4. Expecting understanding and support (vis-a-vis the other parent, a teacher, an adult or boy in the neighborhood, an official or policeman).
5. Interfering with territory (straightening up room).	5. Money problems (not getting monthly allowance and the need to request it, not getting enough money, using parent's account or money without permission).
6. Interfering with privacy (digging in drawers, reading a diary, opening letters, listening to phone calls, talking with boyfriend/ girlfriend).	6. Absence of trust and recognition of adolescent (lack of trust in what he says and of his ability, negation of his views and feelings, not sharing problems with him).
7. Expecting help at home (cleaning house, washing dishes, washing car, errands, looking after siblings, help in business).	7. Lack of self-disclosure and communication by the father.
8. Money problems (allowance not given, must be requested. Not enough money given, use of family's account without permission, borrowing money from friends).	8. Lack of understanding and support outside family (toward a teacher, adolescent, neighbor, official, policeman).

Next, reviewing the 27 conflicts, we prepared a list of 40 general conflicts, representative of the dimensions or scope of the more specific foci described earlier. These were arranged in a random order without numbers and were presented to adolescents in 16 peer groups from various schools. They were asked to rank the frequency of conflicts in descending order from most frequent to least frequent. Table 3-A presents 20 conflicts common to girls and boys according to a composite of all these lists.

Different adolescents in the peer groups were approached and a conversation-interview was held whose purpose was to learn more about the significance of a particular communication pattern of the

Table 3-A (continued)

Girls	Boys
9. Parental interference in choice of boyfriend.	9. Parent's lack of sincerity and reliability.
10. Interfering with sibling relations.	10. Relations between father and mother.
11. Parent's lack of sincerity and reliability.	11. Expecting help at home (washing car, errands, help in house or garden, help in business).
12. Relations between father and mother.	12. Interfering with privacy (opening letters, overhearing conversations, straightening up room, dress).
13. Lack of understanding and support outside home (towards a teacher, neighbor, official).	13. Use of family car (taking it without permission, maintaining it in poor condition, keeping it after the agreed time).
14. Lack of trust in adolescent (in her ability, her future chances, her ability to alter behavior).	14. Interfering with choice of friends or choice of steady girlfriend.
15. Mother's behavior (dominating the father, acting like a teenager, gossiping).	15. Interference regarding choice of major or vocation.
16. Father's behavior (lack of attention, of involvement and disclosure, lack of positive mutual communication).	16. Interference regarding military service.
17. Health (irregular eating, lack of sleep and moods. Under- or overweight).	17. Difference of opinion (politics, music).
18. Use of family car (taking it without permission or returning it late, damaging it).	18. Father offering his past as model ('when I was your age').
19. Interference regarding major area of study or choice of vocation.	19. Use of force (hitting, slaps, expelling from home).
20. Interference regarding plans for military service.	20. Interfering with sibling relations.

*The interviews were conducted with subjects aged 15-22, but in the peer groups adolescents from ages 14-15 to 17-18 participated. Therefore we have limited the age range in the table.

parent, as it appeared in the original interviews. Particularly, the respondents were requested to interpret the message.

From these activities, two additional comments may be made:

It seems clear that the focus of conflict varies with age and historical distance. Just as the combination of factors provoking confrontations differs, so does the influence of a particular event in terms of the adolescent's or parent's sense of hurt. The significance of a conflict at the time it occurs differs from its significance when reported in the interview. It appears, both in the interviews and in the written accounts, that while one adolescent might describe a conflict in a state of agitation, unable to overcome his emotions even in the presence of a stranger, another adolescent might look back and use intellectual analysis, successfully pinpointing the reasons for the parent's behavior and feelings. Thus, there is considerable overlap between conflict headings in terms of areas of content and significance of injury.

Some interviews included descriptions by a particular adolescent of various conflicts, while other adolescents focused on one particularly significant, dominant conflict. This is not to say that additional conflicts did not develop in the same family which were significant when they occurred; however, at the time of the interview one conflict simply obscured previous confrontations.

It is possible to make the following generalizations, according to the raw material we have collected and the information in Table 3-A:

The struggle with the demands of schooling plus parental perceptions vis a vis academic achievement provide a dominant focus of conflict throughout all of adolescence in all population strata. Adolescents recognize the importance of success in their studies, are aware that they live in an achievement-oriented, competitive society and expect it will remain that way in the future. Utopian systems proposing the establishment of a progressive school without competition or grades, have come to nothing. Moreover, forecasts of the future agree that greater selectivity is to be expected in universities due to fiscal limitations, that the need for a higher scientific and professional level will promote the emphasis on mastery learning, and that greater competitiveness for job positions and social mobility will mean greater value placed on recognized achievement. Hence, responsibility for preparing for this future would seem to be a critical function of the school, parents and adolescents, both separately and together.

One possible direction could be to teach adolescents and parents how to transfer responsibility for homework preparation to the adolescent and how to maintain appropriate communication in the area of assessing the coping process. It is clear that the peer group could play an important role, conducting learning experiences which support adolescents in this area. The facilitator could hold parallel, repeated discussions with parents in order to protect the quality of family life, including parents' and adolescents' mental health.

It is clear that sex as a variable has limited significance. The most obvious area of difference is parental anxiety about the daughter's health, her sexual development and the possibility of her being hurt as a result of sexual activity against her will, with her consent or because of social pressure. Perhaps increased, appropriate sex education and the establishing of communication channels between adolescents and parents in this area would help, since neither of those involved can escape from the problem. The subject of additional activities to increase women's security is worthy of discussion in various settings, including peer groups.

Another area of difference between the sexes is conflict regarding territorial autonomy and privacy. Conflicts of this type are extremely dominant in mother-daughter relations in early adolescence and, as described earlier in the chapter, represent deeper issues than is apparent. They clearly arise out of basic individuation struggles between the two women involved, and the severe phenomena, which occur in certain *situations,* may be explained by the character of family relationships and by various factors in the sexual identity formation processes of each woman.

Among boys, adolescent-father relations are dominant. The young man is anxious for his father's recognition, expressions of love and the development of communication based on the positive principle of equal human worth. In contrast, most mothers, even the culturally disadvantaged, manage to fulfill these needs in mother-daughter relationships and sometimes also in a relationship with their sons.

There are certain differences in the ranking order of specific problems in the table, or in how they are expressed, but these are self-evident and need not be elaborated.

How does conflict influence the adolescent's outlook and his expression of feelings, i.e., how does it influence his overall needs?

Analysis of the examples of conflicts in this chapter points to three dimensions or intersecting axes of basic human individuation needs at each developmental stage: *recognition, confidence* and *autonomy.* At each stage they acquire unique significance in terms of adolescent psycho-social maturational tasks. Following, for the sake of clarity, are several examples:

Adolescents who complain about a father who does not disclose anything of himself, does not listen to them, preaches but does not discuss, etc. are actually complaining that the father does not recognize the fact that they are no longer children, that they are of equal human worth; when he does not entrust them with his feelings and problems, he does not impart confidence in them as trustworthy people; when he conditions his love on their behavior (on the street, in school or at home), he does not enable them to see that he loves them for themselves. Similarly, the lack of clarity about his attitude to their activities and plans and the uncertainty of how he is likely to react to their decisions denies them the autonomy to develop their own personal identity.

The parent who repeats "when I was your age—I did, I was, I knew"—is relaying a message that he does not recognize the equal worth of his son or daughter; that he is unsure they are capable of coping with the expected psycho-social maturational tasks, and therefore do not deserve the autonomy to try, to offer interpretations in accordance with their viewpoint and their feelings, or to fashion a personal identity and independent pattern of living.

A mother who infringes on her daughter's privacy, specifically, the daughter's right to freedom within the particular territory of her room; which includes eavesdropping on conversations and reading her letters or diary without permission, is communicating clearly that she does not recognize her daughter's equal human worth. She, thereby, fails to provide her daughter with the feeling that she is capable of grasping things, feeling and expressing herself appropriately even in her private diary, letters and conversations; her impinging on her daughter's domain denies her daughter the autonomy to establish and maintain interpersonal interaction as a natural result of feeling the right and possibility of individuation from an omnipotent mother.

Applying the approach exemplified with these analyses, it is possible to clarify the significance of each conflict from the viewpoints of both adolescent and parent. Once these two perspectives are clear, it is possible to continue investigating how one could avoid such conflicts, weaken their negative implications, or simply learn positive things from the patterns of their development.

Chapter Four

Parent-Adolescent Communication—Learning to Negotiate Transfer of Power and Authority

Introductory Comments

FOUR PRINCIPLE ISSUES WERE DISCUSSED IN THE PRECEDING CHAPTERS:

- that psychological separation of adolescents from parents is essential for the development of modern man. It occurs during the process of personal identity shaping and preparation for responsible coping with psycho-social maturation tasks.
- that conflicts and crises arise during adolescence which may be universal or unique to certain people or certain families. These crises can produce anxiety and pressures, threats, withdrawal into seclusion, the use of physical force and/or flight from the home including escape into premature sexual relations and early pregnancies. Sometimes the difficult reactions aroused may become chronic and irreversible for the adolescent or the parent or both.
- that adolescents and parents need and desire to maintain a tie between them. The universal and/or unique patterns of such connections can be understood within a particular ecological constellation.
- that in a large proportion if not most of the cases communication difficulties, the lack of proper perspective, or the adolescent's and the parent's lack of social skills are identified by adolescents, parents and significant others as the source of problems. In other words, it would seem that those involved in family transactions lack the willingness or the capability to conduct communication at a level appropriate to the challenge facing them, which would enable negotiations, and which would contribute positively to fulfilling mutual needs and expectations.

This chapter will address the task of supporting improved methods of communication and combine the special knowledge accumulated by communications theorists with the conclusions garnered from experience in work with adolescents. It is important to add at this point that although the development of parallel parent groups to encourage adolescents and parents to learn and develop mutual responsibility for family functioning is desirable, the work in Israel and the U.S., has taught us several things:

- Fulfillment of the educational system's responsibility to provide support to adolescents is limited by school-parent cooperation, both in terms of ability and the desire of either side to make such a commitment.

- Lack of parental cooperation, for whatever reason, does not absolve the adolescent or facilitator of his responsibility in the matter.

- It is possible to teach adolescents how to function even without parallel parental activity. School and family are two separate socializing systems; the child can and must learn to act within each of them according to the specific patterns characterizing each system. It is important for the adolescent's individuation development to accept and understand the premise that he is responsible for his own values and behavior, as much as the teacher or parent is responsible for his or her values and behavior. Thus communication and negotiation can be carried out even without the agreement of all parties.

Part of the school's responsibility to advance adolescent individuational development includes the assurance of appropriate support for its students, regardless of the possibility or lack of possibility of holding parallel parental activity. This assumption, however, does not obviate the necessity for guidance counselors or educators to work with parents, in groups or as individuals, to help those who are struggling to balance fulfillment of their own needs with advancing their children's development.

Patterns of Communication: Motivation and Difficulties

It is necessary to state at the beginning that there is a distinction between verbal communication, nonverbal, and meta-communication (Ruesch, 1953). Communication occurs in each interpersonal encounter. Even if a meeting occurs where a message does not effect a reaction, there is nonverbal communication from the one who did not wish to respond to the message. Meta-communication is a type of accompanying communication, occurring along with verbal or nonverbal communications; it may be viewed as a sort of "communication about communication" (Ruesch & Bateson, 1951). When a father raises his voice to give an order or a mother's vocal expression includes sobbing, the communicative content that is added to the verbal and non-verbal expressions is meta-communication. It serves to express the intensity of their feelings beyond the verbal aspects included in the message; hence the actual message transmitted includes verbal, nonverbal and meta-communication. Meta-communication may have the effect of enhancing or reducing the value of the words spoken. In some regards, the true communication may be found in the meta-communicative utterances and additions rather than in the verbal communication forms. Two examples of meta-communication in adolescent-parent relations will illustrate this point.

Many adolescents described the impression received during conversations with their fathers that their father was occupied with important things, that it was forbidden to pester him with everyday, marginal matters, and that such things could be addressed to the mother or coped with alone. Thus, the father transmitted a message, which meaning might be even more important, in addition to the father's direct words; this message had to do with who he is, what he is interested in and what ought to be discussed with him.

Similarly, communications with mothers responding to excited tales of what had happened to the child with "Fine, finish eating, the food's already gotten cold," clearly reveal her disinterest in her child's experiences. What is important to her—in this case, seeing to her child's nutrition—occupies her wholly. Such a message may also include the more general meta-communication about what women and mothers are interested/not interested in.

Role division in the family reflects assumptions about role division in communication and expectations of communication patterns. For example, a script was prepared about what could happen at supper: what topics would be raised, what messages would be relayed, which reactions would be received, etc. after conducting interviews with families in a particular, culturally deprived population. The script was translated into a brief documentary film, and then a parallel group-learning experience was held in which members were asked to compose their own film on the same subject. Afterwards the two films were viewed and analyzed. There was an unexpectedly high correlation between the two films.

In each family there is a unique array of communication patterns: who talks about what and in what way? To whom does one turn for what things and how? From whom are certain things expected? What aspects of family occurrences are related to relatives, friends and/or neighbors and what are not relayed? Which topics are discussed during a shared meal, what is discussed only with the father, only with the mother, or with an older sibling, etc.?

There is a balance within each family in terms of power and authority, and communication patterns are intended to maintain that balance. In traditional culture norms were defined for the whole community: who sat at the table and where had great significance; who began and/ or concluded the meal and with what ceremonies and blessings was an integral part of the meal itself; tradition not only settled what was said at the table and what was left to transact in other settings, but endowed the conversation with additional significance. Informal coalitions, methods of conveying messages, etc. all were brought into play to increase communication within the traditional setting.

Communication patterns continue to exist for modern families, but each family establishes its unique pattern gradually from the point at which the family is established. Some of these patterns reflect patterns previously existing in the father's or mother's family of origin, while others are a compromise between needs and expectations conveyed through meta-communication.

A primary factor in interpersonal communication is the degree to which communicators are aware of their patterns of functioning, like to what extent they realize they do/don't look at the eyes of a speaker, that they do/don't give him a feeling of listening, or even how they relate to what others say: do they begin by rejecting, instead of saying something positive first and only afterwards make critical comments? These situations have been recorded considerably. Adolescents often describe the impossibility of talking with a teacher or adult because "she doesn't let the children speak—she corrects them, makes comments and reacts inappropriately." The problem is more severe in a family, since the stability of the various members playing their roles often creates the feeling of a broken record. For example, one young man commented: "Even before I open my mouth I know what Father and Mother will say, and how my brother will jump to defend Mother and blame me, and I will shut him up; and my little sister will stick her nose in even if she doesn't know anything, so that nothing will come of all the talking. So I decide not to begin. . . ."

Another boy added: "I would say something, because I'm like that, someone who has to speak, which is like my father, who talks even if not to the point, and repeats himself like a record. And my mother sits as if she weren't there, because she doesn't want to make my father mad . . . and afterwards she comes to soothe me."

Although everyone in a family appears to "know" everyone else, such a feeling of knowing and familiarity does not rule out the need for communication. In peer group discussions, just as in therapy groups, there are recurrent expressions of communication expectations and of the need for mutual understanding: such as the assertion "My father never said that he loves me"; or "My mother didn't relate to what actually happened, but to something which was bothering her." Parents echo these expressions, as the mother who remarked: "Johnny doesn't know me at all, he has a picture in his head and talks about a woman who isn't me."

Different people have differing needs for communication; although sexual stereotypes picture men as not talking, there are notable individual differences. Group differences tend to be related to issues of class as well as personality. Interviewees from culturally deprived surroundings in depressed areas, agreed almost totally in terms of communication problems between sons and fathers. One son related: "My father returns from work, takes the evening paper and waits for his meal. He is silent the whole time as if he weren't yet home. He finishes eating, takes the paper to the easy chair in front of the television. Watches until he falls asleep. That's how it is . . ." The father, in a parallel interview, painted a similar picture: "I get up in the morning and am at work in the carpentry shop early. I finish at five, come home, I've finished my part—I have provided the income. Now I want quiet. They don't understand that I need quiet . . ."

Facilitators of peer groups with parallel groups for fathers have found the response to their expressed desire to increase communication in order to help prevent relational tension to be: "Talking creates even more tension."

Experience has taught that clarification of alternatives for fulfilling individual needs within a particular family system can only arise from a systematic process of coping with the significance of mutual expectations of communication. There are no shortcuts or miracle cures. Only gradually do adolescents and parents learn about alternative meaningful communication within the family.

The first step is to realize how a message is structured. Every message is composed of different parts and therefore can be shaped by means of conscious structuring.

Therefore, it is important for a communicator to ask "what is the purpose of the message", and further, "what do I want the listeners (i.e., one's mother or father) to understand?" To that end, the communicator must be aware of his feeling-perceptions of his parent(s), must be able to identify basic traits of the listener's personality, values and social perspective, as well as the balance of power and authority on which the family is based, and must be able to predict what the feeling-reaction might be to new ideas. Thus, the question of "message" takes on various other implications for the communicator including, what it is that he/she desires to send, what it is that he/she thinks will be understood and perceived, and what it is that he/she thinks will actually be received.

Another important part of a message is the actual *pattern* of message transmission. Identical words may be conveyed in different ways and thereby take on different meanings. One can burst out with a message upon entering the room (or at the table) or wait until a time that seems more appropriate. It is possible to declare that the parents' behavior was hurtful and demand why they did it, or it is possible to introduce the topic by asking them for their feelings about a matter which seems to be a source of conflict. One can attack immediately or hold back, ask calmly for their statement of intention, or interpret the facts according to one's own viewpoint. Parents can be approached separately or addressed together, encouraging them to unite as allies under attack. Alternative reactions raised by adolescents in the peer groups were varied, sometimes more useful and more responsible than those suggested by group leaders. It was clear that each individual had to discover the alternative communication patterns appropriate for each of them.

Rather than teaching particular communication patterns, it seems that it would be more useful to teach developing an approach of finding alternatives, a type of meta-learning of social skills. In our approach the peer group learning experiences repeatedly practice seeking communication alternatives appropriate to particular needs and situations, to the significant others involved and to the social conflict embodied in the incident.

The third element of a message is called the "echo component." With each message there is an expectation of a reaction, and once the message is conveyed, a verbal, nonverbal or meta-reaction is received (movement, silence, distancing, etc.), all of which may be more or less the same, i.e., "echo one another." It is impossible to send messages without prior, simultaneous and subsequent reception and consideration of the nature of this echo. Each person involved reacts differently to a particular message. Each also reacts differently to different transmission patterns. Echo variations could stem from different personal traits, from variations in values and attitudes, from the unique emotional quality of a given situation and also from the level of ambiguity of the message received. Different facilitators or teachers conducting identical learning experiences in different groups receive different echoes, different interpretations of the message, and/or differential treatment of the message content and pattern.

Interpersonal communication problems seem to be particularly related to various inhibitions of the message sender as well as those of the receiver. Discussions cite past influences, overt or obscure, of what is considered to be a similar experience which produced unfavorable results. Other aspects brought up include customary distortions, the possibility of impinging on family myths, anxieties about disturbing the balance of family relationships, and particularly the fear of harming the self-image of the message sender or receiver. Lewin (1951) discusses methods of intervening in message patterns in order to try changing values and behaviors. He refers to these methods as strategies for breaking down communication blocks.

All family communication is based on an assumption of mutual dependence. Whether the source of the communication, i.e., the sender of the first message in a particular interaction, is the adolescent or the parent, there is an assumption based on mutual perceptions of each other and on inner needs (conscious or unconscious) to react to one another and acquire something in exchange. An adolescent sends a particular message with prior assumptions about the response he will receive. Therefore, he formulates his message in accordance with his expectations. That is to say, if the adolescent expects a reaction of anxiety, he might well couch the message in such a way as to reduce the emphasis on any element of danger. If he expects a reaction of indifference or evasion, he may choose words which carry more serious or alarming implications and connotations in order to evoke the parent's sense of responsibility. Parents or teachers who accompany their words with nonverbal messages of cynicism will often elicit a similar echo-reaction. They need to realize that the immediate or long range reaction to cultivating cynicism in communication between them and their children is offending the adolescent and undermining the credibility of their mutual communication.

In fact adolescents themselves are often in the position of being accused of cynical communication patterns. In support group discussions or inservice training sessions, parents, teachers, counselors and friends often complain how offensive this is and ask how to respond. In most instances such behavior is an expression of the adolescent's lack of confidence and part of his playing different roles in interpersonal relations in order to get feedback. In a considerable portion of cases adolescents are themselves unaware of the cynical aspect of their behavior, and it may be nipped by simply saying calmly: "I don't understand why you are talking with me in that way; I find it offensive and unbecoming of you . . . and I do not wish to build that kind of tie with you . . ."

One of the most important aspects of communication between adolescents and others—adults as well as peers—is the quality of *authenticity*. A young person's lack of confidence regarding his place in society, a lack of clear self-support arising naturally from his immaturity, his search for self-identity and concomitant need for security in interpersonal ties, all stress the importance of authenticity: first and foremost, that of his parents, next, that of his friends and peers, but also that of his teachers, guidance counselors, youth movement counselors, etc.

Communication with significant others provides the adolescent a means of testing his perception of those others. The process of identity shaping requires the adolescent to free himself from his early image of the parent as an initial identity object. The adolescent's search for signs confirming his perceptions of his parents is characterized by inner anxiety natural to the separation process and a simultaneous questioning of who he is. For example, he may wonder if his mother is really as altruistic as she represents herself and if she really lives just for his sake, as she claims? Does his father really care about him; does he "truly" love him? Are his ties with friends "real?" For the adolescent the statement "only if I know who my mother really is and who my father really is will I be able to begin to answer: Who am I and what do I want to be" has crucial significance. The repetition of such distrustful testing on the part of many adolescents often raises the hackles of their parents, teachers or counselors, and friends. However, this pattern of communication is usually more an expression of an unsettled self needing positive confirmation than any real lack of trust toward others.

Psychologists and experts in communication problems note the need to distinguish between pseudo-communication and mutual communication. In pseudo-communication there is little connection between the message sent and the feedback. A sort of dialogue of "the deaf" develops between the participants, each of whom transmits his message without taking into account what has been already transmitted or reacting. Dina described the following sequence of events to the guidance counselor: "I came home from school and told my mother about what you told me to talk about with her. She said: 'Fine, the food's already getting cold, sit down and eat . . .' I sat down, began to eat, and began again to tell her, and she responded: 'And this morning you didn't straighten up your room again, and I had to straighten·it up . . .' So we ended up discussing straightening up my room and not about what you told me to negotiate with her." Upon inviting the mother for a talk and raising this issue the mother confirmed the existence of pseudo-communication in the relationship structure. She noted how she would talk about one thing and instead of feedback she would receive parallel messages. The counselor brought up the subject for discussion in the peer group and participants presented additional examples of apparently similar situations. Role play was invoked to help learn how to cope with the problems of pseudo-communication.

Another factor which can lead to communication problems is the incorrect reading or discernment of signs. Such misunderstandings usually can be seen against a background of accumulated emotions and expectations arising from previous adolescent-parent experiences. Sometimes this can be traced to a particularly remarkable incident which has left a deep impression on the adolescent's or parent's feelings and memory. Difficulties in reading communications, especially making incorrect distinctions and/or assumptions, occurs in all areas of interpersonal communication. Peer group learning experiences can be useful by creating greater awareness of the need to consider the possibility of incorrect interpretation of a message or situation. In adolescent-parent relations, for example, a common problem is the inability to differentiate between a mother's concern and her desire to dominate, often considered an unwillingness to grant autonomy. In such cases it is important to prevent the young people from speaking in sweeping generalizations which adolescents, especially the intellectuals among them, tend to use as a defense, and concentrate rather on defining and examination of experience.

Adolescents, like adults, build a "myth" or story about the mother or father, consciously or unconsciously. Conscious awareness of this myth can rise following a particular incident or as the result of going for psychotherapy. Examples of such family myths are: "My father never really loved me . . ." "What is important for my mother is only that I be like she wants . . ." "My brother always tried to prove to me and my parents that I was worthless . . ." Any new communication in the family is combined with this fiction, as a confirmation and reinforcement. In many of the adolescent-parent conflicts the adolescent and the parent relate the same facts about the communication. But each of them interpreted these facts differently, relying on the myth he held about the other person, about his personality, feelings, reactions, etc. The reality of these myths is so strong that experts claim that it cannot be countered by arguing that it had never happened.

Since the adolescent holds his family myths as facts, there can be no alternative but to help him understand these myths on the same level as sexual, occupational, racial stereotypes; family myths are in many respects simply personal stereotypes. Even if there might be a grain of truth to the myth, it is insufficient to support generalizations which make up the body of the myth. The true issues are, therefore, from what did the story devolve, what purpose does it serve for him, and how does it intervene in any particular communication. It is important to realize that continuing such myths not only hurt the parents, but also the adolescent; he remains bound by the myth, which governs how he interprets every message transmitted in the family network.

Such myths not only are about parents, but exist about the children as well at every age. It is often difficult for a parent to free himself from the myth he has created, and which serves him as the basis for hypotheses regarding many situations and behavior patterns. When the parents hold a myth that their son is incapable or not studying, they are liable to continue annoying him about his studies despite academic progress and refuse to believe in his ability to advance intellectually. Even when faced with "facts" the father may try to prove that the child has problems in his studies. Such myths may be connected to deeper, internalized experiences of the parents in their own lives as adolescents. It may even express the parent's continuing struggle with his own individuation process.

The topics of misreading communication and personal myths about others lead into an important overall assumption. It may happen that parents, teachers or students may apply a label to someone. Accordingly, we or our partner in interpersonal interaction, become defensive. We retreat; we make decisions about communication patterns; and crucial activities result. For example, I decide that he—my son, my student, my friend/acquaintance is unreliable, I can't believe him, he won't listen/believe me, then I must do something dramatic to prove it to him, make him sit up and take notice, etc.

Until now direct communication has been the topic of discussion. However, we must take into account meta-communications: transmissions expressing an overall perception, based on accumulated, internalized feelings and intended to represent an overview of a situation. Meta-communication includes various components. One common component is a repetitive message about authority: "How can you talk that way to your father"; "You always think about yourself"; "You know you destroy your mother when you argue with her." Another refers to jockeying relations between siblings or other family members:

"Father always thinks that Jack is right"; "They let Jonah do what they didn't let me to do"; "Mother doesn't say anything about it to Debbie," etc. Communication patterns themselves may be part of meta-communication: "You never listen," "You always inflate one incident and make out as if I was always like that."

There are several points which are shared by these and other examples in this category. First, there is continual struggle for recognition of status and authority which is only vaguely connected to the specific subject of communication at hand. Second, the family relationships seem to be disturbed, and this communication can be seen as an attempt to create a certain balance—by identifying with one parent rather than the other or by a direct attack on the parent with whom there is a conflict about something else. Sometimes a message is thrown out—an indirect communication about the current exchange, which is meant as a sort of flanking movement to help cope with a particular issue. One parent, a reserve artillery officer, stated: "Sometimes when I hear my son marshalling complaints about my personality and my behavior in the course of a discussion about preparing his homework, or when I forgot to run a certain errand he had imposed on me, I feel this is like firing off cannon up front for the sake of softening things up, which is meant to make me lower my profile, or retreat from my attempt to attack a particular position of his."

Some parents and adolescents are afraid of mutual, intimate communication. Apparently this phenomenon is common for insecure fathers fearing personal disclosure, the blurring of boundaries, upsetting family-task definitions and the threat of a loss of status within the family or regarding the adolescent. On the other hand some parents simply lack social skills required for mutual communication; they know only how to explain and give orders.

For adolescents, however, such a phenomenon appears when separation-individuation does not progress as it should. An adolescent may have nice, loving parents, who give him what he requests, but do not provide him with opportunities for conflict and thus for confirmation of what is different between him and them. It is as though he were a part of them rather than an independent individual navigating his way to personal responsibility. Some of these adolescents and parents limit themselves to short communications necessary for everyday needs. In such cases the adolescent shapes his personal identity outside the family system, in peer groups, with a boyfriend or girlfriend, in a youth organization, in social activity at school, with the support of a teacher or counselor, etc. Others spend long hours at home and communicate at length with their parents; however, their communications do not center around what is happening at home, but around what is happening in the outside world. The stream of political or pseudo-scientific intellectualization covers up the lack of other communication.

In such instances, it may be necessary to sharpen the problem of dependence in order to advance the individuation process, helping the young person to define the uniqueness of his behavior in contrast to that of his parents. The exacerbation of cognitive dissonance and the emotional crisis may frequently contribute to a more acute social crisis in the family. The assumption is that a sharp separation and emotional and cognitive support during the process will assure the adolescent's preparedness for an accelerated individuation process.

The approach may be summarized by these points:

- There are levels in the development of interpersonal communication just as there are levels in the development of cognition and social perspective. Berlo (1960) described four levels; the lowest level includes the sending of unidirectional messages, and the highest is that which strives toward mutuality and takes the significant other's needs and messages into consideration concomitantly with the needs of the sender.

- **There is no such thing as non-communication** (Watzlawick et al. 1967). Therefore, a person can and should learn to develop communication patterns appropriate to him, to the significant other, and to the various situations. Silence is communication just like speech, and every body movement communicates to the other person, including the avoidance of encounter by leaving. Every person must learn to communicate positively on a high level, first and foremost in his family.

- Communication between adolescents and their parents is loaded with experiences and expectations: internalized images of the past; family myths, created as an expression of unfulfilled needs; the struggle over separation and receiving recognition, and the progress toward personal identity and accepting responsibility, power and authority. Meta-communications appear behind and/ or parallel to the many messages of the participants, reflecting the complexity and intricacy, consciously or unconsciously, of the interpersonal familial relationships.

- In order to clarify problems appearing in particular conflicts which arise in each stage of development and to gradually advance transfer of responsibility-authority and power from parents to adolescent, adolescents and parents need mutual communication and appropriate support. They need to understand the processes emerging in their intercommunication and to develop willingness and social skills required to hold a dialogue and enter into negotiations.

- Some of the problems in communications are universal to difficulties between adolescents and parents; in addition there are also unique problems specific to age, sex and social status. In a traditional society they were dealt with by definitions and rules which ensured observance of the tenets of religious law and of social norms of behavior in the tribe or community. In modern society, undergoing an accelerated process of social change which includes displacement of norms and deteriorating family stability, the necessary support for maintaining positive communication in terms of the adolescent's development and preservation of the parents' values must come from individual and social systems.
- Communication and negotiation processes between adolescents and parents should develop throughout the duration of extended adolescence—from the beginning of the period until completion of the transition to early adulthood, towards the end of the young person's twenties. This process should include individuation culminating in achieving the ability to bear personal responsibility and shaping a pattern of independent living out of a sense of power and authority.

The adolescent expects three things of his parents during this process:

recognition,
equality of human worth and
receiving power and authority.

Traditional societies acknowledged the importance of social "recognition" of the transition from childhood to maturity. Tribal, ethnic and religious rites of passage were intended to express symbolic recognition of maturation. In Judaism the Bar Mitzva celebration became customary, in which the boy is called up to the Torah to read from the weekly Biblical portion as one of the adults, in the presence of extended family and community. The purpose is to affirm for the adolescent, his family and community that the child has passed a milestone of individuation. He has attained initial recognition that he is not a child, and that the responsibility demanded of a Jew has been transferred to him. Therefore, at least symbolically, his equal value as a human being and Jew has been recognized. He may come to the congregation and be counted in the quorum, since he knows how to read from the Torah, has received the ethical heritage and learned the prayers. Therefore, the assumption is that he understands his responsibility, and is prepared to pay the penalty for his sins. His father proudly declares: "Blessed be He who has relieved me of the responsibility for this child."

In various Christian denominations, the recognition and symbolic transfer of responsibility are expressed through the confirmation ceremony, which bestows recognition and affirmation of readiness for responsibility and receiving personal membership in the church.

But the traditional perception of the problem was formulated in the context of cultures dependant on agriculture or animal husbandry or farming the sea—cultures in which the transition from childhood to adulthood was direct. This view existed for thousands of years in societies, where status norms regarding division of roles, power and authority were clearly defined for each social stratum. We, however, live in a period of rapid modernization, in a complex, intricate, fast-changing society which recognizes a multiplicity of values, a blurring of norms and individual permissiveness. It expects every individual to consciously develop his ability to shape his own identity and build an independent pattern of living.

We must guide parents and adolescents toward conducting mutual communications regarding recognition of adolescents' responsibility, in accordance with principles such as those elaborated below.

Principles of negotiation

First Principle—Recognition

The child's normal development in child-parent relationships, from infancy to adulthood, depends on his receiving recognition from the mother and father. This implies that he feels they:
- are with him and by his side, whenever he needs them
- love him, even when they do not identify with his behavior
- believe in his ability to develop and to be responsible for achieving the biological and psycho-social tasks of each developmental stage
- support him emotionally and practically in his individuation process, and gradually transfer power and authority to him for the purpose of forming his identity and building his life pattern.

In the absence of appropriate parental recognition, adjusted to the child's readiness at each developmental stage, the separation process is impaired, delayed or distorted, and difficulties develop in the adolescent's individuation process.

The following examples illustrate the adolescent's perception in behavioral terms and how a change toward a positive approach to expressing recognition would be reflected:

"Usually, when I go shopping with my mother she starts rejecting each of my choices in words which say that I don't have any taste, that I am just looking for noisy colors and forms, and other negative expressions that anger me terribly. Last week I was pleasantly surprised. Instead of rejecting and criticizing me, she was open to listening to me, asked that I explain why I appreciate the color or the cloth we had seen. I suddenly saw that she accepts my right to personal taste, and recognizes that I have reasons to see things differently from her."

"We sat with my father in front of the TV and watched a movie. When the movie was over, I told my father how strong an expression the director had given the child's role, and how weak and unreal the other character was by contrast. My father listened and said: 'You know, Jack, you have a very adult perception of the complex situation they tried to present. I'm not sure whether many adults would be prepared to understand like you did what occurred here . . .' You know, I simply didn't know how to tell him how important it was for me, that he talks to me recognizing that I understand, too."

"So you're asking how the relations between my mother and I have changed in the past year. I think it's because she acknowledged that I also have opinions. She understood that if she wanted me to listen, she needed to explain the reasons for her thoughts to me, and then I also began to think and explain my views to her. I think she agreed that I wasn't a little girl anymore and that I am able to think and feel, just as she is able to think and feel."

"What angered me so terribly about my father is that he was always disappointed by what I did. I was never good enough for him. He's so perfect and everything about him is just right, and I'm always not OK. I want him to know that he's also not 100% and to agree that I'm not like a zero, and then I'll be able to want to be better."

Although some may be prepared to recognize others in interpersonal relations, they may not be ready to participate in the next principle: assuming the equal human worth of the other person.

Second Principle—"Equal Worth"

An adolescent needs recognition of his uniqueness, understanding of his needs and developmental problems, and acceptance as he is. When the parent acknowledges these points a positive connection can develop between them. At that point, even if the adolescent's behavior is unacceptable, it is possible to talk among themselves and to engage in negotiations as do people who accept the principle of each other's equal human worth.

The following examples illustrate both situations where parents are unwilling to accept the principle of equal worth and those where parents actively accept such a principle.

"What angers me about my father is that he talks to me as though from above. I say something and then he immediately rejects it and says that I don't understand; and immediately begins to explain and explain as though he were a grade school teacher."

"For my mother I will definitely always remain her little girl. She always tries to prove that her taste is better, and to poke fun at things that I've chosen."

"The most important thing that happened last month between my father and I is that he acknowledged he was mistaken and I was right, and asked forgiveness for hurting me. It's a long story, but what's important is that he said: 'Marty, you were right, you really saw it more correctly than I did . . .' It's hard for you to see how good I felt and how much I thanked him . . . That's not correct that I was looking for a compliment. What was important to me was that he viewed me as an adult, not as a child."

"You ask what I like to do with my father? All sorts of things when we are together: an excursion, going to the soccer field and watching TV together. And especially when he asks: 'Davey, what do you think? How did you like it?'"

Recognition and positive communication are insufficient to ensure the adolescent's capacity for coping maturely in psycho-social terms. He also needs to gradually experience responsibility, which implies readiness to ask for and get power and authority. Parents must be the source for adolescents to learn how to fulfill their role responsibility.

Third Principle—Negotiating transfer of responsibility— Power and Authority

A basic component of psycho-social maturation is the ability to cope with problems of power and authority. A parent's feeling of legitimacy and obligation to use power and authority over children originates in the extended period of biological, psychological and social dependency of man. In modern society this period is extended even further due to the complex, intricate social system, to the fact that the economy has practically no need for child labor and to the fact that more parents are able to continue supporting the adolescent as long as necessary. Thus, a larger percentage of the population remains in the educational system, continuing to be economically dependent and deferring entry into the outside world.

The young child stands before his omnipotent mother/father, whom he perceives as possessing all power and authority. Later, as he grows, he perceives the existence of intrafamilial struggles involving problems of power and authority—the issue of woman's status vis-a-vis that of her husband in a patriarchal family, the status of a firstborn sibling in a traditional family, sibling relations, parents' attitude toward their children and the parents' attitude toward their own parents. Concomitantly, the child must cope with the teacher's power and authority at school as well as with that of the school principal and other powerful adults. He must cope with children, like his friends and peers, in other classes and with children or adults in the neighborhood. International and inter-ethnic struggles reflect the same dynamics as struggles over power and authority in relations with neighbors and problems arising with children in other community institutions.

The problem of perceptions: perceptions of needs and conflicts, the sense of power and readiness for action is common to all these states of struggle. It is very important for people in general and adolescents in particular to learn to cope with positions of power and authority. They need to undergo an experiential process of confrontation and verification in order to be able to fulfill sex roles appropriate to their developmental stage and to their identity definition in various social constellations.

The struggle over power and authority expresses the problematic nature of adolescent-parent relations in modern society in which a general disruption of traditional controls has occurred. These problems stem from the social changes discussed in the chapter on implications of modernization, especially as concerns the undermining of the various authority figures: parents, teachers, religious leaders, political leaders, etc. This undermining has various sources which are in part based on the factual development of science and technology in which new often replaces or overthrows old, social organization, urbanization, standardized education and its increased scope, increased level of education and changes in patterns of interpersonal interaction. They are also in part a result of changes which have occurred in the perception of human rights, for individuals and groups. Illustrating the first instance is the fact that many young people know more than their parents about various areas of scientific and technological development, and changes in social organization affect interpersonal experiences, such as sexual relations, relations with members of other races and nations, etc. Traditional bastions of authority are being challenged or questioned: adult authority over the young, men vs. women, ruling nations vs. developing nations, ethnic groups or weak classes vs. rulers, etc.

Power should not be equated with authority. Thus, for example, an individual or nation can be accepted as having power while at the same time individuals may deny their authority. On the other hand, a person's authority may be accepted by virtue of a particular traditional view, but, in fact, he has no actual power.

Adolescent-parent relations are augmented by emotions and perceptions which have been internalized and shaped over a period spanning the birth and the lives of all those involved. In 1978 a committee of the American Association for the Advancement of Psychiatry formulated four assumptions regarding the struggle for power and authority in adolescence:

- The intergenerational struggle for power and authority, generally accompanied by conflict, is basic and essential for transition from adolescence to adulthood. This struggle is a normal phenomenon, and should be viewed as an essential characteristic of adolescent development.
- This conflict originates in man's nature as well as in his biological, social-psychological and cultural dimensions. All those involved in the conflict, parents and adolescents, contribute their part to the conflict, according to their function in social role-play, their personal development and their relations with other family members.
- In most cases this struggle takes place in a covert, imaginary or symbolic form, but in other cases overt expressions, sometimes dramatic and even violent, may also occur.
- Although the results of this conflict are many, varied and complex, and are expressed differently at different times and places, one way or the other both generations must adjust to the situation.

Principle Four: Responsible, non-permissive parents

Most adolescents want parental involvement and support and most talk about parental sincerity and authenticity. Girls claim that they do not want a mother who acts like an adolescent or tries to be a friend instead of fulfilling a maternal role. Girls and boys claim that they want a father who talks with them and not at them. Most adolescents want their parents' support vis-a-vis outside parties, and most acknowledge the parent as responsible for maintaining norms and setting behavioral limits. Adolescents do not see that responsibility as requiring them to forego their basic rights to recognition, mutual communication, autonomy and personal responsibility. The experience of the sixties and seventies in the U.S., Europe and Israel has shown conclusively that permissive parenting has failed. Information from various sources has described both adolescents and adults who have come to grief due to permissiveness, which resulted in unwanted pregnancies, abortions endangering future ability to bear children, dissolution of families, drug and alcohol abuse, mental and social deterioration and loss of personal hope leading to crime, suicide and other pathological conditions.

It seems possible to state categorically that parents are responsible for their children's behavior and for nurturing responsibility; furthermore, it is clear that adults are responsible to see that adolescents learn how to accept personal responsibility. Communication exercises in peer groups should focus on the many questions arising from an examination of the significance of this responsibility. It appears that the desirable, positive responsibility of parents may be defined thus:

- Children and adolescents need limits, i.e., defined norms of expectation and behavior. In traditional society norms were defined by religious law and preserved by tribal, communal, class and family traditions. In modern society every couple faces the responsibility of defining acceptable norms for his own home and family in all the areas which should constitute a broader socio-cultural basis for human relations; certain practices and norms of expectations obligate only family members and emphasize their separateness from society as a whole.
- In democratic families adolescents can be partners in the shaping of these norms, jointly sharing responsibility with their parents for assessing the process of their adaptation. A surprising number of adolescents indicated that there were no agreed norms of mutual expectations regarding a schedule, a shared meal, patterns of relating, standards of appropriate dress for holidays, manner of eating, etc. It must be asked if these are not expressions of a lack of responsibility toward children and adolescents who need to fashion a personal identity and who are supposed to shape normative patterns in their own families in the future. It is important to recall that just as adolescents demand autonomy, they also need limits.
- Clarifying needs and intentions, defining limits, elucidating the reasons for the existence of limits and flexible implementation as the result of considering the adolescent's needs and the recogni-

tion of outside pressures on him is necessary even in families where traditional norms prevail and are enforced. Interpersonal interaction should proceed symmetrically instead of one side simply giving orders and instructions according to their perception of their authority and power or according to transient moods.

- The process of parents sharing different areas of their lives with their adolescent children enables the children to feel involved and understand their parents' behavior from a broader perspective. A common complaint of adolescents from various neighborhoods is that they are unfamiliar with the family's economic situation, the father's work problems, or other problems concerning the family. They do not feel involved, but left out. Particularly if a family crisis should develop, adolescents are not babies—they are capable of learning to bear responsibility and contribute to the welfare of the family. Adolescents who are surprised with news of family failures through reading about it in the newspaper, hearing it from relatives, classmates, neighbors or friends understand clearly the lack of confidence and trust in their capability of participating in family crises. There are two issues of the adolescent's socialization and adolescent-parent relations at stake here: the issue of feeling trust and confidence in the parent, and issue of the adolescent feeling that he is considered trustworthy and reliable in the parents' eyes, in other words the development of his positive self-image.

Principle Five: The Responsible Adolescent

The most important factor in bringing up adolescents who are able to cope with responsibility for their own actions is the transfer of responsibility for self-development and coping to the adolescent himself. Expressing the belief that the young person is capable of being responsible, actively transferring responsibility in certain areas, supporting him as he widens the scope of his responsibility, defining appropriate awards and results devolving on successful achievement are all part of educating a responsible person. Some criteria for a positive process of transferring responsibility are:

- Mutual agreement on defined or agreed division of roles; this mutual agreement includes parent-parent alignment as well as adolescent-parents alignments. Such agreement must begin the moment the child shows the least capability of being able to accept responsibility in specific areas.

- Mutual respect with regard to maturity and capability of living up to tasks involving human responsibility. The adolescents must respect their parents and the parents must respect the potential of their children. Any feeling, from either quarter, of impingement of one's human privacy— responsibility, should result in asking for a mutual discussion of feelings, including the expression of a lack of appreciation or recognition of their fulfillment of responsibilities.

- Determining responsibility means setting norms and limits about expectations, demands, expression of feelings, what could be considered unjustified invasion into the other's areas of privacy-responsibility, etc. Included in this discussion should be cases of infringement of one party on these norms, with the aim of discovering ways to enable airing of the reasons for infringement and suggestions of alternatives for improving the situation so that both sides can reach further mutual understanding. Such determination and discussion can include consideration for basic age differences and variation of responsibility and authority prescribed for family members according to age, sex, state of health and responsibility toward parties outside the home.

- Responsibility for implementation of tasks should be levied both in the home and away from home. He should plan when they will be done according to his own daily or weekly schedule. This should relieve him of the feeling being harassed endlessly and that his parents understand his need to have personal planning and privacy. "Run . . ., give . . ., take . . ., bring . . ., why didn't you arrange . . ., you don't care about me, you don't help," etc. do not take into account his own private needs. However, just as the parent is required to be flexible, to advise and help not only when convenient for him but in accordance with other family members' expectations of him, it is also necessary to clearly request that the adolescent act flexibly and with understanding and that he endeavor to adjust to difficulties when necessary. Autonomy is particularly crucial in terms of territory, the private time and the choice of a method of implementation of responsibility.

- The right to seclude himself and be alone. The adolescent needs peace of mind, solitude and to be by himself, and expects others will not bother him at this time. An adolescent spends the major part of his day in school where someone else determines what he will be doing, when he will be doing it, the rules of discipline, study and activity, and obligates him to account for himself formally from early in the morning until late afternoon. Added to this are assignments of homework and test preparation which are often levied by the various teachers involved without consideration of what their colleagues are requiring. In addition, group activities—youth movements, peer groups, formal extra-curricular groups—have almost no time limit in terms of their demands for the young person's time. Individual peers and friends have their own personal needs and they phone or demand their share in various ways. Therefore, the adolescent's home must become a sort of fortress in which mutual responsibility obligates him to contribute to others, but also guarantees him privacy and a protective retreat. To an adolescent free time is the setting in which he may analyze what has been, is and will be in in terms of others' lives and in his own, in reality and in imagination.

Sharing responsibility also necessitates separateness. Children get on their parents' nerves; the routine of housework can make people frustrated, bored and depressed, and even desire to escape. Just as the norm of regular vacation became established in reaction to tensions arising from difficulties in the work situation, so the need for repeated separation from the presence of others, even though they are vital and beloved is a type of vacation from normal tensions. It is essential that periods on the weekends or during vacations and holidays be set aside as times in which adolescents may leave the house—to be with a friend, a relative, at camp or in another framework, to take over exclusive responsibility for some particular activity, to be with someone else or to enjoy solitude.

Contributing or Intervening Variables

In order to stimulate thought about and create learning experiences appropriate for training facilitators it is necessary to identify variables which promote or impede a favorable separation and individuation process. Given the evidence gathered in interviews, inservice training sessions for guidance counselors and psychologists, and clinical and research evidence from the U.S. and England, the following premises can be proposed. Quotations from the interviews will illustrate the discussion of each variable.

Variable 1: National, ethnic and community cultural patterns

In traditional Jewish culture intellectually talented boys were recommended by their local teachers for further study upon entering adolescence at a famous, higher yeshiva in a distant city or in the private school of a particular rabbi. The adolescents lived in a boarding institution or in the homes of wealthy members of the community, eating on different days in different homes of well-to-do local Jews. Providing room and board for such students was considered high service to the community. In the early twentieth century girls of 10 or 11 years were also sent from smaller villages, especially in Poland, to live with relatives in the city in order to study in high school.

Studying away from home at a boarding school was customary also in English society, especially in highly selective private institutions which could hold classes for students as young as age 11. Similar arrangements exist in other societies as well. Neither the adolescents nor their parents felt abandoned or deprived; all believed these choices were ultimately for the good of the young person and his parents.

This is not the forum to discuss the advantages, shortcomings or problems of residential education. Many studies, surveys and even an international workshop have been devoted to this topic; for those who are interested the proceedings of the workshop have been published recently (Kashti & Arieli, 1987).

It is important to keep in mind that in these social environments there is no social stigma in the child's being separated from the parental home; neither children nor parents consider being sent to residential educational institutions as implying neglect or as causing psychological injury. In certain instances, such as when gifted students from culturally deprived backgrounds are sent to residential schools (Smilansky & Nevo, 1979), leaving home bestows prestige. About 20% of the hundreds of parents interviewed for the present study spent some part of their adolescence outside the family —in residential institutions or on kibbutzim—and most describe this experience positively, even if they had encountered difficulties. Reasons for leaving home included ideological stands—their own in contrast or in common with that of their parents, family difficulties which included inter-relational crises and/or financial difficulties, learning problems at a previous school, etc. Many considered leaving home as an opportunity to reorganize and readjust to integration in Israeli society. Various follow-up studies (Smilansky & Nevo, 1979; Marbach, 1980; Zorman, 1989), indicated that in a considerable portion of cases leaving home during adolescence seemed to be a prominent and positive factor in accelerating the individuation process; however, in other cases it created problems and exacerbated adjustment difficulties. There is no doubt that it is important to understand this phenomenon in our efforts to promote a positive separation and individuation process.

Variable 2: The Nature of the Parental Bond

Descriptions of the relationship between the father and mother recur continually in parental testimony of their own adolescence and in that of adolescents regarding their own parents. There appear to be five main phenomena involved in the interview material:

1. Repeated quarreling between parents such that it undermines the adolescent's confidence in the continuing future existence of the family entity, impairs the image of father or mother or both and makes it difficult to identify with them. The parents demand the adolescent identity with one of them and may even get them to act against the other parent; coalitions are established between the adolescent and one parent which may contribute to the adolescent leaving home before he is ready.

2. A severe imbalance of power and authority between the parents; the feeling of a domineering mother turning the father in a doormat or a dominant father imposing his will on everyone around, ignoring the mother's humanity and taking her functioning for granted; the phenomenon of one very active parent contrasted with one very passive parent, etc. Such an imbalance produces negative perceptions of the parents, and negative feelings toward and relations with him or her develop. This also leads to a desire to escape from the parental home as early as possible, influences mate selection and affects the nature of future parenting.

3. Lack of loving relations and authentic involvement between parents. Although there may be no quarrels, no blows and no cursing, relations are characterized by coldness, remoteness and depression. Expression of this state of affairs differs according to the people involved and from family to family. Remoteness from the home and family resulting from involvement in work or activity in volunteer/social organizations may provide an escape for either or both parents. The mother, neglected by her husband, may then try to be her daughter's or even her son's girlfriend; and in some cases the mother may have a male friend, with whom her relationship is likely to be quite platonic, and the father and adolescents accept his existence and position as a fact. As different as these phenomenon are, they have a marked negative impact on the adolescent's individuation process, of which he may be quite aware and capable of defining.

4. Traditional, delineated and active division of roles within the family. In some families the father is the breadwinner, holds power and displays authority toward his wife and children; and the mother is a housewife and/or works outside the home while providing all

traditional services and taking care of everything and everyone. In general acceptance and mutual understanding, a warm social climate and few signs of unwillingness characterized such families. However, it seemed that this pattern has negative as well as positive effects. Sometimes such a situation is characterized by the mother's repressed anger, quiet or sometimes conspicuous attempts to incite her adolescent children to rebellion, and even mutual threats at moments of crisis. Such a social climate is particularly negative for the girls' individuation process.

5. The lack of agreement on role division producing activity of one or the other parent characterized by a feeling, with which everyone has come to terms, of chance, fortuitousness, or even a sort of anarchy. This phenomenon seems to appear primarily in the wealthy classes and is also usually accompanied by permissiveness in the education and control of children's behavior. The difficulties caused by such rearing in terms of shaping identity and in developing adolescent coping ability has been discussed above.

Variable 3: Activities of youth movements or of some other unifying social-ideological body

Many parents of adolescents included in the study were members in an ideologically-based youth movement during their own adolescence; others participated in vacation and/or leisure time activities and received school help within the framework of public organizations, of municipalities or of individual schools. The question arises as to the role of these social frameworks in the separation and individuation processes as well. Many interviews indicated that youth movements served as a positive, basic, central motivational force in the individuation process of a considerable portion of each age cohort. The youth movement offered the adolescent a central ideology with which he could identify; the youth community possessed a set of values and behavior patterns in interpersonal relations; counselors served as active identification models for whoever did not wish or was unable to identify with his parents, or, for that matter, for whomever alternative models were needed to counterbalance the parents' influence; the organization provided a relatively stable peer group in which one could find friendship and cope with development of social perspective and social skills without pressure; furthermore, it was a voluntary framework essentially without admission preconditions, from which one could resign at any time one wished. This framework functioned as the source of a sense of physical and social security for the young people participating. This factor was shared by participants in all the organizations, which may have been vastly different in terms of political values, organization, patterns of activity and efficiency, and overcame those differences. For the most part youth movements also bestowed a feeling of security to the parents. Parents felt that despite the voluntary, half open structure, it was a social framework in which their children would not stray into the margins of society, in which they would make connections of companionship and friendship, in which the prevalent norms would protect them against sexual deviation, drugs and alcohol, and in which there a certain degree of social supervision would prevail, despite the fact that the coordinators and counselors were not professionals.

Today we face the fact that there has been a decline in the scope of youth movement activities. Furthermore, the educational system is charged with ensuring the developing of a similar youth community promoting the social development of each adolescent. How may this be accomplished?

Components may be learned and copied from existing, still successful youth movements; to what degree can institutions like community centers be involved? and what role can social organizations in various high schools play? A properly constituted task force should be formed within framework of the highest policy-making body to deal with these questions with the purpose of defining desirable patterns for the educational system of the future.

Variable 4: The nature of desirable relations between adolescent and parents

A combination of adolescents' perception of their parents and the examination of the adolescent-parent conflicts may be generalized by several assumptions about the array of desirable relations.

Adolescents need votes of confidence. They want to hear, not assume that the father really does love them, believe them, recognize their worth and ability; they need concrete evidence that he is involved in their feelings and needs, does not distance himself because of negative feelings toward the adolescent and does not look down his nose at them, does not push them and test their ability in order to show them up; does not compete with them or set a trap for them to catch them making mistakes. They expect support from their fathers, as necessary, in time of need.

Adolescents need autonomy and recognition. They do not wish to be treated like children, to be followed after, to be checked up on; they do not expect that parents will invade areas considered private; they expect to be able to have experiences appropriate to their development and needs, and at the same time they expect that their anxiety or their ambivalence will not be exploited in order to prove their unworthiness to have freedom in experiencing companionship and friendship; and finally, they need to know that parents are prepared to listen to them and tender advice predicated on mutual communication. Recognition from parents includes their need to be separate, to be encouraged appropriately according to their readiness and needs rather than according to the parents' perceptions and recollections of what used to be or according to their viewpoint of what ought to be.

Adolescents need mutual communication. As noted previously communication is one possible answer in this age of rapid change, overwhelming problems, complex difficulties, pressures from all sides and ambivalence arising from the parental relationship vying with the need to be autonomous. Through communication can all involved sense and express their emotions, needs, values, approaches, behavior and feelings about their experiences and reactions they have aroused.

Adolescents need trust. They need others to believe in him and his ability. Even more than that, psycho-social development must be encouraged by the parent's faith in the adolescent's future. Negative prophecies, warnings of dire disasters, no-win approaches in terms of conflicts discussed earlier have no place here. In order for the adolescent to be prepared to take the risk and embark on the necessary experience, he must believe in the importance of that experience, his parent's belief in his capacity to "learn from that experience" or from experiences in general.

Adolescents need to perceive the existence of alternatives. Since adolescents are tied to parents and enjoy a measure of security and autonomy within their families, it can be a difficult task to take risks with the unknown, with ambiguity, with the possibility of failure. They may need help in understanding that alternatives appropriate to their needs exist and encouragement to explore experiences rather than to be ensnared by the first suggestion offered them. They also need reassurance that opportunities recur and that perseverance in a trial and error approach is the most efficient way to learn what is most appropriate for them, according to their values and needs.

Adolescents need active support. For some adolescents the progress toward individuation proceeds without noticeable difficulties, aided by the support of a youth movement framework or friend. However, a lack of basic confidence aggravated by the effects of school failures and a lack of readiness to enter into relations with a member of the opposite sex, among other reasons, necessitates active support in separation and individuation. Parents bear the primary responsibility for this support; however, not only do many parents not know how to provide such support when needed, but they are often responsible, consciously or unconsciously, for the adolescent's situation in the first place. Therefore, their position vis a vis responsibility towards their children obligates them to seek professional aid. The guidance counselor, on the other hand, located in the educational system, should ensure necessary support for adolescent *and* parents by means of peer groups and individual counseling.

The effect of prior experiences of separation on present readiness. Various difficulties prevent the supply of proper support and should be taken into consideration. The most problematic of these is clinging to past experiences. This may include several possible factors: a mother who relates that she has already made various efforts to promote her daughter's separation, but they failed, proving that the girl is not ready to be separate: "I sent her abroad with friends, I left her with relatives, and I even sent her away to a boarding school, but she returned home because she is dependent on me." Another describes how "in our home, when I was growing up, I was different, and so my mother also related to me differently . . ." Still another recalls her own difficulties in separating from her parents, drawing parallels as an explanation of her daughter's dependence: "That's how I was at her age, although my mother and father had good relations, and they loved me and gave me everything they had." In reality, the only similarity between the mother's situation and her daughter's was their shared lack of basic confidence. Finally, a mother who describes the difficulties which arose with her son with his beginning junior high school, asserted decisively that "despite my efforts it is impossible to change him, and one simply has to accept the fact that he's like that . . ."

These cases demonstrate how past experiences can actually block the parents and adolescents from active and positive coping with the need for change in order to promote individuation. In each of the cases appropriate support and perseverance in coping could have brought about change and development. The mechanism of clinging to past experiences requires an investment in breaking down the young person's unwillingness to experience new things.

Variable 5: Development of social perspective and readiness for active coping

Although the variables discussed above are all important factors, the adolescent is not the object of his development but its subject; thus, the degree of his readiness and activity has a decisive influence, including several significant items:

The situation of adolescents from intellectual homes, who have developed deep level interpersonal communication, and who have reached a high level of social perspective. These young people are potential candidates for understanding parents as people and for rejecting them as the result of judging their values and behavior. They may also be more ambivalent when relating to their parents—replete with admiration on the one hand and anxiety or guilt feelings on the other. They may be prone to conflict with their parents or even rebel against them, but at the same time they may also have profound understanding of the complexity of the difficulty involved in the transition to adulthood and in establishing their own individuation process without overmuch dependence on the parent. One young woman commented: "I knew what I wanted to study to be and which life companion I wanted to choose, who is different from my father, from the age of 15 . . ."

The situation of adolescents from intellectual homes who have reached a high level of social perspective, but have not developed social skills necessary for interpersonal interactions required in the development of relations with a member of the opposite sex or for coping in the working world. Prolonging the interfamilial connection promotes slow, calm development of family relations, but delays the development of psycho-social maturation in areas outside the family. Such young people, too, may be candidates for difficulties and even experience individuation crises, although they will be of a different nature than those of other categories of young people.

The situation of adolescents from nonintellectual homes who have reached a highly developed level of social perspective due to their cognitive level and capacity to establish diversified interpersonal interaction at school, in a youth movement and in other social constellations. Parents of these youngsters were not models for their development in certain senses. Through their own initiative or by means of appropriate support (of a teacher, counselor or friend) they found a "mentor" who provided support and "opened doors" for them. With social challenges aiding them to reach a high level of individuation, these young people will be prepared for a different sort of tie with their parents.

The situation of adolescents who have not enjoyed appropriate nurturing in childhood and suitable support during their adolescence and can, therefore, only reach individuation at a relatively low cognitive level. These youngsters, however, may possess high level social skills which facilitates personal interaction with people who are significant for them; thus, they find appropriate paths for advancement in vocation or career development, reach intimacy and parenthood early, and build an independent life pattern both differing and paralleling that of their parents.

The situation of adolescents whose social perception gives them a high capacity for assimilation, coordination and integration. These are active factors in shaping the separation process from their parents; such process is accompanied by conflict and confirmation which takes into account the parent's image and the state of equilibrium between parents and channels the adolescents' development and the development of relations with their parents.

In most or all the cases cited in the studies, understanding and suitable support from the facilitator can serve the adolescent and his family in their efforts to enhance the quality of family life and to advance the adolescent's individuation process in an optimal fashion.

Chapter Five

Summary: Generalizations, Assumptions and Definition of Facilitator's Responsibility

THIS CHAPTER WILL ATTEMPT TO FULFILL THREE TASKS: SUMMARIZING the variables and topics presented in the previous chapters and inferring generalizations; reviewing ideas or assumptions which have not been included until now; and defining the roles of the facilitator, whether he/she be educator, guidance counselor or psychologist, doing group work with adolescents or parents. The order of presentation does not attest to their relative importance. If certain ideas have been elaborated in other chapters, it seemed unnecessary to reiterate them in full, but we only mention them; newer concepts required further clarification.

Parents as human beings

This volume was written primarily for educators, guidance counselors, youth counselors and others who deal with adolescents and parents. Therefore, the focus was on the adolescent himself, particularly on his need for individuation as examined from various theoretical approaches. Such approaches included that which viewed his parents from the perspective of outside the family, that which took into account his perceptions and feelings which were steeped in conflict with his parents and that which considered communication problems stemming from such conflicts. This book emphasizes the need to support the adolescent when negotiating transfer of responsibility, power and authority as a means of advancing his development in terms of the individuation process.

The positive/negative quality of the separation of adolescents from their parents during the individuation process is a vital and often

problematic issue for parents as well. All parties must try to compre-
hend the adolescent's needs and problems as an individual human
being, to display empathy for his coping difficulties, and to provide
support during the separation process and the transfer of responsibility from parent to adolescent. Without such comprehension, empathy
and support the chances of the adolescent achieving positive individuation may be harmed.

In order to develop social cognition adolescents need to achieve a
social perspective from which they regard the parent as a human being
with a unique biography, personal needs, present-day problems and
dreams for the future. There are two problems which must be met:
providing support to both the adolescents and their parents while
translating cognitive potential into a feeling that such support is not
only legitimate but essential, and facilitating willingness on both sides
to make the effort to attain mutually positive communication which
will, in turn, ensure insight and understanding.

The following material demonstrates the problematic nature of the
parent as human being. Supplementary material may be found in
Rappoport, Rappoport & Sterliz (1977); S. Smilansky et al. (1983).

- *Parents bring children into the world in order to fulfill their needs.* These
  needs are many and varied; some of them are conscious, but most
  are unconscious. Such needs can be discovered by examining
  descriptions from mothers and fathers in retrospect or by analyzing the present situations.

  Thus, for example, a father talks about the respectful treatment
  of his father which characterized the relationships in his family.
  Another father relates that he did not study and expected that he
  would himself assure his son of all the requisites to enable him
  to study and, thus, experience vicariously through him that which
  he did not attain. A third father speaks of his own suffering as
  the son of a father who was depressed, tough and closed to communication; he decided that his child would grow up under conditions of freedom, openness and mutual ties of understanding.
  A fourth father founded a kibbutz and hoped his son would continue his enterprise. Similarly, there is the father who is a political
  leader whose son is remote from him; another father, an active
  Zionist, complains that his son has left Israel. One mother relates
  that her parents did not have spare time to devote to her, and,
  therefore, she decided that she would devote herself to her children; while another mother claims she grew up with a cold, distant, uninvolved mother and as a result, she determined to be her
  children's friend. A third mother describes her feelings of loneli-

ness because her husband does not understand her, and how she seeks compensation in the company of adolescents visiting her daughter. Still another relates how she sacrificed herself for her children, and now her egocentric adolescent daughter is not even interested in listening to her.

A list such as this could continue for pages. What is important is that aside from raising awareness of the situation in the parties involved, there is a need to help both the parents and adolescents understand that some needs cannot be fulfilled through the other party, because he is a different and separate person. The adolescent's basic personality characteristics, stage of development, unique needs and the structure of the social system in which he lives are different from those of the parent. Nevertheless, some needs could possibly be met with the establishment of mutual, positive communication with which those needs are discussed, priorities for meeting them are coordinated and conditions set for their fulfillment.

- *Separation is a complex, intricate process and is frequently problematic for the parent as well.* The basic assumption is that positive coping and parental support in the transfer of responsibility to the adolescent are essential in enabling a positive individuation process.

Several of the parents' problems in this process are:

The problem of dependence.

Since the turn of the century psychological literature has emphasized the child's, and later the adolescent's, dependence on the parent. This book has also described adolescent expectations of parental involvement, their dependence on the father's recognition, their dependence on parental expression of love for them, and their dependence on parental support vis-a-vis the outside world, the other parent or a sibling.

However, parents are also dependent on their adolescent child. Especially once the parent has reached middle age or beyond, he is often dependent on his child for recognition that he was a good parent, even if he was distracted by studies, ensuring family income, military service and the struggle for upward mobility. In many cases the parent's needs include expecting that he will stand by his side when coping with a spouse or with other children in the family. He also depends on his child for fulfilling future dreams. About 75% of the working mothers and more than half of the fathers in the interviews noted that their children were more important to them than their profession or career. This group included many parents who considered their jobs to be very important and to whom their particular career was very meaningful. Such parental reactions were spontaneously voiced, without being asked to compare importance of their children with that of their career.

The problem of competition.

Mothers and fathers always declare they love their children, wish for their maximal development, and are prepared to do everything to ensure their success. Indeed, most parents not only feel this way and declare their feelings, but actually do a lot, even beyond what is expected, for their children's advancement. However, at some point, for differing reasons, a competitive element appears during adolescence, almost always without anyone being aware of it. It can be discerned when girls report interaction with their mothers regarding beauty, dress, friends and when boys describe debates with their fathers about logic, politics and ideology. The issue becomes even more intense during discussions held at a time of crisis, in the treatment process and also in interviews.

There are several bases for such feelings of competitiveness. First of all, there is a biological basis for such a feeling of competitiveness— the parent's stagnation or even decline in body-build or manner of functioning as contrasted with the adolescent's rapid development, robustness and achievements. There is also a sociological basis—our society emphasizes the freshness and beauty of youth rather than the wisdom of years and advanced age. Furthermore, there is a historical basis—most parents grew up in deprived conditions, under circumstances characterized by fewer alternatives and less enjoyment from life (particularly in terms of sexuality, sociability, travel, etc.), and enjoyed less social confirmation. There is an economic basis—the contemporary economic situation of most parents is better than that of their parents, and they can and do provide their children with more entertainment, learning, clothing, vacations and opportunities to plan for the future. And, of course, there is a psychological basis—psychologists, physicians and educators, as well as the media, have made parents aware of factors which in turn enable them to understand their children's needs more. Unfortunately, such increased sensitivity has also made them more conscious of the possibility of injuring their children's sensibilities. As a result, they are more anxious, more guilt ridden, engage more in psychologizing, and are, in fact, more open to being injured themselves. Since children earn social approval by being "victimized" in such a fashion, parents find they sometimes even do more hurting than they might have allowed themselves.

The problems represented by a present which is complex, intricate, and uncertain and a future which is hard to forecast.

In a society where norms in all areas of life, including sex roles, have been destroyed or blurred and permissive values and behavior earn social approval, it is often very difficult for parents to fulfill the role of socialization imposed on them. Upon looking forward into the 21st century the problem becomes even more sharply delineated. When people attempt to forecast the world in which today's adolescents will function, they all agree that it will be different and uncertain. Often adolescents in families from a culturally deprived area or social strata are better educated than their parents, more involved and active in their own social groups, and in certain senses even better prepared to cope with the uncertainty of the future. There are many cases in which there is special significance growing out of the adolescents' socialization, particularly in terms of father-son relations. However, even among those families firmly in the educated strata problems arise originating in lack of readiness for the future, whether considering the developmental process itself or other uncertainties and changes. This lack of readiness may exist for the parents and/or adolescents and may include a perception on the part of one or both parties of the lack of readiness of the other party. A lack of clarity regarding whose responsibility is for what seems to be a prevalent stumbling block.

The problem of anxiety.

Anxiety is a major issue for modern parents. The factors mentioned above plus additional factors connected to the various conflicts discussed, have combined to increase parental anxiety far beyond what used to be "natural." The nuclear family, separated from supportive extended family structures, exists in splendid isolation in its house/apartment. Mutual psychological dependence develops between the adults; the family consists of one or two children for whom there is no substitute. Society's competitively based school sends warnings and threats about the child's situation and his future prognosis. Signals filter back regarding dangers in youth society: automotive recklessness, seductiveness of drug and alcohol abuse and sexual permissiveness blurring into promiscuity; media "specials" warn and tempt in their warnings. All of these factors raise the level of anxiety for both parent and adolescent alike, and increase feelings of a lack of confidence, frustration, confrontations and guilt.

Parents as a family system

Relating to the parent as a human being and individual may give the impression that he was the one facing the adolescent and colliding with him in the socialization process. However, the picture is a great deal more complex and intricate.

The Two-Dimensional Parental Covenant

When a parent functions, he brings with him influences from his family of origin—the "vertical" generation. He has internalized things experienced as a child; he has unconsciously translated his various past experiences into a scale of values, formulating an ability to assess situations and developing a motif for judging the present. This can be considered the parents' historical covenant.

At the same time, there is a horizontal covenant between the parents which is continually, actively working to influence each of them. Parents cannot implement any action without taking into consideration their spouse's feelings, judgment and sphere of activity vis a vis their children. They must ask themselves: What does he feel? According to what standard does he make his judgments? What would he do in my place? What does he expect me to do? What will he think of me if I act in this manner and how will he react? Does he identify with me? Is he angry and does he have misgivings? Will the situation take on the character wherein I will be seen as the "bad one" and he as the "good one?" or will I be seen as soft and loving and he as tough and judgmental? Most of these questions occur as fleeting, internal images. But a portion are expressed as clear, conscious, cognitive and emotional judgments, recognizable to the parent's perceptions and feelings as well as to the adolescent's perceptions and feelings. In many cases, when asked, both parties were prepared to sketch the nature of the transaction as it ran through their imaginations and influenced their assessment and behavior.

The parental covenant, in both its vertical and horizontal dimensions, provides a constant testing ground for each parent beginning from the day his child enters the world and lasting until the denouement of his and that child's life. However, everything characterizing adolescence and adolescent problems clashes in one way or another with the real or potential influences of the parental covenant; in addition to the problems unique to the relationship, the fact is that such parents, generally in the throes of the problems of middle age, are themselves in the midst of a period of transition. Therefore, during adolescence the impact of the parental covenant is unique. The following reactions are just a sample of the many possible:

- a 45 year old mother: "I knew I couldn't have any more children and that increased my dependence on this single child, whose outbursts foreshorten everything I have dreamed . . ."
- a 48 year old father: "I worked so hard, I invested so much, and he is the real test of my life's dream, but he doesn't understand me at all, he doesn't want to continue with kibbutz life at all. Maybe he will travel around or maybe he'll want to live in America altogether. What we have built isn't of interest . . ."

Another factor in the parental corner of the family system involves the relations between the couple themselves. Memories of interrelations of one's own parents as well as their relations with their adolescent child are revived by the relationships between present parents. At the same time, the parent must take into account the spouse's feelings and behavior, the balance of role division worked out between them, and the extent of support each provides the other in terms of intervening in order to modify the adolescent's behavior. Furthermore, the rapid changes and swings in the adolescent's behavior, and rises, falls and changes in parental reactions to adolescent outbursts characteristic of this period put the parental covenant under continual stress. All these factors cannot fail to affect the relationship between the parent and the adolescent.

The ability of the parental covenant to weather all storms and stress influences the adolescent's self-image as a future parent and his feeling of capability and fitness to fulfill a role which is so essential and problematic. Representatives of society—teachers, guidance counselors, psychologists—sometimes exacerbate parental guilt feelings with the tone of their expectations and demands. They often disregard the fact that children with problems can come from homes boasting good, positive couples and good, positive parents. The problems of such children may not stem from parental functioning, either in the past or the present. It is important to remember that parents have additional needs and commitments aside from their responsibilities as parents. Clashes sometimes occur between the father's or mother's needs to maintain equilibrium in their marital relationship, or between maintaining their commitment to each other as a couple and meeting their children's needs, especially if the child may be an adolescent. Support for parents and adolescents alike to maintain open communication between them during such clashes is extremely important. In modern family life, clashes such as these have become frequent and normative for a high proportion of families.

As adolescents' social perspective developed, their descriptions revealed more and more distinctions between the relationships with their mothers and that with their fathers; on certain subjects they continued to relate to them both as parents. The role of an adult facilitator-helper is to help them develop the most intense capacity possible for differentiating and understanding the meaning of the parental covenant, both in its deeper psychological terms and in its daily implications, and especially in terms of its establishing a mutual support structure for the two parents within which they may fortify one another in continuing to cope with the daily demands of their roles and advancing their children's individuation processes.

The component of "siblings" is interwoven in the problematic aspects of the parental covenant in both its dimensions. Horizontally, adolescents compare themselves to their brothers and sisters at the same time that even the most evenhanded parents make comparisons. Vertically, a mother, who had problems related to her sister's behavior in her adolescence and/or due to parents' expectations with regard to her relationship to and behavior with younger or older siblings, may be more sensitive to maintaining a balance between her adolescent daughter with whose expectations or conduct she clashes and more aware of how these things affect her other children. She must also be aware of the need to maintain a balance between the nature of her interaction with this girl as opposed to the father's interaction with the girl and with the family's other children.

Constraints Imposed on Parents by their Past

Psychodynamic and family communication theory and the recounting of various parent/adolescent conflicts have been used to describe how the past influences present situations for people. There are several factors of which parents, facilitators and adolescents should be aware:

- Since childhood, today's parent has internalized various images of what a parent should be like, what he does and what he can expect out of life and his own children. Such expectations are primarily unconscious, but they unquestionably influence the process of shaping his identity and his mode of coping. The development of social perspective on a high level along with an opportunity for appropriate support can help to partially release a parent from his internalized images; however, most people never receive sufficient support which would make it possible for them to develop appropriate social perspective.

- During their own experience as adolescents and young adults, parents observed transactional patterns in their family of origin, consolidated a particular view of the father's and mother's images and roles, and consciously or unconsciously formulated certain assumptions about the division of roles and nature of relationships in their future family. This can be inferred from testimony about mate selection and descriptions of choices made in terms of educating their own children.

- In addition, adolescence is a time for coping with a "life theme." This is the dominant motive of one's life which energizes daily actions, influences dreams for the future and galvanizes the formation of a life-pattern. In approximately 50% of the 300 interviews, parents were aware of the effects of a "life theme," while in other cases it was possible to identify it from the interview albeit with some difficulty. Some of the cases of awareness of such a "force," the individual claims that he is a captive, to one degree or another, of a "compulsion," of a overriding motive to achieve something. In cases where it was difficult to understand the significance of this factor, it was possible that the opportunity to penetrate deeply enough into the motivational feelings and their interpretation had not been sufficiently utilized.

- A considerable portion of parents of adolescents are at the life-crossroads referred to as the "mid-life crisis." Its significance for this discussion lies in the fact that such a period is pervaded with a sense of insecurity regarding the meaning of the past, current distress or expectation of future change. Parallel with this insecurity is a deep feeling of psychological needs which have not been and are not being fulfilled. This feeling of unmet needs has implications for the individual's relationships in various areas, including his role as a parent.

- Throughout their children's adolescence, parents recall (or think they recall) their own adolescence: what they gained, how they reacted and what they felt. Deep emotional memories such as these cannot help but influence their perception of their own adolescent children and the relationship with them. Most parents attest that these memories serve as criteria with which to compare what is happening at present; others, who consider themselves free of such past influences, are often surprised and even skeptical when a group facilitator or therapist suggests interpretations in this direction.

Traditional/Neo-traditional Role Division and the Modern Family

There have been many changes in the modern family in the 45 years since World War II; nevertheless, when we read descriptions of adolescents and parents in Israel (Smilansky, 1984), England (Kitwood, 1980) and the US (Youniss & Smaller, 1985), the picture in terms of traditional role division is very similar to that described by Parsons & Bales (1955) as typical of the '40's and '50's. Both pictures depict a father focused on instrumental socialization of his offspring toward a future in modern society. He intervenes in issues regarding his children's scholastic status, choice of study majors in secondary school, acquisition of a set of values and expression of political behavior, their plans for choosing a vocation and building a family. He is involved in these areas on behalf of both his sons and his daughters in a decisive majority of cases. The mother, however, is portrayed as focused on her children's needs and affective-expressive struggles in the present. She is concerned with the daughter's or son's feelings, their relations with friends or an intimate companion, their relations at school or with other children's social groupings.

Although both parents worked outside the home in nearly 75% of the cases examined, role division in the home and family remained in accord with the above criteria in the great majority of the families interviewed. It is also interesting to note that although fathers, mothers and adolescents were all interviewed separately, there were no significant discrepancies in the descriptions of the role division.

This basic finding was introduced as a topic in inservice training sessions for facilitators and as well as in courses for students; participants were first asked for their confirmation or contradiction of these findings and then for their explanations. Their responses raised several issues which seem significant. First, the great majority of participants confirmed the data findings based on experience in their families of origin. Those who are currently functioning as parents and those who act as guidance counselors, educators and youth counselors also confirmed this situation from their own experience and from their contacts with the families of students.

What emerged from the discussions of most of those participating in the inservice training courses was that although most of them—

women and men alike—would have liked male parents to be more involved in expressive areas, and although some women claimed to be involved and active in instrumental areas as well, it seemed that the current balance of power and authority continues to exist not too different from that of 40 years ago and that most families don't try to upset it.

Most of those who spoke up expressed justifications, to some extent, for the difference existing in role division. They cited qualitative differences in basic personalities, early socialization or social reality. Most of them did not believe that the changes in sex role definitions which have occurred in the past decades would bring about basic change in familial role divisions.

When various facilitators raised this subject in peer groups as part of the learning experience and then discussed it again a month later, most of the young people from grades 10-11 perceived reality as described by the adults in the inservice training groups.

Pursuing the subject further in several differently constituted peer groups, facilitators found the participants' reactions somewhat surprising. It turned out that most of the young people saw advantages to the currently existing role division. They felt that the present situation allowed them space in which to separate and move forward in the individuation process. Although they expressed a desire for increased paternal involvement and self-disclosure, they did not wish him to end up being like the mother. Many of the younger boys (grades 7-8) noted that they enjoyed going with their father to a soccer or basketball game and discussing sports without fearing that he will turn "personal" and "invade their privacy." Others described how they watched TV with their fathers and discussed politics with them. Some spoke positively about the father being the one who stands for [stable] authority, norms and meaning in certain areas, while they are able to discuss, argue and compromise on other issues with the mother.

Many girls also described enjoying the difference between the role behavior of mother and father, indicating that involvement with each parent takes on a different character. This opinion stood despite any criticism of a mother's over-involvement in private affairs or of a father's excessive distance particularly in situations in which they would have liked him to increase his involvement.

Viewing the families over the two or three generations of relations, there is a notable difference in assessment if the sharp transition from traditionalism to modernism occurred in the grandparents' generation or in the parents' generation; at the same time there is marked continuity. Interviews were studded with remarks by respondents such as "my mother did it this way" and "my father was like that." Therefore, it is clear that the parents of today's parents served as models—for identification by imitation or by rejection. They continue the process, frequently fulfilling the very same role toward their children, playing out the same basis for their role formation despite changes occurring in them and/or in the world surrounding them.

Parental Involvement in Children's Socialization and Adolescent Acceptance of Parental Authority

The study results point to the fact that parents maintain certain norms and see to the socialization of their children. It also is clear that the great majority of adolescents do *not* rebel against their parents, do *not* challenge their authority or good intentions, and do *not* describe their parents either as permissive individuals, escaping their responsibility or as using their children to realize their power and authority. Even when adolescents complain about one of the parent's behavior, they do not cast aspersions on their parents' good intentions, challenge their authority or express a desire to break with the family. Cumulative adolescent and parent testimony, taken in separate interviews, paints a positive picture of concerned families who cope more or less successfully with their patterns of communication and actually are symptomatic of a more general problems of recognition, appreciation, empathy, autonomy and responsibility. Some conflicts refer to deep emotions, both those which have been internalized in childhood and are unconscious for adolescent and parent and those which are conscious, but unexpressed because of various insecurities: uncertainty about the real meaning of those feelings, uncertainty about being prepared to convey such an expression, or uncertainty of how the recipient will react. Some conflicts consist of random, symptomatic expressions which predictably burst out at times of excitement. Other conflicts seem to be basic and prolonged and bear a resemblance, in different situations, to a war of terror mutually inflicted on and affecting all the family members concerned.

Psychological interpretations of conflicts also vary. There is, on the one hand, what could be called the "classic psychodynamic description," also known as "Storm and Stress," out of which context the classical generalization of Anna Freud (1958, p. 182), can be understood that at the onset of puberty the adolescent "will live with members of his family as though they were strangers." Few often even receive it. Even in cases when an adolescent is disappointed by his/

her parent's attitude, it must be remembered that the parent's response often reflects difficulties stemming from a situation of contention with parties from the outside. There are different forms of such problematic situations, the most common of which are:

- A gap between the adolescent's values and needs and social expectations—for example, pressure from mass media and/or companions in one's age cohort imposes a standard of sexual behavior for which the adolescent is unprepared and frequently does not really want. However, when the parent sets limits and elicits blame and accusations from the adolescent, that does not mean the parent is incorrect about his warnings and interdictions. In a retrospective examination of their conflicts, many adolescents express feelings of gratefulness that the parents intervened.

- The clash between the need for individuation and the degree of readiness to bear its consequences. Most of the time both parent and the adolescent knows he will need all his strength in order to cope with psychosocial expectations and developmental tasks. Yet, just as these expectations and tasks arouse anxiety for the adolescent, they also arouse anxieties for the parents. Moreover, conflicts seem to develop in situations where one or both of those involved are ambivalent.

- Clashes result from the varying nature of the pressures brought to bear by the different social entities embedded in the complex, multi-institutional society in which we function. The pattern characterized by a slow process of development during the stage of adolescence based on mutual communication and parental support. Factors predisposing one for such deep conflict differ greatly from individual to individual, but coping difficulties with psychosocial maturational tasks at major junctures stand out distinctively. Often these may represent only turning points during the young person's development, but sometimes, in certain cases, they actually signal a severe family-relations crisis. Problems showing up in the transition to adulthood usually involve the young person and his intimate partner, difficulties in selecting a profession and developing a career, difficulties in choosing a mate, resorting to divorce after a brief marriage, entering into an unwanted pregnancy, a crisis relating to and during army service, etc. Problems showing up at the onset of [the child's] adolescence can result from a crisis in the parental relationship, divorce (of the adolescent's parents) or an extreme change in familial life style such as turning to or away from an extreme religious orientation, emigration from one country to another, the main wage-earner's

leaving an army career, financial failure or criminal indictment of
the head of the family.

The views and definitions of various schools of psychology about
the nature of adolescence and its implications for adolescent-parent
relations influence how the adolescent process is interpreted. The
more profound schools, who base their judgment on penetrating into
the deepest levels of personality, are likely to argue that all of the
difficulties described occurring in the later years actually can be traced
to a high number of "unconscious" "Storm and Stress" cases. They
hold that a late onset of the problematic aspects of development attests
to the conclusion of a period of social moratorium.

However patterns of conflict are interpreted or described, it is clear
from the system of factors presented and from the various depictions
of similar, interchangeable traits, that people—adolescents and parents—are faced with needs, problems and decisions which are particularly crucial in the transition stage from childhood to adulthood.
They need to learn methods of communication to ensure shared development and deserve institutionalized, societal support to encourage a
positive developmental process.

It may be more useful therefore to view the functional unit as a triad:
adolescent-parent-society. In fact, one of the more obvious limitations
found in various clinical papers discussing adolescent-parent relations
is the disregard of social context. Educators, guidance counselors,
parents and adolescents must be aware of the fact that the origin of
the great majority of conflicts between adolescents and parents can be
found in problems related to adolescent and/or parental coping with
society's expectations. It is the social context which, after all, serves
them both as the major frame of reference. Mass media, school and
other social institutions, friends—all represent value-oriented expectations to strive to attain. Difficulty in achieving self fulfillment in
social roles kindles frustration. It is noteworthy that in a considerable
portion of cases even with a relatively high degree amount of adolescent-parent contention family members form a united front vis-a-vis a
"threat" from one or another party outside the family. In such situations adolescents expect support from their parents and often even
receive it. Even in cases when an adolescent is disappointed by his/
her parent's attitude, it must be remembered that the parent's
response often reflects difficulties stemming from a situation of contention with parties from the outside. There are different forms of
such problematic situations, the most common of which are:

- A gap between the adolescent's values and needs and social
  expectations—for example, pressure from mass media and/or

companions in one's age cohort imposes a standard of sexual behavior for which the adolescent is unprepared and frequently does not really want. However, when the parent sets limits and elicits blame and accusations from the adolescent, that does not mean the parent is incorrect about his warnings and interdictions. In a retrospective examination of their conflicts, many adolescents express feelings of gratefulness that the parents intervened.

- The clash between the need for individuation and the degree of readiness to bear its consequences. Most of the time both parent and the adolescent know he will need all his strength in order to cope with psychosocial expectations and developmental tasks. Yet, just as these expectations and tasks arouse anxiety for the adolescent, they also arouse anxieties for the parents. Moreover, conflicts seem to develop in situations where one or both of those involved are ambivalent.

- Clashes result from the varying nature of the pressures brought to bear by the different social entities embedded in the complex, multi-institutional society in which we function. The school maintains its norms and demands; the youth movement makes its expectations felt; companions and friends each put pressure on the youth in their own ways. It is almost inevitable that adolescents and parents end up clashing concerning what behavior is either permissible or desirable. However, this question has a double edge: how can the adolescent integrate into society if he has not been allowed to integrate into his peer society? His status and feelings of competence are influenced by meeting or not meeting the expectations and pressures of other social groupings, especially those which are outside the family, but are in fact closely interwoven in the lives of its members.

Clashes originating in the adolescent-parent-society triad come in innumerable other forms; adolescents participating in peer groups seemed quite able to delineate the direction of these problems according to how they felt. It is important for facilitators of such groups to be able to free both adolescent and parent from feeling that they are on a battlefront in a war between the two of them. The clashes do occur repeatedly between them and there are indeed clashes whose source is the parent's or adolescent's readiness/lack of readiness for seeing issues from the broader perspective, feeling empathy and engaging in mutual communication. However, in most conflicts, it is possible to distinguish between intrafamilial contention, which then may be dealt with, and external pressures which demand a family alliance against an external threat.

Principles promoting positive individuation processes

Principle One—Readiness for separation and the gradual transfer of responsibility for coping and identity shaping to the adolescent

Separation involves child separating from parent as well as parent separating from child. Both participants need to be ready for a separate existence, need to work at creating a positive atmosphere around the process itself despite difficulties which arise and need to reach out with support for each other along the way. Some of the implications of such mutuality in the separation process are:

- It is of utmost importance that adolescents feel their parents believe in their capability to grow up and take responsibility for determining their values, attitudes and behavior. An adolescent will see a lack of such a belief as implying that they are incapable and cannot successfully fulfill their role as future parents or adults existing in a modern society, requiring each citizen to shape his unique identity. Furthermore, such doubts convey a metacommunication to the adolescent that he is unfitted to successfully complete the transition from childhood to adulthood; since it is the parents who are responsible for supporting their child's developmental progress, this hurts their own self-image as powerful adults and parents as well.
- Along with this basic belief in the adolescent's right and capability to achieve individuation there must be continual examination of issues of autonomy and support; in which areas is the young person prepared to accept more responsibility/autonomy with concomitantly less support and in which areas is he less prepared, needful of specific support?
- The adolescent needs to know that his parents recognize his right to individuation, are prepared to gradually grant him more autonomy, and are in the process of transferring the responsibility for shaping his identity and developing coping strategies to him.
- The adolescent needs to believe in his capability to gradually take on the necessary responsibility, and will be able to cope with the implications of such autonomy for himself and his family.
- Every member of the family as well as everyone who is in contact with the family must understand the necessity for individuation and the process of its development despite any of the difficulties and recurrent conflicts in various areas which inevitably arise during this process.

Principle Two—Development of parental psychosocial maturity and Separation

Maturation tasks to which each parent should aspire may be defined despite differences in terms of background, ability, basic personality traits, family situation, etc. The following criteria may be used as a basis for an adult education program which would be appropriate at various points in the parents' lives.

A parent must deal consciously and systematically with the issue of his personal identity.

This is not an easy thing to do in a world as complex, intricate and changing as ours, and past influences, present reality and uncertainty regarding the future all contribute to the difficulty. Therefore, help and support should be available to parents in the form of adult peer groups or in special parents' groups. Socialization of adolescents is a difficult enough task to do under the best of circumstances; a person who neither understands nor is at peace with himself will find it well nigh impossible. Adolescents cannot understand or respect a parent who epitomizes rootlessness, obscurity, vagueness and ambivalence. It is precisely a parent who is alert, sincere, and reliable and represents a system of values that an adolescent needs.

A psychosocially mature parent has values which he translates into behavioral norms.

Such a parent expects his children to understand and respect his values and, at the same time, he understands that his adolescent children have the right to develop values and norms of their own and expects them to be responsible for struggling in their fulfillment. Such a parent is open to the fact that a democratic, modern society includes alternative values and behavior patterns and that adolescence is the particular time for examining all the options. He is open to the possibility of experimenting with the meaning of values and of new behaviors, both for himself and for his adolescent children. Furthermore, he communicates with his adolescent children about his feelings in these areas and about the limits of experimentation he is prepared to countenance until the adolescent becomes a totally independent citizen.

A parent must continue his independent development throughout every stage of his life.

He cannot suspend realization of his potential "because of" his children's dependent status. His needs include contact with his children, empathy and support; their understanding, involvement and support, freely given according to their individual capacities provides him with deserved compensation. However, parents and children all have their own basic personality traits, a separate life focus and private dreams for the future. At the very least children will, in the future, be bound by commitments toward their own spouse and children. Not only does a psychosocially mature parent understand that his children's development is not solely dependent on him, but he knows it is often not even in his control. The separation and individuation processes are natural and must be accepted open-mindedly, accepting its advantages, limitations and problems.

Psychosocially mature parents realize there is no age limit to learning and are willing to learn from their adolescent children.

They understand new options, which they had not confronted during their adolescence, face their children as a result of the rapid process of social change. Such adults, open to learning, progress along with or in parallel to their children. Recognizing that they and their children are separate personalities, they realize that mutual understanding, empathy and mutual support can ensure a better world for themselves, their children and the next generations.

Parents must communicate with their children in general, and with adolescents in particular.

Daughters and sons want parents to be open with them, expect their involvement in the affective areas of their lives and want to talk with them. However, dialogue is what is necessary, not preaching or informative lectures; this may need to be learned by all those involved. Although it is clear that change is a very difficult process, with sensitivity, willingness to invest oneself and appropriate support available, changes may very well occur in many cases.

The relationship between parents and adolescent children must be those of equal human worth.

Parents and children cannot be and need not be equal; adolescents, like younger children, expect the care of a mother or father, not another friend. At the same time they need recognition that they are not children; they want to receive a feeling of empathy with their needs and problems; they need to engage in mutual communication about family relationships; they require constructive criticism even regarding negative behavior; they crave that messages transmitted to them be genuine.

Constructive criticism from parents must focus on specific behavior without generalizing or attacking in any way the personality or developmental process of the adolescent.

Many parents, especially fathers, exhibit a hierarchical, cynical and ultimately lethal approach to criticizing their adolescents, often totally unaware of the degree to which their children are hurt. Often adolescents deserve criticism; but it must relate to a particular value and/or a concrete act. Part of the criticism which is expected and accepted includes how it affects the parent, themselves or others, and possible positive alternatives. In any case, words of criticism should be couched in words which leave the adolescent clearly feeling the parent's assertion of trust in his ability to change or to alter his activity in a positive direction.

Principle Three—Separation: Pace and patterns

Three main patterns in the pace of separation and two dimensions interwoven into the process can be seen from early childhood on. Pace refers to the factor of a pattern being either "too slow" or "too fast" in normative developmental terms as opposed to one which seems appropriate. The two dimensions include:

- the child's unique developmental pattern, associated with his/her basic personality traits, and the significance of his/her cumulative life experience;
- the parents' readiness to permit and support development of autonomy.

The pattern of a "too fast" pace in early childhood can be seen in the example of parents who, due to the pressure of their own needs, leave their infants in day care all day; another example can be mothers from culturally deprived backgrounds who, upon the birth of their next child, assume that the toddler-sibling, who may be walking and perhaps even talking, no longer needs them to promote further cognitive development.

The pattern of a "too slow" pace shows up primarily in mothers who find it difficult to reconcile themselves to their child's individuation and is marked by claims made to themselves as well as to others that the child is too small, is not yet ready for separation, needs them, etc.

Most toddlers adjust to the reality of their parents' or caregivers' needs; in fact, observations of the process indicate that sometimes they know better than the adult how much autonomy they need and how secure they are when separated. The cost of accelerated or delayed separation, relative to the child's needs, is often discovered during psychological treatment when adolescents or adults look back retrospectively.

The pacing pattern is, in certain respects, more problematic during adolescence. Those many adolescents who follow the "Storm and Stress" pattern of development tend to undergo internal difficulties in their development during the transition to adulthood and often end up clashing with their parents and sometimes with their teachers as well.

For other adolescents the rapid pace of change occurring within them in addition to feedback such changes engender from significant adults in their environment make it difficult for them to assess their abilities and needs. Such a situation reaches beyond the adolescent's inner difficulties; it raises the question of the partner in their transaction: a rigid father who expresses freely his feelings that, in his day, adolescents did not behave this way; a mother who is unable to accept the new behavior of her daughter or son; a couple who do not know how to conclude an alliance so that they will act as a unit. One or both parent is always acting to maintain the family balance of power, and such action is inevitably accompanied with anxiety lest the other spouse deprive them, etc. Thus, it is possible to see how the unique needs of adolescents and parents commingle and influence the various phenomena of rigidity, lack of openness, rapidly changing responses, feelings of frustration and disappointment, harsh answers and even severing of communication ties, both in general and during negotiations.

A further pacing variation arises out of the parent's fulfillment of his role to assess the child's readiness to receive authority and responsibility. This variation is far more complicated. If the adolescent is intelligent and copes as necessary with the expectations of school and teachers, parents assume that he is ready to bear successfully the responsibility for his functioning. Due to personal needs and limitations many educated, liberal parents have a tendency to leave the adolescent alone, allowing him to work through his struggle in other psychosocial developmental areas according to his understanding as well. When the young person's cognitive development is slower than the norm and his scholastic achievements are deficient, the institution sends the parents repeated messages from various directions that the child needs help; in fact, the parents and child may even be requested to turn to the school guidance counselor or the psychological service. But the intelligent child creates an illusion of maturity and gives the impression he does not need any help. Therefore, even in cases where communication has apparently been established between adolescents and parents, and negotiations are being conducted about the adolescent's or parent's needs and expectations, a problem in a particular area may develop. Thus, for example, parents may avoid discussing an adolescent's lack of readiness for heterosexual social relations for fear of impinging on the child's privacy and behavioral autonomy.

Sometimes problems develop when the adolescent's needs happen to fit the parent's needs. A good example could be in this not uncommon situation: an adolescent girl fears the pressures and problems arising from heterosexual relations and does not feel a strong need for separation from her parents; her parents, for their part, are afraid that their daughter might get into difficulties with sexual relations and are content to see her inactivity as proof of the fact that she is a "good" student and behaves according to the patterns which they consider acceptable. They discount the possibility that her behavior may be expressing problems originating from not separating from them and from fear of experiencing normative heterosexual relations in a peer group. In such cases separation proceeds too slowly and is not accompanied by the struggle required for acquiring a personal, individuated identity.

At the other end of the scale, a problem may develop when the fact of matching interests and needs between parents and adolescent results in too rapid a separation. The adolescent may feel the need for separation at a point when the parents are busy and preoccupied with other commitments. Therefore, the parents interpret the child's need for separation as an indication of his readiness. This convenient interpretation releases the parents from feeling guilty about letting other pressing demands take precedence over demands represented by their child. They tell themselves, and sometimes others involved in the process as well, that their child is coping by himself, studying or working and earning money, and freeing them from involvement. Adolescents, on the other hand, noted in the interviews their very different understanding, stating "my parents didn't care about me."

This situation presents even more serious ramifications when the young person is himself aware of his problems and that they are because of extreme, premature separation; realizing that his parents are immersed in coping with some other area, he accepts their disregard of his condition as a fact of life, maintains the facade that he is indeed ready for adulthood, and thus reinforces his parents' behavior. When such adolescents are hurt by their excessive independence and premature responsibility, they turn on their parents and accuse them as did this adolescent: "it didn't bother him that I was banging my head against a stone wall, every time I chose a vocation which fit the dreams that he had not realized himself."

Some parents cultivate an ideology of early independence, encouraging or confirming it by various reinforcements. An adolescent receiving messages of this type may end up feeling that he can never show a need for dependence or support. In essence, what happens is that the adolescent acts "like" an independent individual . . . in accordance with his parents' orders.

Too rapid a separation can indeed contribute to release the adolescent from physical and psychological dependence on parents; however, its contribution to the development of an appropriate level of psychosocial maturity is questionable. This can affect not only that stage of development, but also the following stages in terms of capacity for intimacy and meeting the demands of parenthood, shaping a professional identity and choosing a career.

It is quite clear from these and other examples presented in the text or reported in the study itself that **the main problem facing parents and their growing children is finding an appropriate balance between seeing autonomy as an essential, ultimate achievement and considering all the various factors effecting a controlled, gradual and coordinated pace and pattern of individuation.**

A balanced process of individuation must be based concomitantly on several components: increasing autonomy from dependence on parents; increasing readiness for positive experiencing in other areas, such as establishing intimate relations with a spouse, readiness for work and experiencing success at work, readiness for military service and succeeding in meeting its challenges, etc. None of the components can be left out or skipped; success in work or military service cannot mask or make up for not progressing adequately to free oneself from psychological dependence on parents or for being unable to enter into intimate relationships and cope with becoming a parent oneself.

In this context, it is important to note that contention generally appears in a social setting, and its expression is influenced by group cultural patterns as well as by the unique array of interpersonal relations existing within each family. An adolescent's struggle with parental authority may be covert, taking on different forms of expression within the constellation of existing possibilities in the particular family, in certain institutions (school or youth movement) or in the peer group. On the surface, it may not even seem to be a conflict. Furthermore, the possible outcome of such conflict varies with different adolescents and is often unclear. Conflict may serve as an incentive for positive development toward self-validation, development of a sense of responsibility and a positive feeling about the separation process and its outcome; however, it may also have negative results of provoking developmental regression and childish rigidity.

In other words, in the long run coping with conflict can lead to greater flexibility and openness, understanding and personal integrity along with an increased capacity for empathy and relating to the needs of others. However, it can also cause over-defensiveness, self-righteousness, isolation, unwillingness to take into account the needs and attitudes of others, and a lack of ability to cope with additional challenges. Therefore, the support provided to the adolescent and his parents during this process is crucial.

Developmental, power and authority patterns evident in transactions unique to various types of families are the source of problematic aspects and crises in current situations. For example, contention arising between husband and wife over issues of power and authority in terms of role definition, division of labor, feelings of equal worth, etc., influences the personality shaping process, the development of expectations and the formation of adolescent patterns of conflict and validation in those families. A conflict which centers around the power/authority axis within the family itself involves a system which is primary, dynamic and vital in the process of adolescence itself. It is within this ecological context that adolescents discover their competence for coping. As such each family has a unique role to play in influencing and shaping the development of its adolescents.

Assumptions concerning work with peer groups

There are several further assumptions on which basis it is possible to work with a peer support group; some of these are general and others are unique to the approach proposed in this work.

- The support of a peer group the members of which are coping with similar needs and problems can aid to advance the adolescent's individuation process as well as help him form new, mature relations with his parents. Members of such a group understand him, suggest alternative coping strategies, and provide him opportunities to act according to his values, his needs and the situation, either obtaining or possible, in his family. At a later stage in his growth, when he is ready to establish a long-term, intimate relationship, he will need to learn how to free himself from involvement in and pressures of these peers. At that point he will be able to return to his parents on equal terms: as a responsible adult.

- A major focus of the peer group is to help the adolescent perceive and understand the parent as a human being at a particular developmental stage, who brings a network of experiences arising from a unique past with him, who must deal with current problems and who is developing his own expectations regarding the future. Thus, for example, while the adolescent girl must struggle with identity shaping issues and problems of coping appropriate to a 17 year old, her mother has problems appropriate for a 40 year old woman: issues of continuing identity formation, changing status and defining her future role(s) in the family and social system.

- Since separation and self validation are interconnected, an important trait a peer group can help the young person develop is readiness to go against his parents and stand up for himself, i.e., readiness to engage in conflict and ultimately self validation when coping with his parents. An awareness of one's own uniqueness is based on achieving an inner feeling of containing something which deserves recognition and esteem. The attainment of others' recognition and esteem is dependent on achieving such consciousness. Thus, such validation, offering support and confirming the individual's right to recognition, esteem, and a portion of power and authority, is the key to individuation and establishing one's unique personal identity. Furthermore, the lack of separation indicates the existence of an adverse pathological situation.

Conflict and validation can and should be expressed by means of a matrix of alternatives. Actually, validation may often be expressed in the following three forms:

a. The adolescent can develop experimental modes of behavior appropriate to his values, feelings and basic personality traits. He may choose a unique, independent life-style which need not interfere with identification with his parents: he is not them. He understands why they are like they are, due to this or that reason, and hopes that they will understand him, acknowledge his right to be different from them, and accept him as a developing person of equal worth. In certain senses his values and behavior will seem similar to those of his father and in other ways similar to his mother's, and in certain things he is likely to differ from both of them.

b. The adolescent declares a moratorium in order to "find himself" as part of moving forward in his separation process. He asserts to himself (and others) that he is learning to understand himself and significant others and that he is perplexed. He does not emphasize contradictions or negatives. He neither makes use of uncompromising statements: "That's that," nor instantaneous decisions which seem to validate his independence, such as fleeing from home, an early marriage, pregnancy out of wedlock, joining an alienated group, etc. in order to escape his uncertainty. Instead, he consciously says to himself and others: "I'm not yet ready for decisions; I need more time and further experiences which will be meaningful to me in order for me to decide about shaping my identity." The flexibility of modern society allows an individual to extend the individuation process while determining his uniqueness.

c. The adolescent need not negate or oppose his parents in order to express his right to be unique; he need only establish a status of relative equal worth for himself within the family entity. Adolescents of all ages and status can be made aware of possibilities for positive advancement toward separation and individuation through cooperation with the parent and by engaging in a kind of confrontation which is conducted by means of negotiation, rather than by total resistance. Such an approach not only has a positive effect in terms of the parents' feelings and the social climate within the family of origin, but also in terms of the kinds of relationships which will be established by the young person in his family-to-come in the future.

It would seem that closeness, intimacy and mutual commitment develop through a recognition of everyone's mutual right to equal worth and a position of independence which does not consist of one negating another. Open communication is necessary in order to satisfy mutual needs of autonomous personalities; a feeling of true independence cannot arise from opposition and total negation. In a considerable portion of difficult family relations, particularly adolescent-parent relations, one side or both feels that there is no chance for independent status except by negating and debasing the other side. Therefore, the major difficulty is encouraging adolescents to forgo the feeling that "no one can tell me what to be and how to do it," "they don't understand," "they think I don't have a personality," etc.

The peer group makes use of an **alternative model of authority and power** in order for adolescents to learn how to conduct negotiations with their parents. This alternative model promotes understanding and mutual help in adolescent-parent relations and is based on the assumption that both parents and adolescents are people located in a particular developmental stage. Each must become involved in extended, mutual negotiations which will produce a positive feeling in the other and which will progress in transferring responsibility, authority and power to the adolescent. With the recognition that parents bring children into the world in order to satisfy their own needs, they may then proceed to support the adolescent's satisfying his own needs, i.e., progressing in his individuation process.

Parents need understanding and esteem, because consciously or unconsciously, they are coping with issues of proving their sexual identities, feeling that they still have some power and authority over the world, and feeling responsible for their children's socialization and individuation. In exchange for fulfilling their needs through raising children they invest a great deal and even forgo many other things they "need."

Both adolescents and parents need to understand how the balance of power affects both parental activity and adolescent activity. Adolescent-parent relations may reflect, to some degree, anxiety about the significance of an anticipated change in this balance. Three factors affecting parental anxiety predominate in the interviews, parent group discussions and in reports of therapists (for the parents):

- An increase in the adolescent's power components and a decrease in parental authority—the possibility that an adolescent will act irresponsibly, contrary to the parents' values and expectations, or contrary to society's expectations
- Influence of the adolescent's age peer in a contrary direction, which will bring about an adverse development in his perception and behavior;
- Gradually increasing dependence of the parent on his child once the adolescent begins to draw away from the family. This may refer to the parents' emotional dependence for families from the middle and upper classes, and for others to economic dependence as well.

Of course, the emotional intensity and behavioral reactions of parents vary from case to case. But adolescents and parents alike need to understand and accept that in certain situations there simply is no congruency between the parent's needs and the adolescent's needs, just as a woman's needs may not always conform to those of her husband, or those of siblings with each other. There needs to be social affirmation of such a lack of congruency, and alternative coping strategies, which are more in accord with the changing needs and reactions of those concerned, should be sought after. It bears repeating that there is no possibility of a psychological break in adolescent-parent relations like the possibility of divorce which exists in relations between a wife and husband. Therefore, awareness of the difference in needs on the one hand and the fact of mutual commitment on the other should enable the individual to learn how to shape his separation, recognize mutual, equal worth and transfer responsibility for authority and power, while still maintaining contact and involvement.

• Children achieve positive self-esteem, to a great extent, through sincere parental acknowledgment of their right to personal autonomy and by parental reinforcement of their feelings of confidence and capacity to validate themselves in their struggle with the environment which leads, in turn, to feelings of inner validation. The achievement of positive self-esteem, thus, encourages the development of responsibility, personal identity, a positive image and goal for their future family, and a desire to maintain positive, mature ties with the adolescent's parents in the future.

Although peer group help in learning modes of validation and conflict with parents may be obtained without involving the educational establishment in what is happening in the family, such parallel activities can provide parents with the very support they need as well as help train them to provide support important for the adolescent's development. Activities of this sort may be done through direct, individual contact or through parents' groups.

• Initially, the task involved in communication and negotiation over receiving responsibility and the subsequent transfer of authority and power consists of repeated testing of the limits of authority and responsibility. This includes the adolescent's perception of his parents' roles and his expectations of them, the examination of methods of mutual involvement and transaction, and determining the limits of authority and responsibility desirable in the present and for the future. Inner and interpersonal conflicts develop during this process, which are often accompanied by feelings of frustration, conscious or unconscious distortions, inabilities to understand, and strong feelings of anger which may even lead to open strife. But in a society where there is no better alternative, one must be prepared for such eventualities: they are the natural result of the lack of confidence everyone concerned feels about their ability to fulfill their expected roles.

Flexibility and *compromise* are two principles which are paramount at this time. Everyone involved needs to learn to be flexible and when and where to compromise. Insistence on maintaining existing patterns is actually contrary to present and future needs. Righteousness, defending one's position are all unnecessary strategies for either adolescent or adult. Believing in oneself and in the truth as expressed by significant others in one's life, expressing one's readiness to relinquish past attitudes for the sake of positive development in the future in the form of negotiations over such beliefs, can only be attained with tools of flexibility and compromise. Peer group support, and when necessary personal support, provides the framework of mutual respect which will allow the adolescent to respect his parent's authority at the time when he is expected to transfer authority and power to the young person.

• The opportunity to be given greater responsibility for one's behavior and encouragement to stop engaging in power struggles results from the negotiating process. Negotiation means an opportunity to search, examine, and to formulate challenges for the parents as well as the adolescent. The process itself illustrates how to acquire power and authority and to equip oneself for decision making. Decisions are implemented initially within the framework of family and later within the social context, either with peers or a mixed group in *the* immediate environment.

Conflicts about authority and power are usually hiding deep personal and interpersonal conflicts which may express a lack of confidence regarding the right to sexual functioning, internalized memories, fear of competition, etc. The negotiation process is a sort of practical test of resolving such issues, and, therefore, it is important that a facilitator contribute his/her help and support to the adolescent and parents involved by clarifying goals, conceptualizing optional responses, and defining the possible limits of each participant's perception.

• It is important to establish that adolescents and parents may "agree to disagree." Although negotiation should aim at reaching understanding, compromises, accommodations and methods of control for realizing responsibility, when mutual accord has not been reached, participants should not feel stripped of authority or having had a solution/personal responsibility imposed on them. Such expectations of mutual consideration do not absolve anyone of the responsibility of conducting an inner review of his behavior. The significance of mutual consideration is its emphasis on the nature of the relationship: one of dynamic, mutual psychosocial dependence. Furthermore, the agreement to be able to disagree cannot be carried to an extreme whereby the adolescent feels negotiation offers him no chance for achieving individuation, or whereby the parents, sensing their failure in their major role vis a vis their children and society, may throw up their hands and abjure their responsibility.

• All participants need to free themselves from sloganeering. The perennial cry of the parent: "You're irresponsible," "You're inhuman," "You don't care if I die"; and the adolescent's plaint, "You don't care about me," "You only want to humiliate me," "You've never understood me and never will," are not only hurtful, but destructive. A response of this type, concentrating on the "you" not only fails to support the development and growth potential of the other person, but actively limits it. Statements such as these invite no response other than denial and therefore cannot lead to any further dialogue or negotiation. Therefore, such response pattern not only does not help but actually can impair the quality of family life.

Especially when participants in the negotiation process get bogged down in exchanges of this sort, but also in the normal run of events, the facilitator and peer group support consists to a great extent in using appropriate learning experiences to evaluate and define the possibility of improving readiness to change behavior. In addition, it is possible through the offices of the peer group to choose alternative areas and approaches in which the next attempt at transferring authority and formulating responsible behavior will be made.

● Just as it is possible to agree to disagree and/or add further areas of authority and autonomy to those under negotiation, it is also permissible to retreat albeit temporarily from previously held "stands." A young person may feel that he wants and is ready to move away into his own "independent" living quarters and still expect parental support. This support may include permission to return and live in the parents' home for a particular period of time or to live near them or even to "want to return home" whether it might be in order to benefit from their practical help, their moral support or simply for the sake of feeling emotional security. A retreat from independence can be easily labelled a failure, especially during adolescence; therefore it is important that the young person and his parents be aware of the permissibility of temporary lapses without changing the overall direction towards separation and autonomy.

● Activity in school must also be aimed at contributing to the adolescent's individuation process.

The message to adolescent students from the school should be: "It is you who are responsible for your development and therefore for your behavior." Just like within the family system, where separation and responsibility are attained through negotiations, the school also must conduct negotiations with its students about their areas of responsibility and about the patterns of transferring responsibility. Such an approach means the school must avoid involving parents in issues which can be resolved through negotiations with the student. Furthermore, schools must be cognizant of the fact that the adolescent's school status has implications in terms of intrafamilial relationships. The issue of the relationship between school, student and parents is discussed extensively in S. Smilansky, N. Fisher & L. Shefatiya (1987).

● The pace and pattern of transferring responsibility to the adolescent depends on various factors: the adolescent's personality, each parent's personality, family values in certain areas (such as religious values, morality in heterosexual relations, etc.), and the ecological reality within which the family operates (school norms, women's sense of security when remaining outside the home). Peer group support (and parallel support in work with parents) may prevent too rapid separation and ensure a balanced individuation process, i.e., the development of psychosocial maturity.

The chapter on the development of the individuation process throughout the life-span is based on the assumption that there is a basic connection between the separation pattern, the pattern of shaping personal identity, and the degree of capacity for initiative and responsibility in building a life model. It seems equally true that when the parent's communication pattern does not grant recognition and/or a feeling of equal worth to the adolescent, and does not enable self acceptance or encourage autonomy with readiness for personal responsibility, it actually impairs the development of shaping a positive personal identity, prevents the building of a positive life model and inhibits the development of future, mature relations with the parents. In short, a deficient communication pattern between parents and adolescents can have adverse implications for choice of a mate and building a family, for shaping professional identity and developing a career, and for readiness to create a mature relationship of trust, empathy and responsibility with the parents.

Part Two

Group Learning Experiences

Shoshana Feldman, Rachel Weiser-Granek, Prof. Sarah Smilansky

Foreword

All of us are presently involved in or have in the past been involved with adolescent-parent relations, whether actively and consciously or passively and unconsciously. Improving these relations may result in a significant improvement in the overall feeling of the individual's well-being as well as an improvement in the family atmosphere. Each individual possesses the resources which are necessary for them to be able to improve.

Involvement in improving adolescent-parent relations requires a willingness on the part of all parties to expose themselves, at least to a certain degree, and the ability to absorb and understand things from his own individual perspective as well as from that of others involved in the process. Therefore, a level of cognitive and emotional maturity is necessary which will enable intensive, responsible work.

An appropriate framework leading toward that end can consist of a consolidated peer support group. It is essential that the facilitator of such a group be familiar with the personal histories of group members, including the family status and norms prevailing in within the families themselves, in order to prevent unnecessary value conflicts between the personal values of the facilitator and his world-view and those of group members, such as statements beginning with "in our neighborhood/in our ethnic group, the custom is. . . ." This can also help prevent unnecessary exposure or unintentional harm from inadvertent revelations of family secrets such as troubles with the law, diseases, congenital defects, cases of orphanhood, etc.

A facilitator leading an adolescent group dealing with the subject of parental relations may react with a sense of blurring of his sense of separate self and with mixed feelings and attitudes. It is therefore important that the leader clarify his current personal attitude toward this subject for himself, based on memories and feelings left over from his adolescence, his present as well as past relations with his parents, his relations with his adolescent son or daughter, etc. Such an inquiry may help the facilitator to distinguish between perceiving the subject from within his own private family system and from the perspective of the needs of his group. He needs to try to avoid projecting values from his personal life and/or norms and stereotypes of his own era onto the norms, needs and values of the members of a contemporary group.

The purpose of learning experiences within the structure of the peer group is to create a stimulus for changing the adolescents' attitudes and behavior. It is, if it fulfills its potential, a change which will promote better understanding of the family system within which they live, will improve interpersonal communication and will foster more efficient functioning within familial roles.

Optimal results may be obtained when working in parallel groups with the "partners" in the familial system, the parents. Therefore, it is recommended that whenever possible meetings of adolescents and their parents should be held jointly or with each group separately, according to the suggestions for learning experiences presented below.

Below are various subjects for group work. The facilitator may choose those subjects and activities according to the needs and levels of the groups participating in the program. It is recommended that the experiences be organized according to preset goals. Some common goals are listed below.

Goals

- To help adolescents become aware of personal and social factors which shape their emotional reaction and behavior toward one or both parents.
- To help adolescents become aware of their parents' needs and expectations, as parents and human beings.
- To help adolescents understand the meaning of separation from parents during adolescence, recognizing that it is an essential stage in the development of a personal identity and a readiness and ability to cope with psychosocial maturation tasks.
- To help adolescents move ahead positively in the process of mutual differentiation, building new, mature, mutual relationships based on the premise of mutual human worth rather than a continuation of the child-parent relationship.
- To help adolescents learn to fulfill needs, resolve problems and conflicts and to ensure continued favorable individuation along with familial integration by means of conducting negotiations based on mutual understanding and support.

Learning Experience No. 1

Goals

- To kindle motivation for dealing with the subject of adolescent-parent relations
- To help clarify and coordinate the expectations of both adolescents and facilitator with regard to this topic. Several alternative activities are suggested below as an introduction to this topic.

Process

Free Association

A. Participants are invited to contribute words which occur to them when they consider ways **adolescent-parent relations** are expressed. The facilitator records all such words on the board. Examples of free associations could be: quarrels, anger, pressure, generation gap, tension, bear hug, worry, jealousy, discrimination, caring, primitiveness, reliability, unconditional love, expectations, disappointments, demands, adjustment . . .

B. Discuss the words brought up around the following points:
   — what are the contexts surrounding these associations? What is behind the quarrels? Why do people quarrel?
   — how can the associations be characterized? good, bad, judgmental, etc.
   — what can be said about the relations as depicted in the associations? can they be changed? should they be changed?
   — do these terms hold in every case? are they valid for you?

Learning Experience No. 2

Watching a film

A. A film or video reflecting relationships between adolescents and parents is shown. The screening may serve the purpose of introducing the subject and showing the various types of problems and conflicts others also have with their parents.

B. After the screening, a short discussion should be held about the issues depicted in the film and the significance of parent-child interchanges. Points for discussion may include:
   — conflicts
   — attitude of participants (parents as compared with adolescents)
   — forms of coping, etc.

Comments: Adolescents have difficulty defining themselves: are they children? adults? etc. The purpose of this experience is to aid in defining personal location along the continuum and to show that most young people are located more or less in the same area along the developmental range, struggle with the same problems, have similar experiences, and are thus able to be of help to each other.

Learning Experience No. 3

Location on the developmental continuum

A. Each participant will receive a diagram of the continuum as illustrated below:

| Infant | child | preadolescent | adolescent | adult | elderly | old |

He/she must place him/herself on the developmental continuum.

B. Each group member presents his personal continuum, and the group compares the self-evaluations of the different members. If there are discrepancies, the reasons for the various choices should be presented. For example, Joe might say: "I placed myself as 'child' because. . . ."
and Danny might note: "I considered myself as 'preadolescent' because. . . ." Participants should arrive at agreed definitions and perquisites for various locations on the continuum.

Comments: These agreed definitions will serve the facilitator and participants throughout the experiences.

C. Then, each member assigns his parents (father and mother separately) a place on the continuum. The discussion which follows should include dealing with the following points:
— what may be said about the parent's location in terms of that of the adolescent? (they are far apart, not so far apart, etc.)
— what are the results of the distance between the two individuals? (there are conflicts; they struggle with different problems; there are other needs, etc.)

D. Discuss the possibility of using the group format to learn how to cope with the "distance" while providing mutual support.

Learning Experience No. 4

"Telephone conversation"

A. The facilitator asks participants to relax in their chairs and close their eyes. The facilitator says:
   — I am at home . . .
   — Mother is busy with her usual jobs . . .
   — I look at her . . .
   — Father is reading a newspaper . . .
   — I look at him . . .
   — I think: Sometime I have run-ins with Father or Mother . . .
   — What are these run-ins about? . . .
   — When does it happen? . . .
   — With whom does it happen more? . . .
   — What makes me angry? . . .
   — What gets Father or Mother angry? . . .
   — Could I prevent the run-in? How? . . .

   Comments: It is important that this be carried out in conditions in which everyone maintains silence, and the facilitator speaks slowly and quietly and pauses between sentences.

B. Participants open their eyes and tell the group which way they would choose to prevent or resolve the quarrel.

C. The facilitator says:
   One common way to resolve quarrels is to have an open discussion with parents. One of the participants holds an imaginary telephone conversation with his father or mother about the quarrel he wishes to prevent or resolve.
   — What would he say to him/her?
   — How does he think his father/mother would react?
   — Could such a conversation really have taken place in his personal situation?

   Comments: Make sure only those who are prepared to expose themselves before the group do so. Emphasize the method of resolution, without relating to the quarrel itself.

D. The facilitator says:
   "The purpose of these meetings is to make such conversations realistic, to turn them into conversations that could lead to conflict resolution and could improve relations between adolescents and their parents."

Expectations
Learning Experience No. 5

1. Life-Worlds

Purpose

To clarify the concepts "adolescent" and "parent" and the life-world of each

A. The facilitator says:
"One of the things separating people from each other is different life experience in the life-world of each individual. Let's see what the various life-worlds consist of." Participants suggest details of different life-worlds while one of the participants (or the facilitator) records them on the board.

Notes: Aim toward raising of issues such as interests, activities, aspirations, outward appearance, concern for children, investment in studies, going out with the gang, earning money, etc. It is important that the list be long and varied.

B. The group splits up into four smaller subgroups and each has to characterize one of the following figures: father, mother, adolescent boy or girl. Each group chooses the items from the list on the board which it thinks are connected with the character they must describe (they may add further points which have not been included) and writes them on a large sheet.

C. The facilitator groups the sheets on the chalkboard (as illustrated below)

| Father | Adol. boy |
| Mother | Adol. girl |

and draws the outline of a house (roof and walls) around the lists.

D. Participants present the problems which typify each of the above characters.

E. A comparison is then made between the content of the life-worlds of each different character.
   — What may be said, overall, about it?
     ● For example:
     Father—occupied with professional advancement.
     Adolescent girl—occupied with her social world.
   The facilitator adds arrows connecting the characters and asks:
   — What may be said about the various connections between the different characters? (expectations, needs, relations, etc.)
     ● What kind of relationship will there be between each of the characters mentioned?

Alternate experience No. 6

A. Participants divide up into four groups. Each group receives a piece of pasteboard and some magic markers. The project is to prepare and make a frontal presentations (sketch, inscription, song, etc.) expressing the concepts **"adolescent"** and **"parent"**; two groups will present "adolescent" and two groups will present "parent."
B. Each group presents its poster to the entire group, with a short written explanation which includes answers to any questions which have been anticipated by the group members. When the presentation is concluded, all posters are displayed on the wall.
C. There is a brief discussion about the significance of feelings reflected in the posters or stylistic means of communicating such feelings.
     ● For example, one group has chosen to present the adolescent using a question mark. It is possible to ask the group: "What does this express? How do the rest of you feel about/identify with this method of presentation?"
D. The facilitator inquires about expectations vis a vis the relationship between the adolescent and his parent based on the works presented. The following folk saying may also be useful (to stir up discussion):

> "May trouble never strike, but how is it possible to get along with parents?"

2. Expectations of Parents and Parents' Expectations

Learning Experience No. 7

Purpose

Clarification of the adolescents' needs and expectations of his parents and his perception of parents' expectations of him

Process

A. The facilitator says: "Each of us has expectations of our parents. Let's each one of us record the expectations he has of his father or mother in these circles."

   Notes: Participants, who wish, may record one for each parent.

Adolescent expectations of Father

B. The facilitator asks participants to take another paper and says: "Parents also have expectations of us. What do you think these expectations are?" Each person records those expectations which he thinks his father or mother have of him.

   Notes: If the participant only dealt with a single parent in the previous part of the exercise, the facilitator should suggest that they relate to the same parent as they had previously.

Father's expectations of the adolescent

C. Participants should examine the two sets of circles and note to what extent expectations match:
   — where do they match?
   — where are there gaps?
   — how could these gaps be closed?
D. Participants who feel prepared to do it may discuss these gaps in a session before the entire group. At that point other group members can suggest alternatives for bridging the gaps.
   • Such as one alternative: verify expectations by interviewing the parents. The various expectations suggested can serve as a basis for preparing a parents' interview such as that suggested below.

Alternative Learning Experience, No. 8

A. Participants divide up into four groups, and each group will represent one of the following characters:

1. Adolescent boy		**2. Adolescent girl**	
Father	Mother	Father	Mother
_____	_____	_____	_____
_____	_____	_____	_____
_____	_____	_____	_____

3. Father		**4. Mother**	
Son	Daughter	Son	Daughter
_____	_____	_____	_____
_____	_____	_____	_____
_____	_____	_____	_____

Groups 1, 2—will discuss and summarize in writing expectations of their parents as an adolescent boy or girl.

Groups 3, 4—will discuss and summarize expectations of their children as father/mother.

B. Each subgroup will present its summary to the entire group.

C. During the summaries, compare the different expectations, emphasizing the existence or absence of differences between adolescents' expectations of parents and their perception of the parents' expectations of adolescents as well as between "sons'" and "daughters'" expectations of parents, and between "fathers'" and "mothers'" expectations of their children as girls and/or as boys.

The facilitator may collect the various lists of expectations at the end of the meeting and bring them to the following meeting to be used as a basis for the parents' interview.

Alternative Learning Experience, No. 9

A. Each participant chooses one of his parents as a topic and fills out the following two questionnaires:

1. My expectations of Father/Mother
2. My Father's/Mother's expectations of me
   "I expect Father to . . ."
   ". . . and Father expects his child to . . ."
   or
   "I expect Mother to . . ."
   ". . . and Mother expects her child to . . ."

Learning Experience No. 10

I expect Father to . . .

Following is a questionnaire that describes expectations of Father. Mark X to indicate how appropriate each expectation is for you.

	Very True 5	True 4	Fairly True 3	Not True 2	Definitely Not True 1
1. I expect my father to appreciate the effort I invest in my studies.	___	___	___	___	___
2. I expect my father to help me choose a vocation or major area of study.	___	___	___	___	___
3. . . . to keep track of which girl or boyfriends I am going with.	___	___	___	___	___
4. . . . to accept criticism of himself.	___	___	___	___	___
5. . . . to guide me about establishing ties with boys/girls.	___	___	___	___	___
6. . . . to share decision making with me if the family has to move to another home.	___	___	___	___	___
7. . . . to know what I am doing in my free time.	___	___	___	___	___
8. . . . to be open with me when the family has financial problems.	___	___	___	___	___
9. . . . to see me as a source of pride.	___	___	___	___	___

10. . . . to be interested in
    things that are
    important to me.   _____ _____ _____ _____ _____

11. Not to object to the way
    I dress or wear my hair.   _____ _____ _____ _____ _____

12. Not to come into my
    room when I am with a
    boyfriend/girlfriend.   _____ _____ _____ _____ _____

13. . . . to rely on me and
    let me be socially
    independent.   _____ _____ _____ _____ _____

14. . . . to be open with me
    when there are health
    problems at home.   _____ _____ _____ _____ _____

15. . . . to treat me as an
    equal.   _____ _____ _____ _____ _____

16. . . . to give me a feeling
    of belonging to the
    family and of security.   _____ _____ _____ _____ _____

17. . . . to accept me as I
    am without attempting
    to change me.   _____ _____ _____ _____ _____

18. . . . to provide me with
    a good, loving home.   _____ _____ _____ _____ _____

19. . . . to confide in me
    when there are
    problems between him
    and my mother.   _____ _____ _____ _____ _____

20. . . . to always be
    available to me.   _____ _____ _____ _____ _____

21. . . . to rely on me and
    put full trust in me.   _____ _____ _____ _____ _____

22. . . . to enable me to
    share my feelings with
    him.   _____ _____ _____ _____ _____

Learning Experience No. 11

Father expects his child . . .

Following you will find a questionnaire describing a father's expectations of his children. Indicate with an X to what extent each expectation is correct for you.

	Very True 5	True 4	Fairly True 3	Not True 2	Definitely Not True 1
1. . . . to know how to take his needs into consideration.	____	____	____	____	____
2. . . . to appreciate the efforts he invests in their education.	____	____	____	____	____
3. . . . to achieve what he himself did not manage to achieve.	____	____	____	____	____
4. . . . to make him feel proud.	____	____	____	____	____
5. . . . to understand him as a person and not only as a father.	____	____	____	____	____
6. . . . to acknowledge that he sacrifices a great deal for them.	____	____	____	____	____
7. . . . to realize the expectations that he has of them.	____	____	____	____	____
8. . . . to allow him to relive his youth through them.	____	____	____	____	____
9. . . . to respect things which are very important to him.	____	____	____	____	____
10. . . . to help the family financially.	____	____	____	____	____
11. . . . to choose a way of life acceptable to him.	____	____	____	____	____
12. . . . to love him unconditionally.	____	____	____	____	____

13. Not to criticize him or to constantly complain to him. _____ _____ _____ _____ _____

14. . . . to structure their lives very differently from his. _____ _____ _____ _____ _____

15. . . . to be independent and always be reliable. _____ _____ _____ _____ _____

16. . . . to be more successful than the children of other family members. _____ _____ _____ _____ _____

Learning Experience No. 12

I expect Mother to . . .

Following is a questionnaire describing expectations of Mother. Please indicate with an X to what extent each expectation fits you.

	Very True 5	True 4	Fairly True 3	Not True 2	Definitely Not True 1
1. I expect Mother to appreciate the effort I invest in studies.	_____	_____	_____	_____	_____
2. I expect Mother to help me choose a vocation or major.	_____	_____	_____	_____	_____
3. . . . to keep track of which girls or boyfriends I am currently going with.	_____	_____	_____	_____	_____
4. . . . to accept criticism of herself.	_____	_____	_____	_____	_____
5. . . . to guide me about establishing ties with boys/girls.	_____	_____	_____	_____	_____
6. . . . to share decision making with me if the family has to move to another home.	_____	_____	_____	_____	_____

7. . . . to know what I am
doing in my free time.   ____ ____ ____ ____ ____

8. . . . to be open with me
when the family has
financial problems.   ____ ____ ____ ____ ____

9. . . . to see me as a
source of pride.   ____ ____ ____ ____ ____

10. . . . to be interested in
things at school which
are important to me.   ____ ____ ____ ____ ____

11. Not to object to the way
I dress or wear my hair.   ____ ____ ____ ____ ____

12. Not to come into my
room when I am with a
boyfriend/girlfriend.   ____ ____ ____ ____ ____

13. . . . to rely on me and
let me be socially
independent.   ____ ____ ____ ____ ____

14. . . . to be open with me
when there are health
problems at home.   ____ ____ ____ ____ ____

15. . . . to treat me as an
equal.   ____ ____ ____ ____ ____

16. . . . to give me a feeling
of belonging to the
family and of security.   ____ ____ ____ ____ ____

17. . . . to accept me as I
am without attempting
to change me.   ____ ____ ____ ____ ____

18. . . . to provide me with
a good, loving home.   ____ ____ ____ ____ ____

19. . . . to confide in me
when there are
problems between her
and my father.   ____ ____ ____ ____ ____

20. . . . to always be
available to me.   ____ ____ ____ ____ ____

21. . . . to rely on me and
put full trust in me.   ____ ____ ____ ____ ____

22. . . . to enable me to
share my feelings with
her.   ____ ____ ____ ____ ____

Learning Experience No. 13

Mother expects that her child . . .

Following is a questionnaire describing a mother's expectations of her children. Indicate with an X to what extent each expectation is correct for you.

	Very True 5	True 4	Fairly True 3	Not True 2	Definitely Not True 1
1. . . . to know how to take her needs into consideration.	____	____	____	____	____
2. . . . to appreciate the efforts she invests in their education.	____	____	____	____	____
3. . . . to achieve what she herself did not manage to achieve.	____	____	____	____	____
4. . . . to make her feel proud.	____	____	____	____	____
5. . . . to understand her as a person and not only as a mother.	____	____	____	____	____
6. . . . to acknowledge that she sacrifices a great deal for them.	____	____	____	____	____
7. . . . to realize the expectations that she has of them.	____	____	____	____	____
8. . . . to allow her to relive her youth through them.	____	____	____	____	____
9. . . . to respect things which are very important to her.	____	____	____	____	____
10. . . . to help the family financially.	____	____	____	____	____
11. . . . to choose a way of life acceptable to her.	____	____	____	____	____
12. . . . to love her unconditionally.	____	____	____	____	____

13. Not to criticize her or to
    constantly complain to
    her.   ＿＿＿ ＿＿＿ ＿＿＿ ＿＿＿ ＿＿＿

14. . . . to structure their
    lives very differently
    from hers.   ＿＿＿ ＿＿＿ ＿＿＿ ＿＿＿ ＿＿＿

15. . . . to be independent
    and always be reliable. ＿＿＿ ＿＿＿ ＿＿＿ ＿＿＿ ＿＿＿

16. . . . to be more
    successful than the
    children of other family
    members.   ＿＿＿ ＿＿＿ ＿＿＿ ＿＿＿ ＿＿＿

B. Participants are divided up into four subgroups. Each group is to examine the questionnaires of its members and discuss the items which received scores of 1 (Definitely Not True) or 5 (Very True). Group members should discuss the significance of these expectations, the significance of the various gaps, differences in father's or mother's expectations, differences in boys' expectations as contrasted with those of girls, etc.

C. One member of each subgroup, representing his subgroup, presents a summary of all the significant subjects which arose in the discussion along with the conclusions reached before the group as a whole. These subjects and conclusions will serve as the basis for subsequent parental interviews.

   Notes: The facilitator should be sure to emphasize that the questionnaires are anonymous.

Learning Experience No. 14

3. Interviewing the parents

Goals

- Practical examination of the adolescents' perception of parental expectations, by means of interviewing the parents
- Practicing the interviewing of parents

I. *Preparing the interview*

Process

A. Facilitator:

"We can see that there is often a gap between the adolescents' expectations of his or her parents and an adolescents' perception of parents' expectations of them. Let's see whether the adolescents' perception really fits the parents' actual expectations. For this purpose we need first to condense the findings from our previous meeting into this table. These lists can serve as a basis for our preparing interviews of our parents."

Notes: If the group raises the issue, expectations may be divided according to sex of parent and sex of adolescent.

Father's expectations		Mother's expectations	
of son	of daughter	of son	of daughter
_____	_____	_____	_____
_____	_____	_____	_____
_____	_____	_____	_____
_____	_____	_____	_____

B. Each participant should copy the expectations and interview his parents— father and mother separately—regarding these expectations. He should elicit from them to what extent they agree with each expectation, why they disagree, and whether they have additional expectations. They should bring the results of the interview(s) to the next meeting.

C. Interview rehearsals can be held: included in the practice session will be choosing the proper timing, both in terms of when and in terms of circumstances (quiet, etc.), how to word the questions, tone of voice, etc.

Notes: Not when parent is tired or hungry . . .
Not when parent is in a hurry to go.
. . . Could you give me a few minutes? I would like to hear your opinions about something . . .
Be sure to plan adequate time to practicing the interview.

This rehearsal should be treated exactly as a role play, in order to examine both the manner of address and also possible reactions and how to cope with them.

Learning Experience No. 15

II. Reporting the interview

Process

A. Participants will report back about interviewing their parents. Initially emphasis should be placed on the following points:
— How did I feel while interviewing my parents?
  • Was it easy/hard to approach them, to get them to talk, to find the right way to get them to talk, to find the right timing, etc.
  • Were there things which came up in the interview (beyond the specific items) which I hadn't expected? which surprised me? which impressed me?
  • How did my parents react to the interview?
  • Has the interview had any influence on our relationship?

At this point compiling results will receive the most attention. Findings should be recorded on the board. For example:

Father's expectations		Mother's expectations	
of son	of daughter	of son	of daughter
_____	_____	_____	_____
_____	_____	_____	_____
_____	_____	_____	_____
_____	_____	_____	_____

Or results may be arranged according to birth order:

  expectations of firstborn son/daughter
  expectations of youngest son/daughter

B. Discuss briefly the following points:
— To what extent do parents' actual expectations fit the adolescents' perception of parental expectations?
  • The adolescent thought his father expected . . . of him, but in the interview it became clear that . . .
— Regarding which expectations do adolescents' expectations of their parents (as raised in the previous meeting) fit parents' expectations of the adolescents?
— In which areas is there agreement and in which areas are the contrasts prominent?
  • The difference between declared intentions and actual behavior.
— What are the reasons for the contrasts? (personality differences, changing expectations, generation gap, etc.)

Learning Experience No. 16

Who are Our Parents?

1. *The parent as human being*

Goal

Differentiating between the adolescent's awareness of his parent **as a person** and **as someone fulfilling a role**

Process

A. The facilitator:

"Each of us perceives his father/mother through their role as parents. Our reactions are thus responses to the parental role as well as to the person behind that role. For example, it is often difficult for us to express certain emotions, particularly anger; it may be hard to feel free to say things which are more personal, to express oneself using "crude" words or slang; it may often be hard to talk about experiences and behavior which are considered normal and acceptable among one's own friends, etc. The parent's image is constantly before us, limiting us."

The following exercise may be used to illustrate this point:

B. This exercise requires the group to work with its imagination. The group should be in a relaxed state; this may be accomplished on an individual basis—by requesting everyone to find a comfortable position and relax or in a group exercise designed to promote relaxation. Everyone should, at the end, by sitting comfortably with their eyes closed.

Facilitator: "Picture your father or your mother—or both of them—in your minds."

pause (about 15 seconds) . . .

"Say the following sentence to Mother (or Father): 'Mother, please give me a glass of milk,' or 'Father, please turn on the light.'"

pause (about 15 seconds) . . .

"Now I will ask you to repeat these sentences, but this time, instead of saying 'Mother' or 'Father,' say their names—'Charlie,' 'Anna.'"

pause (about 15 seconds) . . .

"Now, let's try making some additional requests—ordinary, everyday things—of Father or Mother (using their first names)."

pause (about 15 seconds) . . .

"Now please open your eyes."

pause (about 15 seconds) . . .

C. Facilitator:

"Let's discuss how we felt when we said 'Mother' or 'Father' as opposed to how we felt when we called our parents by their first names?"

Group members share their feelings with each other. Each one says what he wants to and the facilitator reflects their statements back to the participants.

Summarizing Feedback:

Facilitator:

"We can see that calling our parents by their names instead of their titles arouses various emotions: embarrassment, strangeness, repulsion, surprise; but all of these only emphasize that Mother is both 'Mother' and 'Anna,' even though it is hard for us to accept that when confronted with that fact."

Learning Experience No. 17

Alternative II (to B or C)

An open discussion of the fact that it is customary to address a parent by his role, using a universal name (mother, father) rather than by his private first name. The facilitator may present the group with various ways of addressing parents prevalent in different cultures (it is recommended that the following material be prepared beforehand in the form of a poster or transparency).

Means of addressing one's parents, Locale

— Sir

  • customary in European aristocracy; middle to upper classes, 19th century England/US.

— addressing and speaking to parents in the third person.

  • was customary in Western Europe.

— addressing parents as father/mother.

  • generally accepted in our society.

— addressing parents as father/mother with addition of the first name.

  • address prevalent in some societies.

— addressing parents by first name.

  • acceptable primarily in different social classes at certain stages of one's life.

D. Facilitator:

"We have discussed our emotional reactions to Father/Mother:

We get angry when they limit us . . .

We are pleased when they buy us things, etc.

Parenthood is a life role toward which most people focus their energies. In order to know and understand the people who fill this role (their needs, aspirations, struggles), it is important for us to recognize the personal histories which have accompanied them thus far. How well do we really know our fathers and mothers? Let's break up into smaller groups and share what we know about our parents:

— Where does he/she come from?

— What are his/her likes/dislikes (color, food, film, book, etc.)

— What are his/her hobbies?

— What are his/her hopes and dreams?

— What are the thing(s) that he/she finds most frustrating?

— What is guaranteed to make him/her angry?

— Who tells him/her what to do?

— Why does he behave one way rather than another?

Note: Suggest that participants ask their parents (father, mother or both) to tell them a story about their own adolescence, such as, the most embarrassing thing that happened, or the worst fight with their own father or mother, etc. It is also possible to gather stories about parents as adolescents from grandparents or uncles and aunts.

E. The following questions can be discussed by the entire group:

— Do we really know our parents?

— What makes it difficult to get to know them?

— In which areas of life are they less available to "know"?

— What would we like to know about them?

— What could we do to get hold of more information?

Feedback:

When parents are recognized and understood beyond their functioning within the life-role assigned, the way is opened for fuller communication, deeper acquaintanceship, and enriched relationships of all those involved.

2. The Generation Gap

Goal

To enable a more thorough view of the generation gap

General observation

These exercises focus on two aspects of the topic of "the generation gap":
  I. General-social
  II. Personal-experiential.
The facilitator should choose whichever focus he feels is most appropriate for him and his group; however, both aspects could be combined. The facilitator should ask that participants prepare for the meeting by reading and gathering relevant material.

Learning Experience No. 18

Option I

Participants are asked to bring material dealing with the generation gap, such as:

stories	articles
poems	newspaper reports
pictures	reports on films viewed

Option II

Each participant brings an item or items relating to or belonging to the adolescent period of their parents. For example:
  pieces of clothing
  phonograph records
  pictures
  special items or souvenirs

Process

Option I

A. Facilitator:
  "In our previous sessions we discussed how expectations diverge. One of the reasons for this difference is called 'the generation gap.' Let's see what we can find out about what the generation gap really is." Participants present what they have collected about this subject.

B. An open discussion can ensue about how the generation gap is reflected on various levels (cultural norms, expectations, values, behavior, styles) and about its implications for adolescent-parent relations. A film concretely illustrating the generation gap can be viewed and the various significant points which arise can be discussed at this time.

Learning Experience No. 19

3. *Every generation and its rebellion*

Goal

Legitimizing the need for "youthful rebellion"

A. Facilitator:
   "Each generation and each person in his own generation has a need to demonstrate originality or uniqueness. This need may be realized in various ways: in an accepted and adaptive fashion or through rebellion against established conventions."
   "What kind of examples from your own experience can you think of which fit that description?" Participants should contribute examples.

B. "Youthful rebellion" is a common term.
   — what are they rebelling against?
   — when does their rebellion actually take place/begin?
   — are limits set for the rebellion and if so how are they established? who sets them?
   — is this rebellion a wholly negative phenomenon? is it inevitable?
   — against what did your parents rebel when they were younger?

C. View "Rebel without a Cause" with James Dean, and consider the primary messages of the film. For example:
   — youth seems to be characterized as being **"against"** something—against the establishment, against parents, against teachers, etc.
   — the desire to control and impose the adolescent's world-view on adults.
   — the relativistic nature of this view. The more the adolescents mature, the more their views change, and each time there seems to be a desire to adapt the environment to accord with their new perceptions.

Learning Experience No. 20

Relations with Parents
1. Questionnaire on "relations"

Goal

To examine the type of tie between adolescents and their parents

Process

A. Facilitator:
"In one of our previous meetings we tried to get to know our fathers and mothers better as people. Now let's take a look at our relations with them."
Each participant should complete the following two questionnaires, one about the father and one about the mother.

My relations with Father

This questionnaire describes our relations with our fathers. After you have read each item indicate to what extent the statement is true for you with an X.

	Not True 1	Rarely True 2	Some- times True 3	Often True 4	Very True 5
1. My father accepts me as I am.					
2. I am interested in hearing my father's opinion about subjects that affect me.					
3. My father always knows when something is bothering me.					
4. Discussing my problems with my father makes me feel stupid and embarrassed.					
5. Father expects too much of me.					
6. Father trusts my judgment.					

7. Father has his own problems so I don't bother him with mine. _____ _____ _____ _____ _____

8. I don't get a lot of attention from my father. _____ _____ _____ _____ _____

9. My father understands me. _____ _____ _____ _____ _____

10. My father doesn't know or understand what I've been going through lately. _____ _____ _____ _____ _____

11. When Father thinks something is bothering me, he asks me about it. _____ _____ _____ _____ _____

My relations with my mother

This questionnaire describes our relations with our mothers. After you have read each item indicate to what extent the statement is true for you with an X.

	Not True 1	Rarely True 2	Some-times True 3	Often True 4	Very True 5
1. My mother accepts me as I am.	_____	_____	_____	_____	_____
2. I am interested in hearing my mother's opinion about subjects that affect me.	_____	_____	_____	_____	_____
3. My mother always knows when something is bothering me.	_____	_____	_____	_____	_____
4. Discussing my problems with my mother makes me feel stupid and embarrassed.	_____	_____	_____	_____	_____
5. Mother expects too much of me.	_____	_____	_____	_____	_____
6. Mother trusts my judgment.					

7. Mother has her own
problems so I don't
bother her with mine.   _____ _____ _____ _____ _____

8. I don't get a lot of
attention from my
mother.   _____ _____ _____ _____ _____

9. My mother understands
me.   _____ _____ _____ _____ _____

10. My mother doesn't
know or understand
what I've been going
through lately.   _____ _____ _____ _____ _____

11. When Mother thinks
something is bothering
me, she asks me about
it.   _____ _____ _____ _____ _____

A. Each participant evaluates his relations with his father or mother
according to questions like the following:
— In what way are they alike?
— How are they different?
— How could you characterize the type of communication there is
with each of them?
— What is the degree of trust?
— Is there a feeling of stiffness or distance?

Note: The comparison may be carried out in several ways:
an item for the father compared with the same item for the mother.
prominent items (which received scores of 1 or 5) for the father as
compared with prominent items for the mother.

Those participants who feel like doing so may take the opportunity
to share their impressions with group members.

B. Participants discuss the question: "What are the ideal relations that
I would like to have with Father/Mother? Are these realistic?

Learning Experience No. 21

2. True friendship with parents?

Goal

To examine the possibility of having true friendship between parents
and children

Process

A. Facilitator:

"Parents frequently say: 'We want to be your friends.' How is this expressed in practice? Let's examine this point." Participants shall be divided into smaller groups and each group will constitute a newspaper editorial staff, dealing with one of the selections below. Each group should react to the incident (by formulating answers for itself) from the point of view of:

— parent
— adolescent—friend
— counselor
— the adolescent himself
— another adult

Selection 1

"My mother tries to be my friend. Each time I go out with my boyfriend, she waits for me until I return, exploding with curiosity.

She wants to know everything: What did he say? What did I reply? How did I feel? How much money did he spend? What are my future plans?

My life is an open book for her. I don't want to hurt her, but I don't need a 40 year old friend. I want privacy."

Selection 2

". . . I thought that when my daughter, Nina, grew up we could be very close friends. We would go out sometimes to spend time together or to shop, we would share experiences and feelings and have long, intimate conversations. I would be able to tell her about my life and she would share with me everything that happens to her, since my daughter is the person closest to me. The truth is that she has become the most insufferable thing there is in my house. She is totally self-involved, interested only in what is happening to her, without any sensitivity for any member of the household. All of us have the feeling that we exist solely to serve her and must adapt to her moods. The house is a hotel for her, for eating and sleeping and for talking hours on end with her boy and girlfriends, who I don't even know, on the phone. When I ask for details, she answers impudently that it's none of my business. Sometimes I'm insulted to the point of tears by this tone of address. Long ago, I buried the dream about close friendship between us deep in my heart, but a modicum of respect and sensitivity, understanding and closeness—must I forgo that as well?''

B. Each group presents the selection and the various answers in the form of psychodrama before the entire group. In other words, one participant represents the "character" who turns to the editorial staff and the others will respond to him.
C. Discuss the following points:
— what are the advantages and disadvantages of a friendship between parents and children?
— can there be true friendship with parents? why? why not?

Note: It is important to clarify the responsibility of the parent's role, which grants him authority and sets limits.

Learning Experience No. 22

3. Birth Order

Goal

Exploration of the influence of birth order on perception of the adolescent's role in the family and its inner relationships

Process

A. Participants will be divided into four small groups, according to their birth order:

Group A	Group B
Firstborn	Middle Children

Group C	Group D
Youngest	Only Children

Note: If there is only one child in a particular group, he can be placed with a group which is most appropriate, according to logic, e.g., an Only Child would join Firstborns.

Learning Experience No. 23

Alternative for Exercise A

A. The facilitator asks each participant to consider:
"If I could choose my place in my family in terms of birth order, which would I choose?" (firstborn, middle . . .) Participants take turns to relate what they have chosen and will be divided into groups according to their choice (Firstborn, youngest, only child . . .).
B. Each group will discuss the significance of birth order (actual or desired) in terms of the following points, and will summarize them on the chalkboard or a piece of pasteboard:
— advantages
— disadvantages
— their expectations
— expectations of them (by parents, other siblings, etc.).
— problems characteristic of each birth position

Learning Experience No. 24

4. When I feel frustrated . . .

Goal

To learn to overcome feelings of frustration and helplessness in relations with father and/or mother

Process

A. The facilitator asks participants to close their eyes and concentrate on the situation he is about to describe, as if they were actually experiencing it:
"I am in the house . . . in my room . . . preparing for the big final exam in history . . .
There's lots of material to learn and go over . . .
I'm trying to imagine what questions might appear on the test . . .
I am rereading my notes of the material learned in class, including the questions given during the lectures or which appeared in the textbook . . .
I feel I have covered all the material and that I am quite ready for the test . . .

The next day, as the test begins, I receive the sheet of questions and get a sinking feeling—the questions are completely different from what I expected . . .
How do I feel?"

Notes: The facilitator may choose another subject which he feels is more relevant to the participants.

B. Participants open their eyes and share their various feelings with their friends:
— frustration
— anger
— helplessness, etc.
C. Facilitator:
"In the example described, did "I" do everything possible so that the reason for the feelings of frustration and helplessness came from the unexpected discovery that the questions were not what had been predicted? Sometimes a person may choose not to try at all to do anything, since he experiences a feeling of frustration and helplessness from the outset (e.g., a person who feels from the start that he cannot cope with the quantity of material, so he does not even take the test).
"Such feelings are not limited to someone's studies. For example, it sometimes happens that we feel something similar (frustration, helplessness . . .) in our relations with our fathers or mothers as well.
"Try to recall such as instance . . ."
— How was the frustration expressed?
— What did you do?
— How did you overcome it?"
D. Participants pair off and discuss the incident they thought about and what they did.
The "listener" can offer additional suggestions for overcoming these feelings. If no suggestions for the specific instance suggest themselves in the discussion, other methods might be tried, such as role playing the incident, getting the "narrator" to take both sides in another, similar situation, etc.
E. All the various suggestions discussed between the couples should be aired before the entire group.

Facilitator's Summary

Sometimes it is possible to get the other side closer to us, to make him or her soften his views, be more flexible, even to get closer to our attitudes, ultimately to understand us; but this is not always possible. Sometimes, if that last is a true statement for me, if I cannot bring about any change in my father or mother, it may be worth changing myself in order not to drown in a feeling of frustration and helplessness. This—"constructive coping" is very important, especially in frustrating situations; it is learning to see the "half full glass" in every situation.

Learning Experience No. 25

Expressing Feelings Toward Parents

1. Negative feelings

Goals

- To maximize awareness of the existence of vexing characteristics in parents, and to encourage discussion about this
- To legitimize expression of anger towards parents
- To refute the generalization that criticism and anger imply lack of love
- To provide different methods for expressing anger

Process

A. Facilitator:
   "There are things that we like about our parents and there are things which anger us and drive us crazy! We might even find ourselves feeling active hatred in reaction to that trait or behavior. This happens to each of us.
   Let's think about a trait or behavior of our fathers and mothers which we simply can't stand."
   Before the entire group, collect a list from each member of the following items: the most infuriating, hateful, annoying behavior/ trait(s) of my father . . ., of my mother . . .
B. Compare infuriating traits and behaviors of mothers with those characteristic of fathers.
   — do they overlap?
   — does infuriating behavior attributable to the father produce the same fury when done by the mother?
   — does what angers one member of the group anger others?
C. Facilitator's Summary
   "It seems clear that it is perfectly natural to get angry about a parent's trait or behavior. This doesn't have to mean that we hate

the parent or that we have stopped loving him. Some things we find difficult to deal with don't give others any trouble; other things which don't bother us particularly, bother others a lot. In any case, the important thing is to cope with the anger and be able to say to a parent, for example: 'I am angry with what you did,' without saying 'I hate you.'"

Learning Experience No. 26

2. *Positive Emotions*

Goals

- To clarify the concept of empathy for members of the group
- To increase participants' skill in showing empathy in different ways

Process

A. Facilitator:
"We all noticed how difficult it was for us to talk about negative emotions regarding our parents. What happens with positive emotions? Do we express them? In what ways?

"We all like to be on the receiving end of compliments; we all feel good when people express positive emotions towards us. Do we do this towards others? Who can give us some examples of both directions: instances when you were comforted, and instances when you did the comforting. It is not necessary to discuss why the comfort was necessary."

Learning Experience No. 27

B. Facilitator:
"Concern and expression of feelings is a mutual thing. It's not enough that I, as an adolescent, am aware of my parents' needs and take an interest in what happens to them as people. It is also important that I know how to show them, actively, that I care.

"Close your eyes and think as I speak: **"I am in distress . . .** [pause to allow a distressful situation to be imagined fully]
How do I feel?
In what way do I express my distress?
What reactions do I expect?"
[Longer pause.]

My parents are in distress . . . [pause allowing imagination of appropriate situation]

How do I see that they are in distress, what signals their feelings to me? How do I feel about their situation? How do I express my concern (toward my father . . . toward my mother)?"

Notes: Discussion is recommended of the point that concern is essentially empathy. True empathy exists when the message "I care" is conveyed to another person. Empathy is a translation of the German concept *Einfuhlung*. *Ein* means "inside, within." *Fuhlung* is to feel, to sense. Hence the literal meaining of empathy is "to feel within."

Participants will relate various ways to express concern, both from the point of view of expressing concern to someone else and being the recipient of expressions of concern. For example: touching, talking, silence, passing a note, through a third party.

Role play can be used to practice various methods for expressing empathy; scripts could be the situations imagined in the directed fantasy.

Learning Experience No. 28

Alternative experience

A. The facilitator will present the following situation:

"Joey, a 16 year old, found out that his father was having problems with his boss at work. When Joey saw his father that evening on the porch, it seemed to him that he was almost in tears. Joey didn't know what to do—to go and speak with him—or not?

Notes: We recommend including one suggestion out of the three which says: "I wouldn't do anything . . . I would ignore it . . . I would leave the house . . . etc." This kind of suggestion may be dramatized in the following way: The father seats next to an empty chair. Joseph passes by him and leaves the room. Silence prevails for half a minute. Joseph returns to the room.

The participants take a few minutes to record what each would have done had he been in Joey's place. They could record it in the form of a dialogue. Each participant takes turns offering suggestions.

The facilitator selects two or three different suggestions from those offered and asks participants to act them out in a role play.

B. **The actors report back to the group:**
   — What did each, **as Joseph,** try to convey to the father?
   — What did he expect in terms of the father's reaction?
   — Does he think his message was received?
   — What were his feelings about the father's reaction?
   — What did he imagine were the father's expectations?
   — How did he receive the message of concern?
C. A discussion should be held focusing on the following points:
   — To what extent do my parents allow me to inquire into what happens to them, and tell me what is disturbing them?
   — Why do they sometimes avoid this? (the need to maintain the image of perfection and stability before the world; a desire to defend their children at any cost; the fear of appearing weak, etc.)
   — How can we help our parents?

Learning Experience No. 29

Parents—Between Themselves

Goal

To help the adolescent perceive his role in cases of conflict between the parents which do not concern him directly

Process

A. Facilitator: I'd like to read a translation of a short poem from the book, *I Wish that Suddenly*, by Judah Atlas:

> "When Father and Mother argue sometimes and say "Quiet, quiet . . . The children are listening," It's really unpleasant, But I'm not alarmed at all. But when they begin to maintain Long silences, I Suddenly feel that I want to cry."

Participants should relate to the emotions that the poem evokes in them.

B. Facilitator:
   "Conflicts and quarrels between parents happen all the time. Sometimes these conflicts are between the two parents as individuals and sometimes they involve one parent in conflict with himself or with his surroundings. When the quarrel does not directly affect

the adolescent, he may choose from several alternatives in reacting. Let's take a look at them:

"Dafna is in 11th grade and has felt for a long time that there are problems in her parents' relationship. Dafna has several options in terms of what she could do.

Facilitator: Take a look at each of the options available to Dafna and think about these two questions with regard to each one:
— What is the nature of each of these "alternative activities"?
— Which alternative do you feel is preferable and why?
The following five methods have been prepared on separate plac-ards; the Facilitator or members of the group read them aloud and discuss them:

DISREGARD—she acts as though she does not know anything.

REFLECTION—she tells her parents that she knows they have problems, that she cares, but doesn't wish to interfere.

PASSIVE INTERVENTION—she tells her parents that she is aware of difficulties and that they would do well if they were to request help from others.

ACTIVE INTERVENTION—she intervenes actively, trying to help through mediation, reconciliation, justification, etc.

TAKING A POSITION—she clearly supports one of the parents

Afterwards going over the stances, the Facilitator distributes the signs around the room, asking each participant to choose the sign which represents the attitude which is closest and most acceptable

to his opinion, and then to sit next to it. Each group gathered
around a particular sign is to discuss:
— why did they chose this method of behavior?
— what are its advantages and disadvantages?
— what is their attitude toward the other methods?
C. Each group will present its conclusions to the entire group.

Feedback

We can see that parents are human beings and subject to the same
kinds of conflicts and disputations as other human beings. Sometimes
they have problems getting along in general and with each other; there
is often a need to impress upon them the fact that we are aware of
their difficulties, which also makes things hard for us; however, we
are limited in our ability to act without causing harm.

Alternative Experience No. 30

A. Facilitator:
"So far we have focused on conflicts between the adolescent and
his parents. Although we usually relate to parents as a single,
unified entity, we have actually seen that parents are also people—
('the two of us together and each one by himself') with opinions,
wills, needs and different desires. Hence it is natural that conflicts
arise between them, too. In our meeting today we will focus on
this topic and on the adolescent's behavior and response when
conflict arises between parents."
Participants take turns suggesting various possible conflicts
between parents which are not connected with the adolescent.
Possible conflicts could include:
— career vs. family;
— financial problems;
— relations with the family of origin (grandparents, aunts, etc.);
— different customs;
— mutual friends;
— preferred types of recreation;
— varying political views;
— contrast between personal traits, such as neatness, punctuality,
etc.

B. Facilitator:

"Watch the following incident enacted between a 'husband' and a 'wife.' Note how you would react if you were the son or daughter of these parents on a slip of paper."

The facilitator chooses one of the conflicts suggested in part A and asks two participants to present it to the group, taking the roles of husband and wife.

Notes: It is important that the conflict be significant and familiar, such as:

1 The woman wants to go to work, but the husband objects.
2 The man invests a lot at work and returns late. His wife always complains about this.
3 The woman wants to go out at night for recreation and for meeting mutual friends, but the husband is always too tired.

C. The adolescents take turns reacting.
D. "As you can see, there are various possible reactions to conflicts such as these; let's try to characterize these reactions."

Notes: If reactions were not sufficiently varied, or if participants have difficulty in categorizing, the facilitator can suggest further examples to lead them towards the generalizations desired. The intention is to arrive at types of reactions such as:

Denial—there is no conflict at all.
Disregard—there is conflict but I don't interfere.
Emotional reflection—the adolescent shows how the conflict affects him.

Learning Experience No. 31

E. Facilitator:

"Now let's see how the *parents* took these different reactions! We can use role play for this too. Watch and ask yourselves:
— What are they feeling?
— What are all the possible results of each reaction?

One participant will present his reaction and the "parent" will share his feeling with the whole group concerning that reaction (how it affects him), and how he plans to act in consequence of that reaction.

Notes: For example:
Adolescent: ". . . I am no longer able to listen to your fights. Solve your problems when I am not at home."
Parent: "How dare you say such a thing? Who do you think you are, interfering in things which are none of your business anyway?
Another parent: ". . . I'm really sorry. I hadn't thought about what this might be doing to you."

F. Discuss the following points:
    1. What are the advantages and disadvantages of each type of reaction?
    2. What emotions does each reaction arouse in the adolescent as well as in the parent, and why?
    3. What difficulties might the adolescent encounter by entering into a conflict between his parents?
    4. How can he choose the most appropriate reaction to a particular conflict in a given situation?
    The discussion will serve as feedback for the experience.

Notes: The difficulty parents have in accepting the adolescent as a person with his own point of view, equal in value to that of the parents, should be discussed.

Learning Experience No. 32

Alternative experience

A. The Facilitator asks participants to close their eyes and concentrate on the following situation:
    It's late at night . . . I'm in my room . . . in bed . . . I wake up hearing raised voices . . . Father and Mother are arguing and yelling at each other . . .
    — how do I feel?
    — what am I afraid of?
    Participants open their eyes and write down their feelings, fears and thoughts on a slip of paper—anonymously.

B. The Facilitator collects the slips and reads them to the group.
    — anger
    — a sense of guilt and failure
    — fear of abandonment
    — identification with one side
    — shame
    — any others that come up

Notes: It is recommended that the Facilitator read them in alphabetical order to prevent disclosure.

Learning Experience No. 33

C. Facilitator:
"Let's assume that there is an additional participant in our group called Al, and Al wrote:

Recently, this has been happening over and over. I'm afraid this is it. Now they will surely get divorced. I'm not sure that they care about me. What will happen to me?

"What could we tell Al?"
Participants should react freely. Possible reactions:
— Your parents still love you and are concerned about you.
— Your parents are still your father and mother even though they might not live together.
— They won't necessarily get divorced.
— Even if they get divorced, it's not the end of the world.
— It might be better in the long run for them to separate than continue to make each other miserable.
— Your parents aren't the only ones to fight.

D. Participants can offer various suggestions on how to help Al, such as:
— how to talk with his parents
— how to share his distress with the parents
— how to suggest that the parents seek professional help
— that he should seek help himself to overcome the crisis
— to accept and work through the divorce ahead while continuing to function.

Notes: ● Suggestions may be concretized through role play.
Alternatively, instead of Al's letter, the following passage could be discussed:

I have found out that the parents of a good friend of mine are getting divorced. How should I act? What should I say to him/her?

Learning Experience No. 34

Conflicts in Adolescent-Parent Relations

1. Classifying conflicts

Goal

Clarifying the foci of common conflicts in adolescent-parent relations

Process

A. Facilitator:
   "In our meeting today we are going to focus on common conflicts between adolescents and parents."
   Participants will split up into groups of four or five. Each participant is asked to write down two or three primary conflicts he has with his father and two or three primary conflicts he has with his mother.

   Notes: The possibility should be considered that one of the participants will state: "I **don't** have conflicts with my parents." How can this be explained?

B. Each group should discuss the conflicts mentioned, gather the responses and categorize them according to frequency.

C. Representatives of each group summarize their findings to the entire group. The facilitator records the findings on the board so that everyone can see all the groups' results.
   The following format is recommended for recording the overall conflict summary on the board:
   Conflicts between adolescent boys and the **father**

   _____

   _____

   Conflicts between adolescent girls and **the father**

   _____

   _____

   Conflicts of adolescent boys with **the mother**

   _____

   _____

   Conflicts of adolescent girls with **the mother**

   _____

   _____

D. Discuss specific characteristics of the conflicts in each group.
   Facilitator's Summary:
   "We can see that most conflicts seem to be about the same or similar subjects. The next time we get together we will explore them both from the standpoint of adolescents and from the standpoint of parents."

Learning Experience No. 35

2. "Two sides of the same coin"

Goal

To help adolescents see conflicts from both their perspective as well as that of their parents

Process

A. The Facilitator introduces a list of common conflicts either taken from those raised in the previous meeting or from the following list:
   — An adolescent insists on keeping the door to his room closed;
   — Parents' comments about their son/daughter's messy room;
   — Playing music too loudly;
   — Type of music listened to;
   — Debates about style of dress;
   — Parental interference in choice of friends;
   — Prohibition of hitchhiking;
   — Debate about an appropriate hour to return home at night;
   — Struggle over telephone calls—number and/or length;
   — Maintaining privacy;
   — Debates about limits of intimacy.
   One of the participants chooses one of the conflicts and conducts a "dialogue" with himself by playing both roles; thus, he speaks for both the adolescent and for the parent.

   Notes: The goal of this experience is to help the adolescent understand the parent's emotions and his position in the conflict. Thus, it is important that the **same** adolescent take both the role of adolescent and of parent in the given situation. Therefore, we do not suggest role play in which two participants act out separately the roles of parent and adolescent.
   In order to emphasize the role switch and portray it more graphically, two chairs, labeled "parent" and "teenager," may be set up facing each other. The actor moves from chair to chair according to the role he is playing. Of course, other means of illustrating the role switch may be

employed, such as evocative hats or simply labels. It may be necessary to request the participants to try to honestly portray the reactions they probably are quite familiar with rather than be tempted into portraying stereotypical roles.

At certain points in the dialogue, members of the group watching may wish to suggest different reactions from their own experience.

B. This process is repeated with another three or four participants, each choosing different conflicts.

Notes: Although different reactions may be contributed, analysis and discussion should be deferred until the end of the exercise.

C. The **"players"** tell the whole group:
— how did they feel while they were "adolescents"?
— how did they feel while they were "parents"?
— have they changed their understanding of the conflict issues in any way?

Notes: It is important to allow the "players" to report their feelings first.

D. The other participants add their own considerations to the issue; for example, they may express a new understanding of parental anxiety for their children's well-being on the one hand coming up against the adolescents' desire for independence.

Learning Experience No. 35

3. *Conflicts over adolescent sexuality*

Process

A. Facilitator:
"Get comfortable in your chairs, close your eyes and let my voice get into your heads, the voice of your thoughts. "I am a teenager. My body is growing into that of an adult; my personality is developing and is sometimes like an adult and sometimes like a child. I have sexual and emotional needs and I want to be in charge of shaping my sexual behavior. How do my parents see me, at least how do I think they see me, in such a role?
(pause)
What are my parents prepared to **accept** regarding me?
(pause)
What are they unprepared to accept?"
(pause)

Participants fill in slips like these without signing their names:

> Mother/Father are unprepared to accept . . .

> Mother/Father are prepared to accept . . .

B. The Facilitator collects the slips and writes (or reads) all the things parents are prepared to accept as opposed to those that parents are unprepared to accept. The group discusses the individual and varied nature of the limits of prohibition and permission. For example, sexual behavior which is permitted by some parents, such as embracing and kissing in their presence or discussing sexual relations, etc., is forbidden by other parents.
— What do the parents fear?
— What is the source of these fears?
— Why are there so many conflicts in this area?
— What can be done to prevent conflicts or alleviate fears?
Participants should make various suggestions, such as:

Notes: It might be a good idea to record the suggestions as they come up on the board.
— to check whether my own (adolescent) perception is in fact correct. Sometimes I just assume that my parents do not or will not accept certain things.
— To understand my parents' difficulty in initiating a conversation on the above subjects (as a result of education, the generation gap, etc.), and to help them by approaching them directly and frankly.

Mature communication through conversation and dialogue will help my parents learn about me and accept me as an adult.
C. Using role play and role-reversal, participants can illustrate suggestions and/or offer advice. For example:
— Parents who become angry when their son brings home his girlfriends and expects them to sleep over.
— A mother who allows her daughter to have sexual relations with her steady boyfriend, but does not permit him to sleep over in her house.
— Mother-daughter dialogue when the daughter wants support in asking the family doctor for birth control pills.
— Parent-son discussion of what to do when son's girlfriend turns up pregnant.

Learning Experience No. 36

4. Pocket Money

Goal

To help in clarifying and coping with conflicts over the issue of money

Process

A. Below is a list of statements. Each participant should indicate next
   to each statement whether he agrees or disagrees.
   — An adolescent should be given pocket money on a regular basis.
   — If an adolescent is expected to perform special duties at home
     (yardwork, dishwashing, car washing, baby-sitting, etc.), he
     should be paid for them.
   — It is important that the adolescent have his own money.
   — Parents should not interfere with what the adolescent does with
     his money.
   — If the adolescent wants pocket money, he must work and earn
     that money.
   — Parents must provide pocket money.
   — In one sense pocket money develops independence, and in
     another sense it creates dependence.
   — Sometimes pocket money ought to be forgone.

   Notes: The list can be reproduced as a questionnaire, or read out loud
   to the group as a whole with the participants marking down D(isagree)
   or A(gree) on a slip of paper.

B. Participants break up into small subgroups.
   In the subgroups the different statements are discussed with members reacting and comparing each other's responses to the different
   statements. Ask the members to anchor their reactions to specific
   examples from their personal experience of getting or not getting
   pocket money. Group members can exchange suggestions about
   how to cope with these conflicts.

C. Each group chooses one money-related conflict to present before
   the entire group. The presentation should be made as follows:

● description of the conflict
● presenting the attitudes of "significant others"
● suggestion for a solution

5. Dependence/Independence

Goals

- To enable adolescents to experience the conflict each of them has regarding independence-dependence
- To enable adolescents to clarify their preferences regarding independence and dependence in their relations with parents for themselves
- To examine these preferences with the parents as well

Learning Experience No. 37

First Meeting

Process

A. Facilitator:

"In our previous meetings we have dealt with various conflicts between adolescents and their parents. We have seen that a gap exists between the perceptions and approaches to a problem on the part of the adolescent and on the part of the parents. In the next few meetings we will explore this subject in greater depth. One of the most controversial points is the adolescent's desire to move from a state of **dependence** to a state of **independence**."

"Please sit comfortably in your chairs. Close your eyes. Pay attention to each of the muscles in your body in turn and make sure they are relaxed."

Pause.

"Think about the word 'independence.' What pops into your mind when you think about the word? What feelings do you have when those words occur to you? What does it mean to you to be 'independent'?"

Pause.

"Now, hold on to all those associations and feelings having to do with 'independence' and store them away in the RIGHT side of your body."

Pause

"Now, concentrate on the word 'dependence'—what does it mean for me to be dependent on someone else? What sort of feelings and thoughts occur to me?"

Pause

"Now, hold on to all those associations and feelings having to do with 'dependence' and store them away in the LEFT side of your body."

Pause

"When I say **independence**—everybody move his right side in a way which expresses how he feels independence. When I say **dependence**—everybody do the same thing with the left side of his body."

Pause

The Facilitator says 'independence' or 'dependence' several times, alternating them unexpectedly and gives sufficient time between each word to let the participants change positions.

B. The Facilitator asks participants to open their eyes and invites members to relate how they felt and what they experienced during their movements; he/she inquires which feelings were more pleasant, with which feelings and/or associations they had difficulty, etc.

Notes: Reference is to feelings that arose initially upon hearing the words independence/dependence and to the sensations by means of which they tried to express their feelings, as well as to the conflict they experienced.

C. Facilitator:

"Now that we have experienced the essential feelings of dependence/independence, let's try to clarify what is actually meant by seeking independence and how that search manifests itself in terms of behavior."

The Facilitator asks those participants who are prepared to do so to tell the group about and illustrate what independence is for them. Questions can be directed at them to elicit in what way they express their desire for independence and how their behavior in relations with their parents expresses this desire. At the same time, they should be encouraged to discuss their readiness to continue in their position of dependence, including the "advantages," their desire for dependence and the fear of independence.

D. The group should discuss all the different views and variations in defining independence/dependence.

E. Participants offer various possible interpretations for the different variations in terms of the environment, primarily the parents; in other words, they should consider how parents will react to the different types of behavior and how they might respond to them.

Notes: Dialogues can be introduced here to check the various alternative parental reactions to their children's expression of independence and/or their continuing desire for dependence. It might be interesting to repeat a dialogue with players switching roles: the "teenager" to be the "parent" and the "parent" to be the "teenager" and then discuss different feelings of the players when they took on the different roles.

Learning Experience No. 39

F. The Facilitator requests each adolescent to record:
   1. three most important things in which he would like to be independent in terms of his relations with his parents.
   2. three important things concerning which he would prefer to remain dependent on his parents.

G. The Facilitator collates answers from the participants into two lists:
   1. **Aspiration towards independence.**
   2. **Willingness for dependence.**
   Thus, for example, **The issue of money, clothing, etc.** would show up as follows:

   "I am unprepared to report on spending of pocket money"— would come under category 1 "Aspiration towards independence."

   "I am ready to report and consult about how I spend my pocket money" might fit into category 2 "Willingness for dependence."

or

   "I want a new garment although Mother claims I have enough clothing" (independence).

and

   "I am prepared to make do with the clothing Mother decides to buy, because I am not ready to invest effort in choosing clothes" (dependence).

H. Discuss the following points briefly—
   — what can we learn from these two lists?
   — how do you think your parents would relate to each point appearing in the two lists?

Notes: If not enough subjects are suggested, the following items may be useful:
— purchasing clothes or other personal items alone.
— cleaning the house.
— caring for younger siblings.
— shopping.
— sleeping away from home.
— choosing what to wear.
— being responsible for studies.
— talking with teachers about the state of studies.
— setting an evening curfew.
— deciding on the type of recreation.

Learning Experience No. 40

I. Facilitator:
    "We have been exploring our views and wishes on the issue of independence-dependence which is inevitably limited to our own private points of view and according to our subjective perception of parents' views. Let's try to check this directly with parents and make up an interview to help us do this."
    The group will decide on ten items concerning which the interview will be conducted.
    Each participant will interview three sets of parents whom he knows (and who have adolescent children). He will ask them to consider which of the items they might be prepared to allow an adolescent independence, and for which subjects is it important to them to maintain the adolescent's dependence on them.
    The interview will be conducted with each parent separately (the father alone, the mother alone).
    Although interviews will remain anonymous, it is important to indicate the ages of the respondents' adolescent children. The adolescents should bring the interviews to the second meeting.

Process

A. Participants break up into subgroups. Each group will arrange the respondents' answers in a table:

Item	Father		Mother		ages of adolescents
	independence	dependence	independence	dependence	
1 . . .					
2 . . .					
3 . . .					

B. The members of the subgroups discuss the significance of the results, including the following points:
    — for which items are father/mother willing to grant independence?
    — over which items are father/mother willing to maintain dependence?
    — on which items is there accord between ourselves and our parents?
    — about which items is there an "age" or "generation gap"?
    — what does "adolescent independence" mean in the eyes of father/mother?

— what do we feel, as adolescents, towards parents' responses? how do our feelings fit in with our interpretation of independence (in the previous learning experience)?

Learning Experience No. 41

Differentiation and Individuation

1. The Separation Process

Goals

- To increase awareness of the importance of differentiation from parents
- To encourage conveying this message to parents

Process

A. Facilitator:

"One of the most obvious and important needs manifested during adolescence is that of individuation, i.e., the *individuum*, the 'I,' must stand on its own.

In order for the 'I' to be able to stand on its own two feet, it has to be able to distinguish its feet from that of its parents. Therefore, individuation grows out of the process of differentiation from one's parents."

The Facilitator hands out a slip with the following uncompleted sentence on one side:

For me, the process of
differentiation . . .

and this uncompleted sentence on the other side:

For me, the need for individuation is . . .

"Please finish the sentences on both sides of the piece of paper."

Participants should read their answers in turn. Attention should be devoted to the varying expressions of this need by different people and to the importance of differentiation as a source of growth and development during adolescence.

Notes: It is best to avoid verbal definitions in order to enable maximal associative consideration of the concepts of differentiation and individuation.

Learning Experience No. 41

2. *"Time will tell"*

Goals

- To clarify the effect of the time dimension on development of relations between children and parents

- To heighten awareness of the possibility of change in the nature of relations by means of appropriate coping

Process

A. The facilitator presents the following excerpt to participants:

A child of 7 says: "My father is a genius . . . he knows everything"

A child of 14 says: "My father knows, but . . ."

A 17 year old says: "My father doesn't understand anything . . ."

A man of 40 says: "My father knew a lot."

Based on this excerpt, discuss the following points:
  — What do you think about this quotation? Do you agree with what it says?
  — What does this variation in perception attest to?
  — According to this excerpt, what will the nature of relations be at each stage?
  — Can anyone offer examples of conflicts that once were but no longer exist, or the opposite?
  — How does time influence the perception of relations?

Notes: There is a famous Mark Twain story which is very similar about how much has father learned during the time Twain grew from age 17 to age 21. See how many similar stories the participants can come up with which illustrate the same points and ask them to relate personally to the truth which makes these stories "funny."

Learning Experience No. 42

Communication between Adolescents and their Parents

1. Conducting negotiations

Goals

- Becoming aware of gaps concerning perceptions of obligations and privileges of adolescents and their parents
- Using negotiation as a way to solve conflicts

First Meeting

Process

A. Participants are divided up into four groups. Two groups are to write down the **obligations and rights** of adolescents. Two groups are to write down the **obligations and rights** of parents toward adolescents.

Each group will arrange its list in two columns (obligations/rights) and attach the lists to the board.

Notes: It is important to limit the duration of activity to 20 minutes.

B. The lists should then be compared.

C. Facilitator:

"An examination of the two groups of lists shows us that although there are points of agreement, there are also gaps and variations in how the obligations and rights of adolescents and parents are perceived. Let's focus on the points of dissension and see how we might bring the positions closer, without entering into sharp conflicts."

Choosing a particular point from the list of adolescent "rights" about which the parents disagree—such as, for example, keeping a pet against the parents' wishes, the Facilitator invites participants to join in a role play episode, practicing negotiating with parents to actualize this right.

Emphasis should not be on any particular right but rather **on the manner of conducting negotiations.**

Notes: negotiating by shouting or entrenchment behind positions of power, as opposed to an attempt to listen and understand the positions of the other side.

Homework

Each participant should choose one point of contention and negotiate on it with his parents. He will have to report to the group at the following meeting about the way negotiations were conducted, his parents' reactions, his difficulties, successes, thoughts, feelings, etc.

> *Notes:* In order to make reporting easier, we recommend that essential points be recorded. A report sheet could be prepared and xeroxed which would outline the main areas which will have to be remembered.

Learning Experience No. 43

Second Meeting

Process

A. Volunteers report to the group about their experiences.
B. The Facilitator selects several of the examples cited and asks participants to reenact the negotiations before the group using role play. Other participants can join in (using empty chairs placed next to each of the characters), trying out other alternatives.
C. Facilitator:
   "In conducting negotiations the intention is not to change parents, but to produce a solution to the problem."
   The Facilitator chooses another problem from those raised by the adolescents. One participant acts the part of the adolescent, and another is a very **authoritarian** father/mother. Then, a third participant acts out the part of a **non-authoritarian** father/mother (with the same "adolescent").
D. The "adolescent" tells how he felt with each of the parental figures, including how he had planned to conduct the negotiations with each "type." Other participants are invited to contribute their remarks and recommendations.
E. At a certain point a fourth significant figure may be added to the interaction, such as an older or younger sibling, grandparent, uncle/aunt, etc. Discussion could be organized of the effect of this fourth figure on the negotiation process. If time allows, it is recommended that different variations of conducting negotiations be rehearsed, using other characters and events.

F. A summary discussion should be held to answer the following points:
   — Do I think that I would conduct the negotiations differently now?
   — How do I feel about someone else intervening in negotiations with my parents?
   — Even if I didn't succeed in negotiations today, an opening should be left for trying again (ask for examples of this).

Alternative Learning Experience No. 44

A. Participants should break up into groups of four. Each group receives a card containing a description of a conflict between a parent (father or mother) and an adolescent.
   Two participants from each group will take the roles of parent and adolescent and attempt to cope with the conflict. The other two participants will be observers. Each of them is to observe a different character in the negotiation process and write down his impressions.
B. At the conclusion of the role-play process, the observers report on the method of negotiations in the different groups. At that point other participants may suggest additional methods.

Learning Experience No. 45

2. Improving communication between adolescents and parents

Goals

● Getting in touch with our emotional reactions and with those of others
● Practicing altering reaction patterns
A. Each participant writes the typical reactions of his family members during a conflict, whether he does or does not approve.

   Notes: In order to help participants list many reactions, they should be encouraged to recall common situations in the family or altercations which have occurred recently.

Father's reactions . . .

Mother's reactions . . .

My reactions (or those of other adolescents I know . . .

Reactions of brothers/sisters.

Notes: It is possible to make do with the reactions of father-mother and adolescent only (without siblings).

B. Reactions should be arranged on the board (or a posterboard), according to the participants' reports, as follows:

typical reactions of father	typical reactions of mother	typical reactions of adolescent	typical reactions of brother/sister

If the facilitator feels that the list of reactions is too limited, he may also add typical reactions in accordance with a list prepared beforehand.

For example:

— Don't bother me now, I'm busy.

— You and your constant foolishness.

— I haven't the energy to listen to you.

— I have sacrificed my life for you.

— You are always bothering me.

— Now you can shut up and listen to what I have to say.

— Stop treating me like a baby.

— How often do I have to ask you for the same thing?

— Maybe you could stop interfering in my business?

— Slams the door and walks out.

— Cries.

— Gets irritated by everything.

— Yells.

— Shuts himself/herself in room.

C. Attention should be paid to the repetition and universality of reactions in different family systems and by individuals with different roles.

D. Participants break up into small groups. Each group discusses the reactions of only one figure:

— With which reactions am I comfortable?

— Which reactions would I like to change?

— How would I change them?

E. Each group reports to the entire group on
   — difficulties in carrying out the task.
   — reactions they would like to change.
   — suggestions for change.
F. A practice session is held using role play and role reversal for the various suggestions.

In conclusion, the Facilitator states:

— "It is important that we become aware of the fact that our reactions lead to counter-reactions.
— We are able to change our own reactions and thereby to condition different reactions in others.
— Details that sometimes seem to us less important, like manner of address, tone of speech and timing arouse reactions in others which are undesirable ultimately for us.
— Sometimes two sides find it hard to 'break the ice,' and each side waits for the other to make the first move. If we wish to resolve the conflict, it is important to overcome 'prestige barriers' (who will speak first) and address the other side.
— Improving communication can help contribute to conflict resolution and sometimes even to its prevention."

Learning Experience No. 46

Suggestions for Summarizing the Unit

Then and Now

Each participant writes a sentence or two on a slip of paper, expressing his view of relations with his parents. The Facilitator distributes slips which had been written by the participants during the initial session. Everyone compares their slips, looking for the significance of the difference(s) between them—if there is a difference—and shares results with the others.

Suggestion-Round

Participants produce an "advice column" to adolescents for improving communication with parents including explanations of their suggestions.

Do's and Don'ts

Participants break up into small groups. Each group prepares a "Ten Commandments" of do's and don'ts for relations with parents.

Composing a script

Each group composes a script which focuses on two or three points which had been discussed during the learning experiences. Any group prepared to do so will present its script to the entire group. Instead of a script, a dramatization might be prepared to summarize the topic.

Open letter

An "open letter" to the parents is proposed. What would we like to say to them?

Personal application

Each one should tell about something from the various activities he has applied personally:
— How was this received?
— How did he feel?

Alternative

"A friend told me about a problem he has with his parents.
— What did I advise him to do?
— What were the results?"

Learning Experience Nos. 47-50

Meetings with Parents

Why do we need to hold meetings with parents?

The transition from childhood to adulthood is not an easy or a straight path; it contains many ups and downs. The resulting difficulties and conflicts are reflected in all areas of life and in various relationships. Parents may be more aware of the broader meanings, reasons and changing conditions of the adolescent. They have experience in other life-contexts and may bring this experience to bear on the situation at hand.

Bringing parents into closer proximity to the adolescents' life-world—through sincere understanding and inquiry and by increasing awareness of both adolescents' and their own needs and difficulties in facing modernity can actually help adolescents in their differentiation and individuation process.

However, even with proximity, it is important that parents be aware of the adolescent's need for distance from them and for maintaining the

boundaries of privacy. This need neither abrogate the value of proximity spoken of above nor be considered as a threat to parental authority and position.

In order to change attitudes and improve communication between
parents and adolescents, it is desirable to work with both sides, either
together or separately. This is not an easy task, as it invites much
resistance on the part of both adolescents and parents. But given the
importance of this subject, the facilitator should make an effort to cope
with this resistance.

The parents' group is meant to form a (parent) peer support group
with goals similar to the goals of the adolescents' group. Parents will
find mutual support in such a group ("this doesn't only happen to
me at home . . ."); the group will also help them to develop skills for
conflict resolution and for requesting help when necessary. Group
work will increase parents' awareness of the distress and crises which
adolescents experience, and will encourage them to open channels of
communication which will enable adolescents to turn to them in times
of trouble.

Work with parents can also constitute an opportunity for creating
better ties between the school and families, beyond that of reporting
grades and disciplinary problems.

Planning sessions

Planning sessions is predicated on several factors:
- willingness of parents to attend sessions
- the number of sessions that can be held
- proper physical conditions (e.g., an appropriate place, lighting,
  proper timing, convenient hours)

Meetings must be carefully planned and realistically organized, both
technically and content-wise, in order to prevent disappointments and
false hopes. It is preferable not to hold a meeting at all rather than
have something superficial.

It is up to the Facilitator to decide, according to circumstances whether
to hold a onetime session with parents and adolescents in the middle
of the course of activity of the adolescents' group or at the end, or to
hold a series of meetings. Meetings may be for parents only or combined, part for parents only and part for.them together with the adolescents. It is recommended that light refreshments be provided for
each meeting to create a warm, informal atmosphere. Depending on
ultimate numbers of participants, it might be a good idea for the facilitator to arrange for a colleague to assist him or her in both planning
and carrying out the meetings in order to reduce tensions and to help

cope with the various problems associated with conducting such meetings. Following are examples of proposals for meetings with parents.

Details of a proposed model

We have chosen the option of four meetings. According to the recommended sequence, the first two meetings will be with parents only, partially theoretical and partially experiential; the remaining two meetings will be held jointly with adolescents and parents.

Operative Goals

- Clarification of the goals of the meetings
- Getting acquainted with typical problems of adolescence
- Recognizing and understanding the "other side"
- Methods for coping with conflicts and improving communication between adolescents and parents

First Session, No. 47

Parents Alone

A. Getting acquainted
B. Clarification of session structure and goals
C. Content:
   1) Information about typical problems of adolescence
   2) Information about stages of family development
   3) Description of each person's place in family transactions and understanding mutual patterns of influence.
   — Using information garnered during previous group work with the adolescent children of these parents, the Facilitator will establish relevant discussion points in this meeting.
   — The Facilitator may speak himself or invite a colleague.
   — Different modes of presentation which could be used include:
      • lecture
      • film and discussion
      • information sheets and work in small groups (buzz sessions)
      • questions and answers

Second session, No. 48

This session focuses on clarifying the parent's place in the son's/daughter's adolescence and the significance of the process for the parents.

The sample suggestions included below may be applied using various experiential, small group dynamic techniques as well as discussion with the full group, role play, descriptions of incidents, etc. It is recommended that active experience be combined with cognitive discussion, as was done in the adolescent peer groups.

Happiness Profile

1. Noting conflicts that parents have with adolescents and ranking their severity.
2. Each parent should rank himself on the scale below as he remembers himself at different ages, and connect the points for a profile.

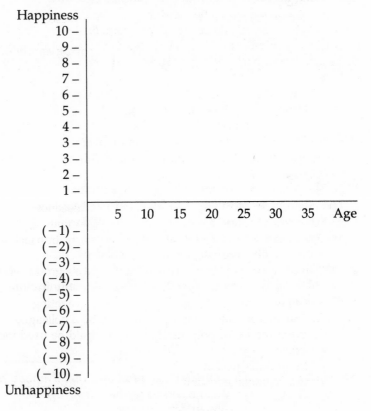

In smaller buzz-groups each person will present his profile; focus should be directed toward the feeling of happiness or unhappiness between the ages of 10-20.

Then each parent should try to place his own adolescent on the same scale; any similarity and/or variation should be discussed.

We recommend suggesting that parents ask their adolescent son or daughter at home to place himself on the profile and compare the parents' placement of him with his placement of himself. This comparison may serve as an opening for dialogue and discussion.

3. Parents' report of incidents and conflicts with their parents, and how they resolved the conflicts.
   How would they feel were their son/daughter to resolve the conflict in this way?

4. Clarification of parents' needs and their perception of their role as parents, and its consequences for the adolescents.
   — What do "they" expect of me as a father/mother?
   — What do I expect of myself as a father/mother?
   — How would I like to be viewed by my son/daughter?
   — What are my needs at this stage of my life?
   — How do my needs merge with my son's/daughter's needs?

5. Realization of parental expectations and dreams through the adolescents.
   — I always dreamed about . . . so I want my son/daughter to be . . . to do . . . to receive . . .
   — I didn't have it and so . . .
   — It's important to me that my son/daughter succeed at . . .

6. "True friendship" between parents and children.
   — For and against.
   — The price required for each of these positions.

7. The meaning of "respect" in adolescent-parent relations:
   — What does it mean for me to respect my parents . . .
   — What does it mean to me that my children will respect me . . .
   — Am I capable of apologizing to my children?

8. Development of the subject of "listening" and awareness of various parental reactions which foster or impede communication.
   For example:

Impeding reactions: command, warning and threat, moralizing, judging and accusation, investigation, scorn, comparison to others . . .

Fostering reactions: encouragement, praise, calming, sharing feelings, understanding needs and problems, counsel . . .

— How do I usually react?
— What is the mode of communication between me and my child?
— What can I do in order to change?

9. Dealing with the problem of limits:
— What does "no limits" mean for children (I deserve everything)
— What does "no limits" mean for parents (giving everything)
— If they give everything, what do they ask for in return? (the right to interfere, to dictate, to make conditional)

10. Work regarding sample incidents on different subjects, chosen by the Facilitator, such as:
— violence in the family
— exploitation of children by parents and exploitation of parents by children
— how do I feel when my son/daughter fail? How do I react?
— exaggerated demands by children
— lack of consideration for others' needs
— conflicts between siblings and parental intercession
— comparison made by parents between siblings or others.

11. Discussion of the sending of distress signals:
— Do I relate seriously to my son's/daughter's adolescence, and am I attentive and sensitive to their upsets?
— Am I capable of ascertaining that my son/daughter is distressed?
— My son/daughter is in crisis—what do I do?
— When and how do I determine that something is sufficiently important to constitute a crisis?

A relevant film could be shown followed by a discussion of its meaning and specific points which arise from it; for example:

It Can't Happen to Me (the drug problem)
When Jenny, When (sexual relations)
Phoebe (pregnancy)
Amilia (incest)
Daddy's Girl
Pulling Strings (group pressure)
Anorexia

Note: The Facilitator could suggest to parents that, before the joint meeting with the adolescents, they prepare a list of topics and problems they would like to have considered. These requests should, preferably, be recorded anonymously on slips of paper like the one below.

> A problem with my son/daughter is upsetting me and I would like
> to receive help or a suggestion, namely

A list such as this might also be requested from the adolescents:

> A problem with my father/mother is upsetting me and I would
> like to receive help or a suggestion, namely

These slips can be held in reserve for use in the discussions held in
the fourth meeting.

Learning Experiences Nos. 49-50

Joint Meetings of Parents and Adolescents (Third and Fourth Meeting)

Preliminary Notes and Clarifications

- Both adolescents and parents must be prepared for the joint meetings, while clarifying the importance of the encounter. Resistance to holding a joint meeting can arise from a fear of revealing conflicts in the family, fears about an unexpected clash in public, or feelings of embarrassment about parents. In such instances resistance may be abrogated by disproving the fears and noting the advantages of a face-to-face meeting. Establishing the "program" of the meeting at the outset and "warm-up" activities can contribute to a feeling of well-being and the reduction of anxieties.
- The adolescent should be encouraged to attend the meeting even if his parents cannot come.
- It is important to recall that adolescents, unlike their parents, are experienced in group work; therefore, the variation between the parents' group and the adolescents' group is likely to be expressed by a different pace and work-style. The Facilitator should keep track of such differences, controlling the right to speak, maintaining limits, quickening the pace when necessary, etc.
- The Facilitator could co-opt a few adolescents as "assistant facilitators" to help him conduct the meeting. For example, when dividing up into groups, they can serve to maintain the principles of group work by explaining things to parents, preparing signs and cards, writing on the board, placards, etc.

- Although, as noted, the goal of the meeting is to elicit confrontation and validation between the differing views of parents and their adolescent children, this is not necessarily between a specific parent's views and the views of his own adolescent. Therefore, **it is important to ensure that parents and their own adolescents *not* be in the same small group.** Also, it is important to maintain **heterogeneity**, i.e., not to have separate groups composed of all parents or all adolescents.

- Buzz-sessions, role play and simulation are particularly recommended work techniques in a meeting of this type. Role play and role reversal help to concretize conflicts and enable viewing the situation from various angles. **It is important** to allow parents to experience the role of "adolescent." Simulation allows transfer of various family situations to the group, and practicing different alternatives for coping.

In order to work intensively and productively, we suggest beginning with comprehensive views of the parents' and the adolescent's life-worlds; then, it is possible to continue with a definition of the clash between these two worlds and the conflicts arising from it. The work can propose alternative methods of coping as well as definition and conclude with integration and generalization.

Three possible focuses are suggested below, from which the Facilitator may select the topic which seems most appropriate:
- obligations and rights of adolescents and their parents
- the struggle over dependence and independence
- parents' expectations of adolescents and vice versa

When working on one of the above topics, the Facilitator may bring in the effect of the time dimension, the problem of "double messages," the parents' desire to protect their children, one side disregarding the other side's needs, etc. After a comprehensive discussion of the topic selected, it is recommended that he choose one significant conflict to focus on which has come up in a previous group meeting or earlier in the discussion of this group. Other possible conflicts from which to choose are listed below:

> choice of profession
> sexual development
> clash of values
> scholastic achievement
> differing life style

Suggestions for illustrating conflicts and coping methods

1. Analysis of a case (in small groups)

Analysis of a case which demands decision making:
- what is the parents' position?
- what is the adolescents' position?
- how can a decision be reached which will satisfy both sides? Sample case:

An 11th grade student wants to leave school and go to work.

---

2. Family meeting (simulation in the full group) Sample topic:

Preparation of a family agreement about dividing house chores.

Other participants will play the roles of family members: father, mother, brothers, sisters, etc. Each family member will indicate his complaints, preferences and wishes, and the family must reach a mutually acceptable agreement.

Alternative

Participants may be divided into small groups; each group constitutes a family and must reach an agreement on the issue of task division or on any other relevant issue. Afterwards, a comparison will be made between the solutions suggested in the different groups.

3. Intentions and directions

Am I really able to stand behind my declarations? We often threaten things we don't intend to do or say things we don't really mean. For example:

"I'll throw you out of the house"

"I don't care what you do . . ."

"I'll run away from home . . ."

"There are no secrets between parents and children . . ."

"Dad is my best friend . . ."

"**Your** best friend is me, your mother . . ."

"Whatever you decide is absolutely fine with me . . ."

Participants should contribute examples of similar statements from their own experiences. If time allows, they should also explain why these declarations cannot possibly be carried out. Afterwards, the following questions can be discussed:

— what happens (how do I feel) when such a declaration is disproved?
— in my opinion, what does the other side think and feel?

Points like these should be emphasized:

— the importance of reliability and consistency in establishing relations on a basis of mutual equality.
— the danger of making idle threats.
— recognition of the implications of our various declarations and how they are perceived by the other side.
— the efficacy of stopping for a moment before an emotional outburst (mental "counting to ten").

4. Collection of problems

Adolescents and parents, separately and anonymously, write down various problems which disturb them in their interrelationship. One participant draws a slip at random from the pile and reads the problem aloud. The group suggests solutions or coping methods.

Bibliography

Ackerman, N.W. "Prejudice and scapegoating in the family." In Zuk, G. E. & Boszarmanyi-Nagi (Eds.), *Family Therapy and Disturbed Families*. Palo Alto: Science and Behavior Books, 1967.

Adelson, J. "Adolescence and the generation gap." *Psychology Today*, 12 (9), 33-37, 1979.

Adelson, J. & Doehrman, M.J. "The psychodynamic approach to adolescence." In Adelson, J. (Ed.), *Handbook of Adolescent Psychology*. New York: Wiley, 1980.

Bateson, G. The challenge of research in family diagnosis and therapy, summary of panel discussion: I. Formal research in family structure. In N.W. Ackerman, F.L. Beatman & S. Sanford (Eds.), *Exploring the Base for Family Therapy*. New York: Family Service Assn., 1961.

Bell, D. & Bell, L. "Parental validation and support in the development of adolescent daughters." In Grotevant, H. & Cooper, C.R. (Eds.), *Adolescent Development in the Family*. San Francisco: Jossey-Bass, 1983.

Berlo, D.K. *The Process of Communication*. New York: Holt, Rinehart Winston, 1960.

Blos, P. *On Adolescence: A Psychoanalytic Interpretation*. New York : Free Press, 196 2.

The Adolescent Passage: Developmental Issues. New York: International Universities Press, 1979.

Boszarmanyi-Nagi, I. "A theory of relationships." In Boszarmanyi-Nagi, I. & Framo, J. (Eds.), *Intensive Family Therapy*. New York: Harper & Row, 1965.

Boszarmanyi-Nagi, I. & Spark, G.U. *Invisible Loyalties: Reciprocity in Intergenerational Family Therapy*. New York: Harper & Row, 1973.

Bowen, M. "Theory and practice in psychotherapy." In Guerin, P.J. (Ed.), *Family Therapy, Theory and Practice*. New York: Gardner Press, 1976.

Bowlby, J. *Maternal Care and Mental Health*. Geneva: World Health Organization, 1951 .

Attachment and Loss (Vols. 1 & 2). New York: Basic Books, 1969.

Ckzenmihalyi, M. & Larson, R. *Being Adolescent*. New York: Basic Books, 1984.

Coles, R. and Stokes, G. *Sex and the American Teenager*. New York: Harper and Row, 1984.

Cooper, C.R., Grotevant, H. & Condon, S. "Individuality and connectedness in the family as a context for adolescent identity formation and role-taking skills." In Grotevant, H. & Cooper, C.R. (Eds.), *Adolescent Development in the Family*. San Francisco: Jossey-Bass, 1983.

Damon, W. *Social Development and Personality*. New York: Norton, 1983.

Douvan, E. & Adelson, J. *The Adolescent Experience*. New York: Wiley, 1966.

Dreyfus, E.A. *Adolescence, Theory and Experience*. Charles E. Merrill Pub., 1976.

Dusek, J.B. & Flaherty, J.F. *The Development of Self-Concept during the Adolescent Years*. Chicago: Society of Research in Child Development, 1981.

Elder, G.H. *Children of the Great Depression*. Chicago: University of Chicago Press, 1974.

Erikson, E.H. *Childhood and Society*. New York: W.W. Norton & Co., 1950.

Identity, Youth and Crisis. New York: W.W. Norton & Co., 1968.

Freud, A. "Adolescence." In Eissler, R.S. & al., *Psychological Study of the Child*, Vol. 13. New York: Int. Universities Press, 1958.

Freud, S. "The transformation of puberty." In Strachey, J. (Ed.), *The Complete Psychological Works*. New York: Norton, 1905.

Galbo, J. "Adolescents' perceptions of significant adults: A review of the literature." *Adolescence, 16*, 951-970, 1984.

Gilligan, C. *In a Different Voice*. Harvard University Press, 1982.

Goldberg, S. and Lewis, M. "Play behavior in the year-old infant: Early sex differences." *Child Development, 40(1)*, 21-31, 1969.

Gould, R.L. *Transformations: Growth and Change in Adult Life*. New York: Simon & Schuster, 1978.

Hall, G.S. *Adolescence: Its Psychology and its Relations to Physiology, Anthropology, Sex, Crime, Religion and Education*. New Jersey: Prentice Hall, 1905.

Halpern, H. *Cutting Loose*. New York: Simon & Schuster, 1977.

Havighurst, R.J. *Developmental Tasks and Education*. Longmans, 1953.

Hetherington, E.M. "The effect of father's absence on child development." *Young Children, 26*, 233, 1971.

Hetherington, E. "Effects of father absence on personality development in adolescent daughters." *Developmental Psychology, 7*, 313-326, 1972.

Jackson, D.D. and Satir, V.M. "Family diagnosis and family therapy." In N. Ackerman, F.L. Blatman & S.N. Sherman (Eds.), *Exploring the Base for Family Therapy*. New York: Family Service Assn., 1961.

Josselson, R.L. "Psychosocial aspects of psychosocial maturity in adolescence." *J. of Youth and Adolescence, 6* (12), 25-55, 145-165, 1977.

Josselson, R.L. "Ego development in adolescence." In Adelson, J. (Ed.), *Handbook of Adolescent Development*, New York: Wiley, 1980.

Kantor, D. & Lehr, M. *Inside the Family*. San Francisco: Jossey-Bass, 1975.

Kashti, Y. & Arieli, M. "Residential schools as powerful environments." *Mental Health and Society, Vol. III*, No. 3-4, 1976.

Residential Settings and the Community: Congruence Conflict. London: Freund, 1987.

Keniston, K. *Young Radicals: Notes on Committed Youth*. New York: Harcourt Brace Jovanovich, 1968.

"Student activism, moral development and morality." *American Journal of Orthopsychiatry, 40*, 577-92, 1970.

Kitwood, T. *Disclosures to a Stranger*. London: Routledge and Kegan, 1980.

Kohlberg, L. "Stage and sequence: The cognitive developmental approach to socialization." In D.A. Goslin (Ed.), *Handbook of Socialization Theory and Research* . Chicago: Rand McNally, 1969.

Krosnik, J.A. & Judd, M. "Transitions in social influence at adolescence." *Developmental Psychology, 18*, 359-368, 1982.

Lasch, C.H. *The Culture of Narcissism*. New York: Norton, 1977.

Levinson, D.Y. & al. *The Seasons of a Man's Life*. New York: Knopf, 1978.

Lewin, K. *Field Theory in Social Science*. New York: Harper & Row, 1951.

Lewis, M. "State as an infant-environment interaction: An analysis of mother-infant interactions as a function of sex." *Merrill-Palmer Quarterly, 18*, 95-121, 1972.

Mahler, M.S. *On Human Symbiosis and the Vicissitudes of Individuation: Infantile Psychosis* (Vol. 1). New York: International Universities Press, 1968.

Maier, H.W. "Challenge of child development." *Child Welfare, 61*, 72-74, 1982.

Masterson, J. *The Psychiatric Dilemma of Adolescence*. Boston: Little, Brown, 1967.

Minuchin, S. *Families and Family Therapy*. Cambridge: Harvard University Press, 1974.

O'Connell, A. "The relationship between life structure and identity synthesis in traditional, neo-traditional and non-traditional women." *J. of Personality, 44* (4), 1976.

Offer, D. *The Psychological World of the Teenager*. New York: Basic Books, 1969.

Offer, D. & Offer, J.B. *From Teenage to Young Manhood: A Psychological Study*. New York: Basic Books, 1975.

Osherson, S.D. *Holding On or Letting Go*. New York: Macmillan, 1980.

Parsons, T. & Bales, R.F. *Family, Socialization and Interaction Process* . Glencoe, Ill.: Free Press, 1955.

Piaget, J. & Inhelder, B. *The Psychology of the Child*. New York: Basic Books, 1969.

Rappoport, R., Rappoport, R. & Sterliz, Z. *Fathers, Mothers and Society: Perspectives on Parenting*. New York: Basic Books, 1977.

Rubin, L.B. *Worlds of Pain*. New York: Basic Books, 1976.

Ruesch, J. "Synopsis of the theory of human communication." *Psychiatry, 16*, 215-243, 1953.

Ruesch, J. & Bateson, G. *Communication: The Social Matrix of Psychiatry*. New York: Norton, 1951.

Rutter, M. "Individual differences." In Rutter, M. & Herson, L. (Eds.), *Child Psychiatry: Modern Approaches*. Oxford: Blackwill, 1977.

Sabatelli, R. & Mazor, A. "Differentiation, individuation and identity formation: The integration of family systems and individual developmental perspectives." *Adolescence, 20*, 79, 1985.

Satir, V. *Conjoint Family Therapy*. Palo Alto: Science and Behavior Books, 1967.

Schaefer, R. "Concepts of self and identity and the experience of separation-individuation in adolescence." *Psychoanalytic Quarterly, 42*, 42-59, 1973.

Schaefer, H.R. & Emerson, P.E. "The development of social attachments in infancy." *Monographs of the Society for Research in Child Development, 29*, 3, 1964.

Selman, R. *The Growth of Interpersonal Understanding: Developmental and Clinical Analysis*. New York: Academic Press, 1980.

Sheehy, G. *Passages*. New York: Bantam Books, 1977.

Smilansky, M. & Nevo, D. *The Gifted Disadvantaged*. New York: Gordon and Breach, 1979.

Smilansky, M., Kashti, Y. & Arieli, M. *The Residential Education Alternative*. East Orange, N.J.: The Institute for Humanistic Studies, 1982.

Stewart, W. *A Psychosocial Study of the Formation of the Early Adult Life Structure in Women*. Unpublished doctoral dissertation. New York: Columbia University, 1977.

Stierlin, H. *Separating Parents and Adolescents*. New York: Jason Aronson, 1981.

Teyber, E. "Effects of the parental coalition on adolescent emancipation." *J. of Marital and Family Therapy, 9*, 89-99, 1983.

Thomas, A., Chess, S. & Birch, H.G. *Temperament and Behavior Disorders in Children*. New York: New York University Press, 1968.

Thomas, A. & Chess, S. *Temperament and Development*. New York: Brunner-Mazel, 1977.

Vaillant, G.E. *Adaptation to Life*. Boston: Little, Brown, 1977.

Vogel, E.G. & Bell, N.W. "The emotionally disturbed child as the family's scape-goat." In Handel, G. (Ed.), *The Psychosocial Interior of the Family*. Chicago: Aldine, 1967.

Wallerstein, J. & Kelly, J. *Surviving the Break-up*. New York: Basic Books, 1980.

Watzlawick, P. & al. *Pragmatics of Human Communication*. New York: Norton, 1967.

White, K.M. & al. "Young adults and their parents: Individuation to mutuality." In Grotevant, H. & Cooper, C.R. (Eds.), *Adolescent Development in the Family*. San Francisco: Jossey-Bass, 1983.

Winnicot, D.W. "Adolescence: Struggling through the doldrums." *Adolescent Psychiatry, 1*, 40-49, 1971.

Youniss, J. & Smaller, J. *Adolescent Relations with Mothers, Fathers and Friends*. Chicago: University of Chicago Press, 1985.